"Though Mr. Cogley is a professio̶[...] he has pressed two of the main h[...] What *was* the American Church like in the past, and how has the present situation come about? Accordingly, the first half of *Catholic America* is a fresh survey of the high spots of American Catholic history from the first 'Romane Catholiques' of Lord Calvert's Maryland to the post-*aggiornamento* assimilated suburbanites. The second part is an analytical conspectus of the varieties of Catholicism, the dying 'ghetto culture,' the schools (a particularly good chapter), the clergy, and the changing church-state issues.

Along the way there are excellent but brief pen-portraits of important figures, the magnanimous and the narrow, heroes and true menaces . . . It is a marvelous procession . . .

Not the least of [the book's] merits is to enable one to consider the future of Catholicism in America calmly and steadily and with some expectation of new life, despite the obvious dissolution of the old." *New York Times Book Review*

"Few authors are better equipped to tackle the subject of contemporary American Catholicism than John Cogley. He has not only reviewed so much recent history . . . but also helped make some of it. . . . As a result, he has produced a refreshingly clear and well-researched history and critique of the American Catholic Church." *The Sign*

"A highly readable, unfootnoted history of the Catholic experience in America. . . . Thoroughly interesting and highly recommended, especially to Protestants lacking knowledge in this area."

Christianity Today

"Cogley's book . . . has all the excellences of the best in the journalistic tradition—objectivity, a dispassionate stance, a telling selection of facts and events, a swift-moving, attention-holding style and, finally, intelligent interpretation." *Washington Post*

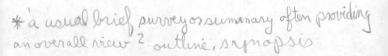

*a usual brief survey or summary often providing an overall view 2 outline, synopsis

Also by John Cogley

RELIGION IN A SECULAR AGE:
THE SEARCH FOR FINAL MEANING

RELIGION IN AMERICA (ED.)

CATHOLIC AMERICA

BY

John Cogley

IMAGE BOOKS

A DIVISION OF DOUBLEDAY & COMPANY, INC.

GARDEN CITY, NEW YORK

1974

TO THE MEMORY OF A FRIEND
JOHN COURTNEY MURRAY, S.J.

The Catholic may not, as others
do, merge his religious and his
patriotic faith, or submerge one
in the other. He must reckon
with his own tradition of thought,
which is wider and deeper than
any that America has elaborated.

J.C.M.
1960

IMAGE BOOKS EDITION

BY SPECIAL ARRANGEMENT WITH THE DIAL PRESS

IMAGE BOOKS EDITION PUBLISHED FEBRUARY 1974

ISBN: 0-385-08916-3

Contents

FOREWORD   6

ACKNOWLEDGMENT   6

PART ONE

1. THE FIRST ROMANE CATHOLIQUES   7

2. THE IRISH INVASION   27

3. A PEOPLE OF PEOPLES   45

4. MORE STATELY MANSIONS   66

5. *AGGIORNAMENTO*—AND BEYOND   95

PART TWO

6. VARIETIES OF CATHOLICISM   116

7. THE GHETTO CULTURE   135

8. THE SCHOOLS   154

9. THE CLERGY   172

10. CHURCH AND STATE   200

AFTERWORD   216

BIBLIOGRAPHY   228

INDEX   231

FOREWORD

The story of American Catholicism has to be an account of historic events, but more than that it should be concerned with the life of a community called to work out its salvation, spiritual and temporal, within the larger community that is America.

In the hope of doing justice to both these aspects in this panoramic view of American Catholic life, I have divided this book into two parts. The first is concerned with some of the high points of an historic experience; the second is an attempt to provide an insight into the character of the Catholic community in the United States by looking at the Church's own institutions, its leadership, and the changing attitudes that were dominant in it during the past two centuries.

ACKNOWLEDGMENT

This book is the work of a "mere journalist," as we are affectionately known in the Academy. It will surprise no one then that the author benefited from the seminal labor of certain hardworking scholars; their books are listed in the Bibliography. I am particularly indebted to the deans of American Catholic history, the late Father Thomas T. McAvoy, C.S.C., author of *A History of the Catholic Church in the United States,* and Monsignor John Tracy Ellis, author of *American Catholicism.*

None of these writers bears any responsibility of course for the opinions set forth in these pages or for any inaccuracies that may have crept into the text. They are mentioned here simply to be thanked, as is my patient secretary, Patricia Cathcart.

J.C.

Part One

CHAPTER ONE
THE FIRST ROMANE CATHOLIQUES

When the nation began, Roman Catholics in the United States accounted for less than forty thousand in a population of four million. Most were descendants of the original English settlers of Maryland; others were found in scattered Irish and German settlements in Pennsylvania; here and there in the remaining states isolated Catholics lived quietly and obscurely in order not to arouse the furies of religious prejudice that bedeviled the age. If all the Catholic families who had emigrated to the colonies had kept faith with the Church, their number would have been significantly larger by the time of the Revolution; but in the face of the penal laws* against Catholicism throughout the colonies many had drifted away, some into religious indifference, others into Protestant churches.

* These laws were based on the idea that Catholicism was not only an "enemy of the true Christian religion" but a political conspiracy. A New York law, drafted in 1700, for example, decreed that any priest ordained by the Pope who practiced Catholic rites "shall be deemed and accounted an incendiary and disturber of the public peace and safety . . ." and was to be banished from the colony. Four years later, priests in Maryland were forbidden by law to baptize children; twelve years after that, the same colony imposed severe penalties on public officials who attended a Mass. Religious restrictions of this sort, not all of them directed against Roman Catholicism, were commonplace in the colonies. In 1774 Alexander Hamilton wrote: "There are at this time in the adjacent county not less than five or six well-meaning men in close jail for publishing their religious sentiments. . . . I have squabbled and scolded, abused and ridiculed, so long about it to little purpose, that I am without common patience. So I must beg you to pity me, and pray for liberty of conscience to all."

*2 a person who excites factions, quarrels or sedition: agitator

1

Anti-Catholicism has been called America's oldest and most abiding prejudice. In early New England it went unquestioned. It was rooted in the theological narrowness then dominant in the Western world and, perhaps more powerfully, in the history of the mother country. From Elizabeth to George III, stringent No Popery laws had been passed in Britain, not only to counter the feeble efforts of the remaining Catholic nobility to restore the faith but to eradicate what remained of the old loyalty to Rome among Englishmen.

The spirit of the anti-Catholic laws, and sometimes the letter, were unabashedly exported to the New World. By and large, the colonists shared John Cotton's view that "it was toleration that made the world anti-Christian."

Anti-Catholic feelings among the colonists were also tied into the popular hatred then felt by Englishmen for their threatening enemies, France and Spain. Because of their strong ties with the papacy, both of these nations were identified with the Church of Rome, as were their settlements on the new continent—New France and the outposts of Spain in the far West. These colonies were established through the efforts not only of explorers and soldiers but of Jesuit and Franciscan missionaries. Among the priests of the two orders, Louis Hennepin and Jacques Marquette, explorers of the Middle West, and Junipero Serra, who established the California missions, have found their way into American schoolbooks. Most lived and died in obscurity, and after death they remained unknown to all but professional historians.

The American outposts of Continental Catholicism would later be incorporated into the Union, but to the men of the thirteen colonies they seemed as foreign as the European powers that ruled over them. At a time when the heirs of the Puritans were still determined to establish a *Novus Ordo Seclorum* on American soil—a promise still memorialized on the dollar bill—everything reminiscent of the age of despotic popes and lordly Roman prelates represented not only a theological abomination but a danger to internal security. Even the powerlessness and practical invisibility of the first American Catholics did not diminish their fears.

The first American Catholics by and large supported the Revolution—at least in the same proportion as other colonists,

'prel ǝt or 'prē͜lāt -- an ecclesiastic of superior rank

though there were partially successful attempts to raise a Roman Catholic regiment of Loyalists among them, principally in Pennsylvania. How many Catholics served in the Continental Army is not known. We have John Carroll's word that "their blood flowed as freely, in proportion to their number, to cement the fabric of independence as that of their fellow citizens" and George Washington's general commendation of Catholics who served under his command; but with the small proportion of Papists among the colonists, the number could not have been great. Among them, only the name of John Barry, "father of the Navy," has found a prominent place in history.

At first the Catholics in the colonies had only slight hopes that complete religious freedom would follow independence. Most agreed, however, that there was nothing to look forward to were the British rule continued. This fact, and the additional circumstance that Catholic France and Polish friends like Kosciusko and Pulaski supported the revolt, had by the end of the Revolutionary War improved what would now be called their public image.

President Washington himself gave an indication of the softening attitude when he told a Catholic group who called on him shortly after he took office, "I presume that your fellow citizens will not forget the patriotic part which you took in the accomplishment of their revolution and the establishment of their government; or the important assistance which we have received from the nation [France] in which the Roman Catholic religion is professed." Earlier, as General of the Army, Washington had outlawed the "ridiculous and childish custom of burning the Effigy of the Pope" during a celebration of Guy Fawkes Day. But anti-Catholicism was too deeply rooted to be banished by such gestures. It hung on for decades.

The recurrent fear that Catholicism would gain a foothold in the young nation did not arise out of thin air. It was based, among other things, on the fact that the Church had developed its own political theories and notions of Church-state relations in the predemocratic past and clung to them tenaciously while the world beyond its reach was changing radically. This would remain the source of religious tensions in the United States right up to the presidency of John F. Kennedy. For it was not until the Second Vatican Council in the early 1960s that the Church formally relinquished an abstract claim to prohibit the public profession of other religions in places where the followers of the Pope constituted a clear majority.

At the time of the American Revolution, the Pope was still a temporal lord ruling his states like any other monarch, as he remained until the papal rule was overthrown by Unification forces in the 1870s. There was, then, substance to the charge that Catholics the world over were subject to "a foreign prince." American Catholics themselves earnestly distinguished between the Pope as Vicar of Christ and the Pope as secular ruler; yet, as long as the Pontiff remained a political sovereign in Italy, their arguments were never very convincing to their fellow citizens.

Through the years the leaders of the Church in the United States sang the glories of the American system, but most Vatican pronouncements, almost until the Second World War, strengthened the impression that followers of the Pope could at best be ambiguous in their support of democracy; earlier papal statements were so full of caveats and qualifications about free speech, freedom of religion, and liberal thought in general as to suggest something less than a blessing on the experiment being made on the other side of the ocean. Add to this the misunderstandings of Catholic beliefs and religious practices which were promulgated by Protestant polemicists, and it is not hard to see why Americans held Catholicism in contempt for so long.

John Adams probably summed up the general opinion of his time in a letter he wrote his wife Abigail in 1774. Adams found a Catholic service he attended in Philadelphia ". . . most awful and affecting: the poor wretches fingering their beads, chanting Latin, not a word of which they understood; their Paternosters and Ave Marias; their holy water; their crossing themselves perpetually; their bowing and kneeling and genuflecting before the altar." The whole scene might have been expected in a European peasant setting, but it must have struck the patrician Adams as a disturbing sight in a

nation founded on the principles enunciated in the Declaration
of Independence.

Inevitably the antipathy to religious practices taken bodily
from the Latin rather than the pre-Reformation Anglo-Saxon
traditions of Catholicism were exploited by Protestant zealots
in the colonies. In a pre-ecumenical age, when the bitterness
of the Reformation struggle was not as far away as it is today,
"Papist," "Jesuitical," and "idolators" carried as much emotional force in the Protestant lands with which the first Americans identified as "heretic" and "sectarian" did in nations
loyal to the papacy.

The memory of past persecutions was still a powerful force.
John Foxe's *Book of Martyrs*, recounting the persecution of
Protestants in gory detail, was widely read throughout the
colonies. Educated Catholics for their part honored Englishmen like Thomas More, John Fisher, Edmund Campion, the
Carthusian monks, and the simple layfolk who went to their
deaths rather than accept Henry VIII or Elizabeth as head of
the Church. As a consequence, in the colonies as in the mother
country both Protestants and Catholics were inclined to look
upon each other as potential tyrants whose recent forebears
had murdered saints and scoffed at the true Gospel. Given
the opportunity, however, neither party seemed loath to practice the oppression it abhorred in the other.

The spirit of the times was such that had Catholics founded
the original colonies, the record might now be one of Catholic
intolerance and Protestant victims. As it happened, though,
Catholics were a helpless minority in New England, and their
early history is one of shameless exclusion and disability. The
measures taken against them included banishment, the out-
lawing of priests, and the prohibition of divine services and
of religious training for children. Even after the Revolution
only four of the original states allowed Roman Catholics full
equality with other Christians—Pennsylvania (with its long history of Quaker toleration), Delaware, Virginia, and Maryland.
The constitutions of the other nine established one or more
of the Protestant sects—or Protestantism in general—as the state
religion, and provided that anyone who held public office accept the truth of the Protestant faith. South Carolina did not
lift the laws against Catholics until 1790; Georgia held out

until 1798; New York, until 1806; Connecticut, until 1818; Massachusetts, until 1833; North Carolina, until 1835.

The attitude that gave rise to such laws was exemplified in the 1774 Suffolk Resolves of the Continental Congress concerning the English Parliament's grant of religious toleration to the French in Canada. The act seemed harmless enough. It gave the Canadians the right to "have, hold, and enjoy the free exercise of the religion of the Church of Rome." Yet the American Congress held that it was "dangerous in an extreme degree to the Protestant religion and to the civil rights and liberties of all Americans: and, therefore, as men and Protestant Christians, we are indispensably obliged to take all proper measures for our security."

According to Congressman John Jay, later Chief Justice of the United States, such a concession established a religion "fraught with sanguinary and impious tenets"; it threatened to turn the Catholics of Canada into "fit instruments in the hands of power to reduce the ancient free Protestant colonies to the same state of slavery with themselves." Bob Jingle, the "poet laureate" of Congress, put it less elegantly:

> *If Gallic Papists have a right,*
> *To worship their own way,*
> *Then farewell to the liberty,*
> *Of poor America.*

The colonists' charge that, in granting religious liberty to Canadians, Parliament was endangering the liberty of Americans was later used to enlist popular support for the Revolution. In his *Full Vindication of the Measures of Congress,* even the comparatively tolerant Alexander Hamilton, for example, wrote, ". . . they may as well establish Popery in New York and the other colonies as they did in Canada. They had no more right to do it there than here. Your lives, your property, your religion, are all at stake."

The pioneering American Catholics, however, were really more sinned against than sinning. There is no record of any attempt on their part to subvert democratic liberties. As members of a persecuted minority, their leaders had reason to appreciate the benefits of religious tolerance. Perhaps for that reason more than any other, they practiced it somewhat better than most.

There is a kind of paradox in the fact that the first colony to establish a measure of religious toleration—for Christians of all persuasions though not for Jews or nonbelievers—was founded by men who accepted papal authority as a religious principle. Yet, American Catholic history—leaving aside the French and Spanish territories later incorporated into the United States—begins with the founding of Maryland. There, too, begins the history of religious liberty in the United States. But even in Maryland, which was a model of toleration compared to all but Rhode Island among its sister colonies, the wisdom of its founders was soon undone.

The Maryland experiment with religious tolerance later became a source of pride to American Catholics. The colony was originally planned by Sir George Calvert, a wealthy Yorkshireman, who was converted to Catholicism in 1624 at the age of forty-four. After he changed his religion, Calvert was obliged to resign his office as Secretary of State, but he remained in favor with King James I and was named the first Lord Baltimore. Two years before his conversion, Calvert had sponsored a short-lived colony in Newfoundland. As Lord Baltimore, he visited it in 1627 with his second wife and two young children. Disappointed with what he found, he set sail for the South in search of a more hospitable climate. When he reached Virginia, the authorities there insisted that he take the Oath of Succession (with its anti-Catholic provisions), even though he had been exempted by the King from taking the oath at home. Calvert refused and returned to England, but with still another colonization scheme in mind.

On his voyage to America he had taken note of the Chesapeake Bay region, which promised to support a body of transplanted English gentlemen comfortably and also provide him with a tidy income. When he got back home he applied for a charter to establish a colony there, to be called Maryland, after the reigning Queen Henrietta Maria. The charter was not formally granted until shortly after his death, which was due, it was said, to grief over the death of his second wife and their children, who had perished at sea on their way back to the mother country. The deed, along with the title of Baron, was inherited by Cecil, the eldest of Calvert's three grown sons. The second Lord Baltimore, as shrewd a businessman as his father, was at least as interested in profits as he was in establishing a refuge for religious dissenters.

Carrying out his father's plan, Cecil Calvert set up a feudal barony in the new colony. Under his patronage a small group of Roman Catholic "gentlemen" and about two hundred workingmen, some of them Protestants, set sail on the *Ark* and the *Dove* on November 22, 1633, and landed at St. Clement's Island the following March. The expedition, led by Leonard and George Calvert, the founder's younger brothers, included two priests and one lay brother, all Jesuits, who did not come as official chaplains or authorized missionaries but traveled at their own expense as "gentlemen." As such they were entitled to share in the division of the land.

Before the party left England, Cecil Calvert cautiously instructed its officials that "they suffer no scandall nor offense to be given to any of the Protestants whereby any just Complaint may hereafter be made to them, in Virginia or in England, and that for that end they Cause all Acts of Romane Catholique Religion to be done as privately as may be, and that they instruct all the Romane Catholiques to be silent upon all occasions of discourse concerning matters of Religion; and that the said Governor and Commissioners treat the Protestants with as much mildness and favor as Justice will permit."

The colony was carried on in this spirit until civil war broke out in England and the King was deposed. Then a conflict erupted between Calvert and one William Claiborne over disputed territory on the Maryland shore. In 1645 Claiborne, a powerful Virginia Puritan, led an invasion of the colony and took over the property of its Catholics. The Virginians held Maryland for two years, when they were finally driven out by a Catholic force led by Leonard Calvert.

During the "occupation," two of the five Jesuits then in the colony, Fathers Andrew White and Thomas Copley, were sent back to England, where they were promptly arrested for violating the law prohibiting priests who were ordained abroad from entering the realm. They were later released by arguing successfully that they had not returned to the mother country willingly, but had been brought back as prisoners. The three remaining Maryland Jesuits fled to Virginia. All three died in exile, leaving the colony without priests until Father Copley, accompanied by a Father Lawrence Starkey, was sent back in 1648, after Leonard Calvert pleaded with the Jesuit Superior in England to send priests to replace those who had gone.

The next year the Maryland Religious Toleration Act was enacted into law. The Act, ordered by Lord Calvert, formalized what had been practiced from the beginning by providing that no one was to be molested for his religion who professed to believe in Jesus Christ. It would hardly be considered a model of toleration today, but it did mark a kind of breakthrough. Undoubtedly it also affected the American Catholic understanding of religious liberty for the next two centuries.

Two years after the act was passed, Parliament, now controlled by the Puritans, established a commission led by Calvert's old enemy, Claiborne, to get pro-royalist Virginia to submit to the new English government. Claiborne, going beyond the letter of his instructions, proceeded to subdue Maryland as well. For three years, from 1655 to 1658, his commission was in virtually complete control of the colony. Under Claiborne's instigation the General Assembly of Maryland revoked the short-lived Act of Toleration and formally outlawed Catholicism—withholding toleration of "popery . . . prelacy . . . [and] such as under the profession of Christ hold forth and practice licentiousness."

Calvert, if nothing else a shrewd politician, however, managed to get himself reinstated as the proprietor of Maryland within two years, on condition that the original Act of Toleration would be restored. It was, but its second chance at life was brief. During the Revolution of 1688 in England, a man Calvert had appointed governor of Maryland, one Josias Fendall, plotted with a fellow Puritan, John Cooke, against the proprietor and took over the colony. The anti-Catholic laws were immediately put back in force.

Maryland Catholics were angered by the setback; yet, with nowhere else to go, they had to remain where they were. Gradually, though the discriminatory laws remained on the books and Catholics were still denied suffrage and the right

*adj: lacking legal or moral restraints esp: sexual
2 marked disregard for rules

to hold political office, and were also obliged to support the established Anglican Church, a kind of practical toleration was worked out as a "gentleman's agreement" between them and their neighbors. The leading Catholic families were permitted to carry on as if some of the laws did not exist. A number of them grew rich in time and freely sent their sons to Catholic colleges in France, though it was actually against the law to do so.

Among the young men who went abroad were the two leading Catholics of their time, Charles Carroll, who exercised more direct influence on the American Catholic community than any layman before or since, and his distant cousin, John Carroll, the American Catholic Church's first bishop.

The Carrolls had long been the first Catholic family of the colony. They were so eminently acceptable that even their religion was not seriously held against them. They farmed, hunted, danced, and entertained as social equals with the colonial aristocracy. Like a few other affluent Maryland Catholic families who had attained the power that inevitably accompanies wealth, they were generally regarded as untouchable by most of their Protestant neighbors.

The founder of the American branch was an earlier Charles Carroll, who arrived in Maryland in 1688 with a writ signed by the third Lord Baltimore appointing him attorney general. A personable, capable young man, Carroll prospered in the colony, not only as a popular lawyer but as a successful dry-goods dealer and landowner. In the time-honored manner, the young man used his money to make even more by giving out loans to fellow colonists at a high rate of interest. In short order he became one of the wealthiest men in Maryland, the owner of large stretches of land, lord of a comfortable manor, father of four sons, and the leading spokesman for his beleaguered coreligionists. The sons in their turn increased the family holdings. By the third generation, Charles Carroll of Carrollton, as the first Charles's grandson chose to be known, was probably the richest man in America.

Though other Catholic families fell by the wayside under the pressure of the times—including the English Calverts—most of the Carrolls remained loyal to the Church. Their homes, along with the Jesuit manors in the colony, were used for the celebration of Mass and religious instruction, and their fellow Catholics looked to them for leadership and protection. When, as happened from time to time, Catholic colonists were charged with plotting against the Crown, the colonial government, or the established Protestant faith, it was taken for granted that a Carroll would answer the accusation.

For example, the father of Charles Carroll of Carrollton protested successfully against a discriminatory bill "to prevent the growth of Popery" which was presented in the Upper House of the Maryland Assembly in 1751. After the proposed legislation became known, the governor was promptly presented with an "Humble Petition and Remonstrance of Charles Carroll on behalf of Himself and all other Roman Catholics of the Province of Maryland." Carroll argued in it that he was born and bred in Maryland and that "in thirty years of Manhood" he never even heard that "the Roman Catholics as a body have given any just complaint to the Government." A few years later the governor of Maryland, writing about Carroll, naturally referred to him as the "Head of that Sect" (the Roman Catholic Church), though Carroll was a layman. Actually the ecclesiastical superior of the Maryland Catholics was an English bishop, the Vicar Apostolic of the London District, who delegated his authority to the Maryland Jesuits; but such canonical niceties meant little at the time, and the Carrolls were regarded by all as the foremost Catholic spokesmen in the colony.

For all their respectability, however, even the devoted Carrolls knew moments of discouragement. At one point in 1757, when a new law was passed doubling Catholic taxes, the second Charles Carroll entertained the idea of moving his family to Louisiana. Happily for the Church in America, and for the nation itself, he later changed his mind.

This Charles Carroll's son and namesake, who was to be the most distinguished member of the family, was in Flanders at the time, finishing his studies at Saint-Omer's, a Jesuit college favored by the wealthy Catholics of the colony. He and his cousin John, the future bishop, were friends and classmates, as they had been earlier at Bohemia Manor, a little school the American Jesuits conducted in Maryland.

After their schooldays the two Carrolls went their separate ways. Charles returned to the colony within a few years to settle into the traditional life of the manor. John, who left America at the age of thirteen, did not return until he was past forty. In the meantime he had joined the Jesuits, was ordained a priest in Belgium, and taught in schools run by the Society of Jesus on the Continent. After the Jesuits were suppressed in 1773—by a Franciscan pope who sacrificed the order to what he believed was the higher welfare of Catholic Europe—Father Carroll, disheartened, discouraged, and more than a little bitter, returned to Maryland to live quietly in his mother's home in Rock Creek. He did not join the priestly association formed by the ex-Jesuits of the colonies but confined himself to serving the pastoral needs of Catholics in the Rock Creek area. Father Carroll's long life, however, was only half over, and his most productive years were still to come.

Charles Carroll was born to be the leading Catholic layman of his day; he became a member of the larger American establishment by gambling on freedom. Like most of the Founding Fathers, he was a man of conservative temper; since, in addition, he was very wealthy, the decision to throw in his lot with the revolutionaries could not have been taken lightly. Carroll's emergence on the national scene began inauspiciously enough in 1773 with his entry into a public controversy over the imposition of "fees," a euphemism for taxes ordered by the colonial governor against the wishes of the Maryland legislature. The governor's action was resented by the colonists and brought on angry charges of taxation without representation—an opinion Charles Carroll shared.

To sweeten the resentment of the unpopular tax, a man named Daniel Dulany, a lawyer who was known locally for his skill in controversy, came to the governor's defense in the *Maryland Gazette* by writing a dialogue between a witless opponent of the measure, called First Citizen, and a brilliant defender of it, called Second Citizen. Another dialogue appeared in the paper a month later, this one written by Charles Carroll, in which First Citizen's case was more convincingly set forth. The new "First Citizen" argued that his views had been so mangled by the original presentation that they were scarcely recognizable as his own. Though both writers remained technically anonymous, readers throughout the colony knew who they were.

Carroll's contribution accurately reflected the view of the restive colonists. It won immediate popular approbation, enough to spark an answer from Dulany (writing now as "Antilon"). Dulany's reply then drew a fresh response from Carroll, still nominally shrouded as "First Citizen." The argument Ping-Ponged back and forth until Dulany allowed himself to slip into a disastrous *ad hominem* remark: He charged that Carroll, or First Citizen, was clearly incompetent to discuss political matters because, as everyone knew, he was "disabled from giving a voice in the choice of representatives on account of his principles which are distrusted by these laws. . . . He is not a Protestant."

Inadvertently, Dulany handed Carroll victory on a platter. Like many controversialists before and since, he had misjudged the mercurial mood of the public. The political and religious climate had so changed that what might have scored a point for Dulany a few years earlier carried the day for Carroll, who in his response turned the tables by comparing Antilon to a Spanish inquisitor. The anti-Governor platform which Carroll supported was upheld overwhelmingly in the next election and Carroll was lavishly credited with the triumph.

After the election the happy winners flooded the *Gazette* with letters praising First Citizen and thanking him for his assistance. Through Charles Carroll, then, the Catholics of Maryland, probably about one-twelfth of the colonists at the time, achieved their first solid social and even political acceptance. The crude anti-Catholicism that had gone unchallenged for so long became—at least temporarily—passé.

Carroll went on from there. He was elected to various patriotic committees, including the prestigious Committee of Correspondence; later he won a seat in the Maryland legislature. Finally he was sent to the Second Continental Congress, where, on his first day in office, he signed the Declaration of Independence, joining twelve Congregationalists, twenty-nine Episcopalians, eight Presbyterians, three Unitarians, a Baptist, a

Quaker, and Benjamin Franklin, who styled himself simply as a Deist.

Carroll not only supported the Revolution with his private fortune but put his tested diplomatic skill in the service of the young nation. He was elected to the United States Senate after the war but later gave up the seat in order to have full time for the Maryland legislature, which he regarded as a more important post. He lived to be ninety-five, "the last of the Signers"—long enough to see the land of his birth change from a place where men of his religious convictions were deprived of ordinary civil rights to a nation where the practice of any faith or none was protected from governmental interference by a constitutional provision.

John Carroll played a smaller part in the Revolutionary cause but was destined for a more formative role in the history of American Catholicism. As its first bishop, an honor he finally received in 1790, it fell to him to organize the American Church, shape its character, and set the style that would later distinguish it as at once devoted to the Papacy and loyally American.

John Carroll's support of the Revolutionary cause was unequivocal, though as a priest he was always loath to engage in political activities. "I have observed," he once wrote, "that when the ministers of religion leave the duties of their profession to take a busy part in political matters they generally fall into contempt and sometimes even bring discredit to the cause in whose service they are engaged." In spite of this caution, in early 1776 he accepted an invitation offered to him by the Continental Congress to join an ill-starred diplomatic mission to Canada. Its purpose was to win Catholic support for the colonists' cause—a bold undertaking in view of the adverse American reaction to the granting of religious liberty to the Canadians only two years earlier.

Father Carroll had been added as a kind of afterthought to a distinguished committee which included Charles Carroll and Samuel Chase, a Maryland Protestant, and was headed by the suave Benjamin Franklin, whose gift for diplomacy was already becoming legendary.

The group never stood a chance with the Canadian Catholics, who were still smarting from the Americans' recent show of disdain for their religious rights. Franklin's party was received with a frigidity unmatched in the history of diplomatic receptions. Father Carroll was regarded by Bishop Briand, the head of the Church in Quebec, as disloyal to the cause of religious freedom because he was serving the Congress that so shortly before had shown its contempt for Canadian Catholicism. The priest in the party actually felt the cold blasts more than the others. It was a measure of Briand's hostility that he later suspended a Canadian priest merely for allowing Carroll to say Mass in his home.

Franklin, who was suffering poor health at the time, was particularly distressed by the fiasco. It yielded one lasting effect, however. Father Carroll had been highly solicitous for the older man's comfort throughout the trip, and he and Franklin became lasting friends. Back home, Franklin told friends that the priest had actually saved his life. Eight years later, when Franklin, in Paris, was sounded out by the Vatican on how he felt about the appointment of Carroll as leader of the Church in America, he gave the Maryland priest an unqualified commendation.

"The Pope's Nuncio called," Franklin wrote in his *Private Journal*, "and acquainted me that the Pope had, on my recommendation, appointed Mr. John Carroll superior of the Catholic clergy in America, with many of the powers of a bishop; and that probably he would be made a bishop *in partibus* before the end of the year. . . ."

The question of appointing a superior for the Church in the new nation had been brought to the Vatican's attention soon after independence for the "thirteen states in America" became an established fact. The Select Body of the Clergy, the organization of American priests, made it clear to Rome that it would no longer accept the authority of a British prelate and requested that some new arrangement be made.

Carroll, who originally organized the Select Body, was not the priests' first choice when they decided to ask the Vatican to name a leader for the American mission. That honor fell to Father John Lewis, who had been the last superior of the Maryland Jesuits before the order was suppressed. Lewis, however, was already old and had grown so infirm that the authorities in Rome decided against him, naming Carroll in his place. Carroll was not eager to assume the responsibility. He did so out of a concern that if he turned it down, the post would go to a foreign bishop, probably a Frenchman; he believed that would be a mistake of the kind which the Vatican, in its ignorance of the temper of the American people, might easily make.

In the beginning, the priests themselves were opposed to the idea of naming an American bishop. Some twenty of them had sent a letter to the Pope in 1784 arguing that "we are convinced that [naming a bishop] would be much more detrimental than otherwise to the interests of religion." All prelates, whatever their ecclesiastical allegiance, were hated figures in the colonies, and the members of the American Catholic clergy were quite aware of that fact. The Anglicans had also long avoided arousing sleeping dogs by holding out against naming a bishop for the colonies, but in 1787 they moved. Following the consecration of an American, Bishop Samuel Seabury, in Scotland, the Archbishop of Canterbury consecrated bishops for Pennsylvania and New York. Surprisingly there was no general outcry; actually the prestige of the American Episcopal Church (which had been at a low ebb during the late colonial period) rose. The Roman Catholic clergy consequently became less hesitant about the full establishment of their Church in the United States. By then Carroll himself favored the idea. He had learned from experience that without episcopal consecration not only was he unable to ordain new priests but was otherwise hampered in his dealings with the Vatican.

The American Catholic clergy agreed that their first bishop should be one of their own number and should not be proposed by the Holy See but nominated by them, in order to dissipate as much as possible the notion that American Catholicism was under foreign control. Carroll passed on this recommendation to the Roman authorities, who reluctantly agreed to it.

To no one's surprise, John Carroll was chosen when the vote was taken. Rome was notified, and on November 6, 1789, Carroll was named Bishop of Baltimore, a diocese which then took in the entire territory of the United States. He traveled to England for the consecration. In August, 1790, it was carried out in the private chapel of Thomas Weld, one of the remaining English Catholic gentry, by a Bishop Walmesley, an elderly Benedictine monk who was Vicar Apostolic of the Western District.

A few years earlier in a report to his superiors in Rome, Carroll had described the extent of Catholicism in the States. There were, he wrote, about 15,800 Catholics in Maryland, about 3000 of them Negro slaves. Another 7000 Catholics resided in Pennsylvania, 200 in Virginia, and perhaps 1500 in New York. The Marylanders were comparatively well served by the ex-Jesuits who were still vigorous enough to work; the Pennsylvanians, on the other hand, were visited by a priest only four or five times a year; there were no priests in New York, though Carroll reported that he had heard rumors about the recent arrival of a Franciscan friar.

In all, there were less than thirty priests in the country. More were needed immediately. The shortage meant that the new bishop and his immediate successors would be forced to deal with some questionable clerical characters in the years ahead.

Most of the European priests who came to the States after independence were dedicated, hardworking men fired with missionary zeal. Others, unfortunately, were the kind who could not get along with superiors at home and had crossed the ocean set upon enjoying maximum freedom from authority. As time passed, Bishop Carroll and his successors had to handle more than their share of clerical adventurers, malcontents, troublemakers, alcoholics, and neurotics. This was only one of the difficulties connected with laying the foundations for the Church that two hundred years later would be the largest religious body in the United States.

Many of Carroll's problems were connected with his inability to get a sympathetic hearing in Rome. Over the years the Church had learned a great deal about how to get along with monarchs and dictators, but in the eighteenth century Catholic authorities had little or no experience with democracies. The word itself was associated in the Roman curial mind with French anticlericalism, skepticism, and irreligion. The

~ Catholic governing system

idea that a government could be neutral toward the Church, rather than either supportive of or inimical to it, was still novel and difficult for the conservatives in the Vatican to grasp, and the reigning theologians of the time still looked upon the privileges traditionally granted to the Church by civil law as a divine right, either dutifully granted or maliciously withheld. They made no distinction between the anti-Catholic governments of Europe and the "neutral" government in far-off America.

The very newness of the American situation complicated Bishop Carroll's difficulties. His requests for necessary dispensations from the canonical norm sometimes struck the Roman authorities as unreasonable and dangerous. Some of his opinions, for example that in the Anglo-Saxon culture of the New World the liturgy should be carried out in English rather than in the traditional Latin, were looked upon as outrageous—as the idea still seemed to some of his successors when it was first put forth at the Second Vatican Council almost two centuries later.

Because Carroll was looked upon as an obscure bishop in an unimportant missionary outpost, neither his actions nor his ideas were taken very seriously in the Vatican, which at the time was preoccupied with the effects of the French Revolution on the Church in Europe. In the total hierarchical setup, the Bishop of the "American States" counted for little. Certainly no one in Rome suspected the importance he would have in the subsequent history of worldwide Catholicism. Carroll himself undoubtedly underestimated his own importance, both as an American and as an ecclesiastic. In retrospect, however, he must be counted among the greatest of post-Reformation Roman Catholic bishops.

He was neither a zealot nor a church reformer, but with his Maryland background, he understood the virtues of tolerance and the wisdom in government's making no claim to competence in theological matters. (Again, it took more than two centuries for the Universal Church to catch up to him on this.) His sympathy for the new kind of government found in the United States was apparent to all. As both a patriot and the spiritual leader of his flock, he made a point of sending letters of congratulations or condolence to the nation's political leaders on appropriate occasions. He studiously maintained cordial, though never intimate, contacts with the President and the leaders of Congress. Political figures in turn frequently turned up when he presided over the dedication of new churches and other Catholic institutions. It is a measure of Carroll's success in lessening the suspicion of Catholicism that, when Saint Peter's, the first Catholic church in New York, was dedicated in 1786, President Washington and his cabinet, along with members of Congress, attended a public dinner held to mark the occasion.

In his monumental *Church and State in the United States,* the Episcopal scholar, Canon Anson Phelps Stokes, summed up Carroll's immediate contribution in these words: "The patriotism, breadth, and character of Father Carroll, as first bishop of the Roman Catholic Church in the United States, from 1789 on, probably did as much as anything else to create a more favorable attitude [toward Catholicism] during the first two decades of the new century." Canon Stokes went on to describe Carroll as "one of those to whom we are most indebted for our religious freedom in this country."

Carroll served as Bishop, later Archbishop, of Baltimore during a period of growth for the Church. Through immigration, the number of Catholics increased steadily, and the original small band of American priests was augmented by Irish missionaries, groups of Dominicans and Augustinians sent from abroad, and, following the Revolution in France, by a band of French refugee priests. Among the Frenchmen was a group of Sulpician Fathers, a teaching order which played an important part by educating the next generation of American priests and setting a model for clerical piety that would hold on for many years.

At Carroll's request, the original diocese of Baltimore was elevated to an archdiocese with four suffragan sees in 1808. In addition to Carroll's own Auxiliary, bishops were named for New York, Philadelphia, Boston, and Bardstown, Kentucky, the last named a diocese vast in territory but small in the number of people to be served. There were French Catholics in the Kentucky territory before it was admitted to the Union in 1792, but they had gone so long unattended by priests that only a few remained even nominally in the Church. By the time the diocese was set up, their number had been increased to about 10,000 by a group of venturesome Marylanders who had moved westward seeking their fortune.

An American, William Du Bourg, became the Bishop of Louisiana in 1817, after the Louisiana Purchase. Carroll remained the leader of all the American clergy, though he was never named Primate, in the European manner. It was he who called the first synod which laid down the rules and regulations under which the Church in the United States operated. He nominated priests for the new bishoprics, sent missionaries beyond the Eastern Seaboard when they became available, and reported regularly to Rome on the overall state of what was known there simply as the American Missions.

His own diocese, even after it was subdivided, included Maryland, the District of Columbia, North and South Carolina, and Georgia. The archbishop not only built parish churches but encouraged the Sulpicians to conduct a seminary for native clergy—Saint Mary's, which still exists in Baltimore.

From the small Sulpician Society came a number of the pioneer prelates, including Benedict Joseph Flaget, the first bishop to venture into the Middle West. After the Society of Jesus was fully restored in 1814, Carroll helped set up a novitiate and scholasticate for American recruits to his own order, the forerunner of Woodstock College of Maryland, which was transferred to Morningside Heights in New York City only in the 1960s. He also accepted a group of Carmelite nuns from Europe and sponsored the establishment of several other convents in the archdiocese. A number of academies and schools, the most important of which were Mount Saint Mary's (still in existence) and Georgetown, the present Jesuit university in Washington, were founded under his direction. All this of course was done without state subsidy or significant grants from abroad. The "brick and mortar" bishops of American Catholicism were to come later, but it was Carroll who set the mold for them.

By the time of his death in 1815, there were one hundred Catholic parishes in the land served by as many priests. The penal laws against Catholics were gone, never to return, though the spirit that brought them into being would soon be revived. Almost all political offices and appointments were constitutionally open to members of the once-despised Church; yet it would be 145 years before a Roman Catholic would sit in the White House.

Along with these massive accomplishments, Archbishop Carroll left two serious problems for his successors to deal with. One involved nationalistic rivalries among Americans from Ireland, Germany, and France, which soon threatened Catholic unity; the other was the system of lay trusteeship that he allowed to get a foothold in the parishes established under his direction. The controversies and squabbles over the trustee system between bishops and laity, on the one hand, and among members of the Catholic clergy, on the other, would later cast a shadow over the American Church.

John Carroll was not a superman nor even a superbishop, but his record as the original builder of the Catholic Church in America has yet to be outshone by any of the hundreds of Americans who have followed him in the Catholic hierarchy. He was not particularly charismatic, nor even conspicuously pious. His biographers draw a portrait of a somewhat aloof, aristocratic gentleman of kindly, dignified manner, who might have lacked great gifts but was intent at all times on doing his duty and meeting each crisis as it arose, blinded to possibilities neither by discouragement nor extravagant vision. There had been no real enthusiasm for him when he was first appointed Superior of the American mission, but it is clear two hundred years later that he was the right man in the right place at the right time.

CHAPTER TWO

THE IRISH INVASION

During the fifty years following Archbishop Carroll's death, the Church in the United States kept pace with the rapid growth of the country. More than a half-million Europeans poured into the United States between 1830 and 1840. The number was tripled in the next decade. A high proportion of the newcomers, altogether too many for the comfort of the native-born, were Catholics, most of them Irish.

Many of the Germans, the French, and other groups of newly arrived Catholics moved westward after they reached America. The impoverished Irish, though they were a rural people, stayed in the seaboard cities, where they found work as common laborers, lived in crowded tenements, and seemed all the more formidable as a "foreign" element because of their obvious presence in places only recently homogeneously Protestant. Their crude peasant ways, combined with their easy acceptance of the idea that, because they spoke English, the new nation belonged to them as much as to those who had arrived on American shores long before them, were, to say the least, disconcerting to older settlers.

Both state and Church, it was soon clear, had to come to terms with what looked like an Irish invasion. It was not easy for either. Only with difficulty had Protestant America made adjustments to conform to the presence of Catholics as a tiny minority; it was now faced with a vast number of them who were not averse to demanding what they took to be their God-given rights. The Church, which had been established according to English Jesuit and French Sulpician patterns of genteel behavior, was thrown into turmoil. The source of the worst grievance of the Irish was that, while they outnumbered all other immigrants, the American Catholic hierarchy of the time was unmistakably French, as were most of the lower clergy.

John Carroll's immediate successor had been his Auxiliary Bishop, Leonard Neale, already a septuagenarian when Carroll died. Neale lived just about long enough to secure the succession of Ambrose Maréchal, a French-born Sulpician, to the Baltimore diocese. For a short period the only Irish bishop in the country was Henry Conwell of Philadelphia, an incompetent prelate who lost any influence he might have had after he was reproved by Rome for allowing laymen in his diocese to get an upper hand over the clergy. Maréchal, then, was the undisputed leader of a small hierarchy which included Cheverus in Boston, and the Sulpicians, Flaget in Bardstown and Du Bourg in Louisiana. The dominance of these men lent a certain credence to the Irish charge that the French were turning the American Church into a Gallic preserve. Some of the Irish, egged on by resentful members of the rustic clergy they had brought with them, were determined not to let this happen. A few went as far as to threaten schism.

Wherever Irish Catholics were settled, but particularly in New York and Philadelphia, there were recurrent complaints that the French clergy did not understand them or even the English language. One critical priest, a leader of the New York clergy, said of his own Bishop, John Dubois, that Dubois had spent thirty-six years in America, but "when he attempts to give common instruction, only thirty-six out of three thousand can understand a word of what he says. Hundreds leave the Church and go into the Rum Shops while he is speaking." Theodore Maynard, who quoted the priest, Father John Power, in his study of American Catholicism, suggested there might be some exaggeration here, since Dubois as a young man took English lessons from no less a master of the language than Patrick Henry.

It would not be unheard of in the future that American Catholic congregations would complain bitterly about the slapdash preaching in their churches; the difference in the early nineteenth century was that, with the trustee system in force, dissatisfied parishioners had the power to do something about it.

Under the system, the parish lay vestry owned Church property and doled out the pastors' salaries. The system worked well enough until some lay groups began to claim the right to hire and fire their priests without the approval of the Bishop. When, for one reason or another, a priest displeased his flock it was easy enough to starve him out and replace him with another or to establish a new parish altogether and let the Bishop make the most of it. With Church property held in the congregation's name, they had the legal power to do so.

The trustee system went all the way back to the beginnings of Catholicism in the colonies, when priests were as scarce as saints and the laity had to set up their own churches. Archbishop Carroll had always insisted that a bishop could never surrender his spiritual authority to the whims of a lay congregation, but he did not hesitate to approve the idea of laymen controlling parish property. The practice seemed to be thoroughly in keeping with the spirit of the new nation. The Archbishop, however, would certainly not have gone along with the later claim that priests were merely the employees of their parishioners. He would undoubtedly have been aghast at the idea that the authority of the laity extended to first naming and later dictating to their bishops. Yet, even this right was claimed as the controversy grew and relations deteriorated between clergy and laity and between priests and bishops. In addition, in Philadelphia and certain other places, there was open dissension between Irish and German Catholic laymen. Both intensely nationalistic, the two communities found it impossible to unite even at the altar, and separate national parishes were established for them by rival trustee groups.

The trustee issue came to a head when a vexatious vestry in Norfolk, Virginia, brought its grievances to the attention of Thomas Jefferson in a letter later circulated to members of Congress.

The vestry stressed that though immigrants from Ireland were the largest group in the Catholic Church, only one-twentieth of the American clergy were Irish. They hinted darkly at the possibility of royalist domination of the Catholic Church in America through the influence of foreign governments on the bishops. In passing, they charged both the native-born American Jesuits and the French Sulpicians with sheer covetousness. The presbyterian form of ecclesiastical government, they claimed, was not only proper for a church operating in the United States but was in keeping with the true character of Catholicism, since it had been practiced by the early Church. The vestrymen's letter was long, angry, bitter, and carefully designed to appeal to Jefferson's well-known distaste for dogma and ecclesiastical hierarchies.

Jefferson prudently stayed out of the controversy. But the public complaint drew a firm response from Archbishop Maréchal, who soon issued a *Pastoral Letter to the Roman Catholics of Norfolk*. In putting down the Irish claims, Maréchal invoked Church history and the Council of Trent's doctrinal teaching on the authority of the hierarchy. He added that nothing in the Constitution of the United States conflicted with the proper governance of the Church as it was understood by the Roman authorities. There was more than a hint in his letter that the headstrong Irishmen were really seeking hireling priests to do their will.

Later, in a letter to Rome, Archbishop Maréchal minced no words about the Irish priests under his supervision—in his view the least trustworthy of the American clergy and the cause of practically all the scandals of the day. He would welcome English priests in America, the Archbishop wrote, but in the future every Irish priest would be carefully scrutinized before he was accepted into the diocese.

This was not Maréchal's first sign of displeasure with the Irish clergy. For years he had made no secret of his opinion that they were poorly educated, uncultivated, troublesome, and all too often intemperate in their use of alcohol. Needless to say, his view of priests from the Auld Sod did not endear Maréchal to the Irish members of his flock.

One incident in the Irish-French struggle was a clear threat to Catholic unity. After a bitter disagreement with Archbishop Maréchal over the suspension of two Irish priests—one of several such cases—a group of laymen in South Carolina wrote to the Pope asking him to divide Maréchal's archdiocese and set up a new bishopric in Charleston. They proposed that one of their favorites, Thomas Carbry, an Irish-born Dominican friar, be named Bishop. Maréchal had already made it clear that he regarded the rebels as schismatics. When he heard of the letter to the Vatican, he warned Father Carbry that, if he continued to minister to them, he would be suspended from the priesthood. Carbry ignored the warning.

Later, with the connivance of the laity, the Dominican got in touch with Father Richard Hayes, a Franciscan in Ireland who was having difficulties with Rome at the time. Carbry invited the Franciscan to go to Utrecht for consecration by a schismatic Jansenist bishop and then proceed to America, where the disaffected Irish would accept him as their bishop. Carbry added that after Hayes got to Charleston he would be expected to consecrate new bishops, chosen by the laity, for other Irish communities in the States. If Hayes refused to do so, Carbry stated frankly, he would probably be denied financial support.

Had the plan worked, the rebellious American Irish would have had their own independent Church in the United States, and the subsequent history of American Catholicism probably would have been quite different from what it turned out to be. Actually, the scheme came to nothing because Father Hayes would have no part of it. Whatever the trouble he was having with his superiors, the Franciscan was a loyal son of Rome. Carbry's proposition struck him as outrageous, and he immediately brought it to the attention of the Vatican. The authorities in Rome took no official notice of the intrigue, but, realizing how much was at stake, they moved quickly.

Several Irish priests of unquestioned prudence and ability shortly thereafter were named bishops and assigned to American sees. Among them was John England, a priest from Cork, an Irish nationalist, a friend of Daniel O'Connell, and probably the most brilliant Irish cleric of his day. In Cork, Father England, then ten years ordained, had already distinguished himself as a Cathedral preacher, rector of the diocesan seminary, a professor of philosophy and theology, and a friend of the poor. England was sent to the newly erected diocese in South Carolina.

England was only thirty-two years old and a freshly consecrated bishop when he docked in Charleston shortly after Christmas in 1820, with his devoted young sister, Johanna, and Father Dennis Corkery, a youthful secretary, ready to take charge of a flock still torn with dissension. Neither of his first companions lasted long in the New World; Father Corkery was soon fatally stricken with yellow fever, and Johanna died of another illness a few years later. The Bishop himself lived to be only fifty-six, but for twenty-three years he dominated American Catholic life, though he never moved on to one of the larger dioceses where his extraordinary talents would have been given full scope.

England upheld the basic notion of clerical authority which Maréchal and his fellow Frenchmen had long defended, but he shared the general Irish view of French ecclesiastics. In a report to the Vatican, he wrote on one occasion: "I am daily more convinced that the genius of this nation and the administration of the French are not easily reconciled. . . .

The French can never become Americans. Their language, manners, love of *la belle France*, their dress, air, carriage, notions, and mode of speaking about their religion, all are foreign. . . . The French clergy are generally good men and love Religion, but they make the Catholic religion thus to appear to be exotic and cannot understand why it should be made to appear assimilated to American principles."

England ended the trustee controversy in his own diocese by writing a constitution which provided for a polity similar to that governing the Protestant Episcopal Church. The Bishop, according to the scheme, would have ultimate control over Church finances; thus the possibility of congregations repudiating clerical authority and yet claiming rights over parochial property would be eliminated. England also set up a general diocesan fund for a local seminary (to avoid sending future priests to the French Sulpicians in Baltimore), schools, charitable institutions, missionary projects, the erection of a cathedral, and the establishment of new parishes. A board of trustees to include the Bishop, his vicar general, five elected clergymen, and twelve elected laymen, all of whom were obliged to observe the regulations of the "general convention of the Church," was charged with distributing the fund.

In addition, the constitution authorized an annual convention of the Bishop, a house of clergy, and a house of lay delegates elected by the various parishes and districts in the diocese. The convention was to keep a watchful eye on the Catholic institutions of Charleston and recommend changes, but the Bishop alone was authorized to take action.

The constitution worked well, and the once-turbulent diocese settled down. Charleston might well have become something of a model for other dioceses then plagued with dissension over the trustee issue, but the plan was not adopted elsewhere, probably because England was not quite trusted by his brother bishops. They respected his zeal, yet looked upon him as a dangerously innovative and imprudent man. Even Bishop Conwell of Philadelphia, his fellow Irishman, urged Rome not to approve of the Charleston Constitution lest it be demanded elsewhere. Rome was not enthusiastic about England's novel ideas, but was so pleased that tranquillity had been reestablished in Charleston that it allowed his constitution to stand, though there was no support in the Vatican for putting it into effect elsewhere.

The constitution unfortunately did not survive England's episcopacy. His successor abolished it, arguing that it had only led to financial irresponsibility. It was not until after the Second Vatican Council that similar efforts to give the Catholic laity a voice in diocesan affairs were even attempted.

Bishop England succeeded in extending his influence throughout the American Church by means of a paper called the *United States Catholic Miscellany,* the first periodical of its kind in the United States. The *Miscellany,* which was edited by Johanna England until her untimely death in 1827, did not shy away from any of the controversial issues of the day, whether in Church or state. England, its chief contributor, was particularly outspoken about Catholic affairs beyond his own diocese; this did not always go down well with his fellow bishops, who, characteristically, resented "interference" from outside.

In addition to his writings in the *Miscellany,* England found time to teach in his tiny seminary, to preach and lecture incessantly, travel widely, and carry on a vast correspondence. His diocese never consisted of more than a few parishes, but the Bishop's influence extended far beyond them. He accepted a steady flow of invitations to speak to Protestant congregations and frequently delivered sermons in three different non-Catholic churches in one day. He gave hundreds of public lectures, often on the basic compatibility of the Catholic religion and American democracy, and was quick to respond publicly to attacks on the patriotism of his coreligionists.

Our fellow-citizens have been misled in our regard [he told one audience]. It requires patience, kindness, candor, and the friendly communication of truth on our part to gain their affections. We have not exhibited those who have assailed us in false and odious colors. We have not gathered up the calumnies of which the old world has grown ashamed, to cast against them in the new. We have never imputed to them disaffection to our State and National institutions and hostility to our civil liberties that we may excite suspicion and hatred against their persons and their creed. We never sought under the pretext of patriotism to prevent the naturali-

zation of their kindred, that we might deprive them of the just
weight of their numbers, and keep them in helotage and degra-
dation.

England's most notable address, delivered only one month
after he received his own citizenship papers, was given to a
joint session of Congress. In it he argued that the Catholic
Church was not committed to any one form of civil government and stated that Catholics could be good citizens under
any government which respected human rights. "You have
no power to interfere with my religious rights," he told the
legislators. "The tribunal of the Church has no power to interfere with my civil rights." He added, more pointedly, "I
would not allow to the Pope, or to any Bishop of our Church,
outside this Union, the smallest interference with the humblest
vote at our most insignificant ballot box." The Congress responded with thunderous applause.

Before he had celebrated his silver jubilee as a bishop, John
England was exhausted. On his deathbed, in 1842, he delivered
his last oration to the clergy gathered around him, pleading
with them to carry on the work of reconciliation that he had
begun. Without any additional honors from the Church, he
died simply as the Bishop of what he himself, with only slight
exaggeration, once described as the poorest diocese in Christendom.

His successor, a mediocre churchman, could not be counted
among his admirers. The pattern and pace Bishop England
had set for Charleston were immediately changed. Soon even
the *United States Catholic Miscellany* ceased to mention his
name. It was not until a later generation of scholars began
to dig into the history of American Catholicism that his story
was told. As Peter Guilday, one of his biographers, suggested,
had he lived longer "he might have prevented much of the
animosity toward a Church of which he was then the honor
and the pride."

When he first arrived in Charleston, England urged Maréchal, the official leader of the American hierarchy, to get the
bishops as a body to settle on a policy for all the dioceses
regarding the trustee problem. Maréchal loftily ignored the

suggestion. Instead, he turned to Rome where he found his solution by persuading the Pope, Pius VII, to send an admonition to the American hierarchy about the dissension in the American Church. In his letter the Pontiff set down some general rules which should govern the control of ecclesiastical property. For trustees to override the decisions of their Bishop (as had happened in Philadelphia when an excommunicated priest was accepted by the trustees of St. Mary's Church as their pastor) amounted to a usurpation of the Bishop's rights, the Pontiff declared. The American hierarchy was enjoined to draw up regulations on the ownership and maintenance of Church property. Such rules had to provide that all property acquired in the future would be held in the name of the Bishop of the place. The church buildings could not be blessed until such an arrangement was made.

The Pope's intervention settled the theoretical question once and for all. Yet there was strong resistance to putting the papal decree into effect, especially in Philadelphia, where the issue was brought to the civil courts. But within a few years the Vatican policy was universally accepted and the present system of episcopal control over all diocesan property was firmly established.

The bitter controversy had one unfortunate lasting effect. For generations thereafter every proposal to enlarge the role of the laity in ecclesiastical affairs was rejected out of hand, mainly because of the American Church's unhappy early experience with lay trusteeism. Later bishops, recalling what happened in the nineteenth century, were generally agreed that laymen could not be trusted with such matters, nor did they feel any obligation to issue financial reports on their own stewardship of Church property.

The trustee controversy unquestionably caused bitter divisions within the Church, but soon enough American Catholics were reunited by a threat from outside, for, with a spectacular increase in immigration, feelings against the Irish escalated rapidly among native-born Americans and were quickly extended to all Catholics. The era of good will following the Revolution had definitely come to an end. The Catholic presence in America was now so marked that rumors about a papist take-over again became credible. Anti-Catholic preachers and agitators found it possible to get a wide hearing for almost any charge they could invent, however wild, and some of them were wildly inventive indeed.

Life in America was changing rapidly and older settlers did not like the way things were going. They resented the heightened tensions in the cities, the spreading squalor of lower-class neighborhoods, and what they took to be a lamentable decline in morals. Resentments were focused particularly on the hard-drinking, raucous Irish, who still had a great deal to learn about urban amenities. In addition to their offensive manners, these newly arrived immigrants represented a serious economic threat to native-born workers by their willingness to work for coolie wages. Since the Irish were practically all Catholics, it was easy enough to transfer antipathy toward them into a crusade against the Church with which they were conspicuously identified.

The first serious outburst took place on Monday evening, August 11, 1834, in Charlestown, Massachusetts, a town on the Charles River, facing Boston. After weeks of rising tension in the area, a nativist crowd gathered at the Ursuline Convent there to shout abusive remarks at the nuns. (In picking this symbol of Catholicism, the leaders had chosen oddly since the pupils of the nuns were almost all Protestant children from wealthy upper-class families.) The nuns were frightened, but their Mother Superior summoned the courage to come out and beg the crowd to disperse. Her presence only increased the fury of the demonstrators. The Superior then foolishly tried bravado. "The Bishop has twenty thousand Irishmen at his command in Boston," she shouted to the crowd. Such a threat was not only injudicious but empty. There probably were not that many Irish males in the city at the time, even if, most improbably, the Bishop were really imprudent enough to order them into battle.

The only effect the nun's words actually had was to turn the crowd into a mob. When, on signal, the leaders of the demonstration ignited several barrels of tar in an adjoining field, the excitement grew. At midnight a group of about fifty men entered the convent, as the sisters, now thoroughly intimidated, led their sixty pupils to safety by a rear entrance.

The invaders then set fire to the convent and a farmhouse on the nuns' property. As the buildings went up in flames, hundreds of frenzied people clapped and cheered to celebrate their costless victory.

Later, eight men involved in the incident were charged with arson. At their trial seven of the eight were acquitted and the eighth was quickly pardoned after a group of prominent Catholic Bostonians, in the hope of effecting a reconciliation with their fellow citizens, signed a petition requesting clemency. Reconciliation, in the atmosphere that had grown up, was not to be so easily achieved, however. After the burning of the convent brought anti-Catholicism out into the open, it became clear that the arsonists in Charlestown had thousands of staunch supporters across the land. Soon enough, anti-Catholicism became a favorite theme in letters to the newspapers, on the political stump, and in speeches and public lectures throughout the country.

The ugly mood of America which emerged from the shadows after the Charlestown incident insured the success, five years later, of *Awful Disclosures,* a lurid account of life in a Montreal convent supposedly written by a former nun. The book was later described, quite accurately, as the *Uncle Tom's Cabin* of the nativist movement. *Awful Disclosures* went through twenty printings, sold an unprecedented 300,000 copies, and was kept in print long after its author had been exposed as a consummate liar.

The book was purportedly the work of a young woman named Maria Monk who claimed she had attended a convent school in Montreal, had been converted to Catholicism while there, and had then been cajoled into taking the veil. As a novice, she said, she was told to obey every order given to her by a priest. She soon learned, she claimed, that such obedience meant she was expected to engage in "criminal intercourse" with members of the clergy, as all the younger sisters were required to do. Those who refused were summarily murdered and their bodies carefully disposed of. The babies resulting from the unholy union of priests and nuns were baptized as soon as they were born, immediately dispatched to heaven, and then secretly buried in the convent basement. She herself, she wrote, escaped from the place in order to save the life of the child she was carrying while the book was in preparation.

Maria became an overnight celebrity. Under the auspices of a ministerial group, she told her story again and again to audiences across the country and was widely hailed as a heroine.

It was the girl's own mother who finally exposed her. The mother testified that Maria had not attended the Montreal convent as a pupil nor had she ever entered it as a nun. She had, rather, been the inmate of a Catholic home for delinquents which she ran away from, with the help of a boyfriend, who was probably the father of her child.

That might have been the end of the Maria Monk affair, but a number of diehards simply chose to ignore the testimony of the girl's mother and continued to circulate her book as definite "proof" of what was really going on behind convent walls. When Maria became pregnant a second time, one religious journal insisted that, again, she was a victim of priestly infamy; the Jesuits, the journal claimed, had arranged for this latest seduction in the belief that another pregnancy would cast final doubt on her story. But Maria found few supporters as staunch as this after her mother's testimony, and she rapidly disappeared from the limelight. Years later, after being arrested for pickpocketing in a brothel, she was sentenced to prison, where she died.

Even after Maria's death her *Awful Disclosures* continued to be circulated throughout the United States. The book was revived briefly during John F. Kennedy's presidential campaign in 1960, but by that time Americans had become too sophisticated to be taken in by it, even in areas where anti-Catholicism was still thriving and was again at a feverish pitch.

The most violent incident in the nativists' battle for America took place in 1843. The nominal cause was the decision by the school board of Philadelphia to honor the request of Bishop Francis Kenrick to allow Catholic children in the public schools to read the (Catholic) Douay rather than the (Protestant) King James version of the Bible in class. The Bishop had also asked that Catholic children be dismissed from religious instruction, which of course was based on Protestant teaching. The nativists claimed that the Bishop's request amounted to interference in political affairs by a "foreign prelate" and foreshadowed more outrageous demands to come. A massive protest meeting based on this idea was held in Independence Square to protest the change in school policy.

In May 1844, a nativist group called for a second protest meeting, this one to be held in Kensington, a suburb heavily populated with Irish workingmen. Inevitably, the meeting ended in a brawl, and the nativists were driven back to Philadelphia by a group of tough Irish street fighters. The next day the nativists announced that a third protest meeting would be held a few nights later in the same place. This time they called upon the general public for support. They got it. The volunteers for the second charge on Kensington were a much larger force than the one which made the first attack, and the fighting was notably bloodier. One man was killed; dozens of others were injured during three days of rioting. Blocks of Irish homes were set afire and two Catholic churches were burned to the ground.

A few weeks later fighting broke out in Southwark, another Irish suburb. The pastor of the Southwark Catholic Church, with more apprehension than prudence, had stored rifles in the basement of the church—as a precaution against a possible invasion by a hostile mob, he said later. When the protesters got wind of the cache, they demanded that a search be made of the church. The searching party found no less than eighty-seven guns and stores of ammunition stashed away. The angry crowd gathered in the square outside the church refused to leave after they learned of this. Their anger grew by the minute, and finally the governor of Pennsylvania felt it necessary to send in the militia to keep order.

The state troopers stood on guard in front of the church for two days and nights. Then someone in the crowd fired upon them with a cannon. When the troopers returned the fire, a full-scale riot broke out. For several hours the battle continued between the militia and the angry crowd in the square, while other groups of nativists went up and down the streets seeking out Irishmen. Hundreds of Irish families, fearing for their lives, fled hurriedly from the city. Priests and nuns went into hiding. In all, thirteen persons were killed and more than fifty were wounded before order was established.

The news of what had happened in Philadelphia was enough to cool the fervor of many of the nativists' less militant supporters. But the movement survived. There was no falling off of nativist societies, publications, and propaganda throughout the next decade. Anti-Catholic books appeared by the dozen and "exposures" of the Pope's plans for America became a publishing staple, keeping the old legends and hostilities alive. A favorite charge was that the Papacy, planning to take over the Midwest and West, was the guiding force behind the growing movement toward the frontier.

In 1854, the nativist movement, turning to politics, organized the American Party—or the Know-Nothings, as the party was popularly dubbed by reason of its members' habit of saying "I know nothing" when inquiries were made about their activities. The American Party enjoyed a remarkable early success, though its hour of glory turned out to be brief. In the early 1850s it put about seventy-five members in Congress, all pledged to save the Republic from the Pope and his followers. By 1860, however, political life had taken another turn, and the party found itself abruptly powerless.

The cause for which it stood, though, remained vigorous for years. There were sporadic outbursts of violence between Know-Nothings and Catholics in New York, Philadelphia, and other cities, right up to the Civil War.

The persistent tension between Catholics and nativists was particularly exacerbated by an ill-timed visit to the United States of one Archbishop Cajetan Bedini in 1853. Bedini, an Italian then serving as Papal Nuncio to Brazil, had been sent by the Holy See to report on the condition of the American Church and to settle certain difficulties the clergy were having with the immigrants still pouring in. He was also asked to sound out the possibilities of establishing a papal nunciature in Washington.

Protests against his presence in the country began almost at once. Everywhere Bedini went there were inflammatory letters in the press and in some places angry demonstrations on the streets. In Cincinnati the prelate was burned in effigy for the edification of a large crowd gathered to protest his presence in their city, and after fighting broke out following a similar meeting in Philadelphia, policemen fired on the demonstrators, seriously injuring some. In New York, Bedini was threatened with assassination. In Washington, Congress solemnly debated about what his real purposes were and finally concluded that they were precisely what he said they were; but this did not quiet the attacks on him. An Italian ex-priest who had turned radical claimed, on a very skimpy basis, that Bedini had earlier been responsible for the execution of a group of socialists in Bologna. This aroused the special fury of American social reformers.

The American bishops had not invited the hapless prelate to their country, but after he arrived they had accepted him with the courtesy due a representative of the Pope. Not one American bishop, however, came to his defense publicly during his turbulent stay. When he was secretly put aboard his steamer and had sailed out of New York harbor, almost to a man the bishops sighed with relief. His visitation had made at least one thing clear to them: the United States was not ready for a papal nuncio and probably never would be.

In Rome, Bedini filed a lengthy report on Catholicism in America. It was not overwhelmingly favorable by any means. He found that the Irish priests were deeply devoted to their parishioners and in turn were venerated by the people. However, the Irish clergy were poorly educated, he noted, and tended to be greedy for property and position; the better-educated German priests were several cuts above them; most of the French priests were engaged in seminary education, which they did well; there were very few Italians among the clergy. The churches in America were poorly decorated but were generally well administered, though the Archbishop singled out a few members of the hierarchy for some gentle criticism on this score. The charge bruited about in European clerical circles that American priests were an immoral lot was simply not true: he found only a few cases of clerics who were no better than they should be. The pioneering religious orders of teaching nuns and brothers in the States had to work under severe handicaps, and he found them altogether admirable.

In spite of his experiences with protesters, Bedini favored setting up a nunciature in Washington, at least on a temporary basis. One of the nuncio's main tasks, he suggested, would be to reply to the fantastic lies being circulated in America about the Pope and the Church.

Unfortunately, he reported, the only Catholics most Americans had contact with were poor, ignorant, lower-class Irishmen. This explained to a great extent the widespread antipathy to Catholicism. Very few Catholics had achieved any position of importance in America. For example, there were no Catholic officers in the Army and only a few in the Navy. One Catholic, Roger Taney, was Chief Justice of the United States, but very few were established in the legal profession. Until American Catholics achieved more education and a higher social status, Bedini contended, the Church in America would be seriously handicapped and its members would continue to suffer discrimination.

There were at the time of his visit less than two million Catholics in the United States, or one for roughly every eleven Americans. Of the twenty-two million Protestants, only about five million were actually church members, and they were divided into numerous sects, which he thought were unlikely to draw many Catholics into their ranks. Yet he predicted that the fanaticism of many Protestants was such that Catholics would probably suffer social disabilities for some time to come.

The two million Catholics Archbishop Bedini counted were still heavily concentrated on the Eastern Seaboard, but smaller groups were scattered throughout the country. By 1850 there were three bishoprics on the West Coast. The Bardstown, Kentucky, diocese founded in Carroll's day by the intrepid Bishop Flaget had been divided and subdivided as the nation moved westward. Life on the frontier was much different than in the turbulent cities of the East: more difficult, harsher perhaps, but actually a great deal more tranquil.

Because of the tendency of the Irish to stay in the cities where they first landed—which was due above all to their financial inability to move on—the number of Catholics was comparatively small among those who ventured into the new states, which were once French and Spanish mission territories. But there were enough of them to lay the American foundations for what would later be such thriving Catholic sees as Chicago, Cincinnati, Saint Louis, Cleveland, Los Angeles, and San Francisco.

The pioneering French priests who came after Bishop Flaget were generally zealous, hardworking missionaries, strengthened by poverty and hardship. (Few of the troublemaking clerical adventurers who made life difficult for the Eastern bishops were willing to brave the uncertainties of life out West.) The nuns who served in the backwoods had to forego many of the niceties of convent life, but they did what was to be done, with small assistance from outsiders, and set a tradition of hard work, simplicity, and directness that would last a long time. As their orders grew in number, they established schools equal to those in the East, as well as hospitals, orphanages, and houses of prayer.

By 1860 there were forty-three dioceses and two lesser territorial divisions in the United States, served by forty-five bishops and slightly more than 2000 priests. In the Middle West parishes multiplied rapidly and in many places there were serious attempts to build a school for each of them, following the German tradition.

German Catholics were the backbone of early Middlewestern Catholicism, particularly in Saint Louis, Cincinnati, and Milwaukee. Most of the Germans came from the Rhineland and brought their priests with them. They generally stayed to themselves, living within their own cultural orbit, speaking their native language, and transporting to their new homeland a bucolic, almost monastic piety which was notably different from the devotional patterns being developed among the urbanized masses in the East. Typically, the Germans put more emphasis on the intellectual aspects of their religion than the unlettered Irish. They supported four German-language periodicals of their own. Their parishes carried on the tradition of Rhineland Catholicism, and their religious services, in contrast to the hurried Masses and sentimental pious exercises favored by the Irish, were stately and richly liturgical in spirit.

Though few if any of the Germans were really prosperous, they were never as desperately poor as the Irish, either in the old country or the new. In coming to America, more often than not they had been escaping militarism rather than hunger.

* rustic: pastoral

Many of them arrived as experienced farmers or skilled workmen and quickly settled down to till the rich soil of mid-America or serve the needs of its cities, towns, and villages, with persistence, energy, thrift, and the kind of industry that their Calvinist fellow citizens could admire. Archbishop Bedini had criticized them for being too nationalistic, but because they were not crowded into the cities, their persistent pride in the *Vaterland* was never so widely exposed that it aroused the nativist furies Irish clannishness unleashed.

German Catholicism, then, grew much more tranquilly in its Middlewestern stronghold than its explosive Gaelic counterpart in the East. Over the years, among other monuments, it produced the thriving Saint John's Abbey in Minnesota, which would grow to be the largest Benedictine monastery in the world; hundreds of well-run parishes and schools; and a dozen religious orders of men and women who maintained the schools and other Catholic institutions the pioneers established.

The Germans, however, were smaller in number (most German immigrants were Lutherans), less obvious in their scattered rural and small-town enclaves, and more withdrawn from the mainstream of American society than their Irish co-religionists. Consequently, it was probably inevitable that the Catholicism of the Eastern Seaboard should set the tone and shape the more lasting image of the Catholic Church in the United States.

CHAPTER THREE

A PEOPLE OF PEOPLES

In the years between the Civil War and the First World War, the Church in America became a significant force not only in the United States but within worldwide Catholicism. Immigration rarely let up, and the number of Catholics increased with every boatload of new arrivals. By 1880 there were six million in the United States; thirty-five years later that figure had grown to about fifteen million.

These new Americans came from all the old Catholic nations of Europe. More than a million Poles and a comparable number of Italians were in the New World by the time the Great War broke out in Europe. Over the years millions more —Frenchmen, Spaniards, Germans, Dutchmen, Austrians, Czechs, Hungarians, Lithuanians, and other Catholics from Eastern Europe—had been added to the prolific Irish, who continued to dominate the Church in America though they were soon outnumbered by the later arrivals. The clergy grew proportionately. Almost 20,000 priests and several times that many nuns were serving the Church in America at the outbreak of the First World War.

Only a decade after the United States officially ceased to be treated as a missionary territory by the Vatican (1908), the American Church was among the two or three most prosperous centers of Catholicism in the world. Rome still held to its theoretical reservations about the separation of Church and state, but even the most reactionary Curial cardinals could not deny that Catholicism had waxed strong and healthy under the protection of the American Constitution.

The English priest-historian Philip Hughes later wrote that "by 1790, outside the States of the Church and the new United States of America there was not a single country in the world where the Catholic religion was free to live fully its own life, and not a single country where there seemed any prospect but of further enslavement and gradual emasculation." As it actually turned out, the Church in Europe later fared better than anyone thought was possible at the beginning of the nineteenth century, but nowhere was there a richer fulfillment of hopes than in America.

To be sure, even in America there were disappointments and setbacks, but no more than might have been expected. On its pilgrimage through history, the Church is always affected by the ups and downs of the temporal order, and Catholicism in America was never exempted from the turmoil outside or recurrent dissension within its own ranks. Neither was ever lacking for very long.

The Church could not, for example, escape the shattering

experiences of the Civil War which divided the young nation, setting American against American for four bitter years. During those years the ties uniting Northern and Southern Catholics were severed, as were so many other bonds. The American bishops, North and South, split on the issues. Catholics served in both armies, and priest-chaplains and nun-nurses went forth to meet the human needs of both sides. Though individual Catholics of every rank were ardent partisans throughout the war, the Church itself remained above the fray, favoring neither one side nor the other.

Many in the generations of Americans who followed would look back on the Civil War as a struggle over a single moral issue, human slavery. When the war began, however, the issues seemed typically political, involving sectional and economic interests, with neither side having an overriding claim on the Christian conscience because of the moral character of its aims. But even if slavery had been the only issue, Catholic teaching at the time would have been too ambiguous to put all Catholics in the same camp.

The Church had not gone on record as condemning slavery as per se evil, and the "peculiar institution" was ardently defended by some of the leading Catholics of the day. The Jesuits in Maryland owned slaves, as did the Ursuline nuns in New Orleans and some members of the hierarchy, and there were no objections raised by ecclesiastical authorities. Conscientious laymen among the slaveholders, knowing this, had some reason to believe that the Church actually favored the institution or at least was indifferent. The few Catholic theologians who addressed themselves to the subject had concluded, in their characteristically bloodless fashion, that while slavery was not desirable it was possible to support it without denying basic Christian teachings on human dignity and the brotherhood of man.

The slave as man, these theologians taught, was the spiritual equal of all other men, beloved by God and redeemed by Christ. He had a right to religious instruction and to the Sacraments and other means of salvation. His marriage was no less sacred or indissoluble than that of his master. Slaves had the same claim on life as other men; they were not to be treated cruelly or overworked. They had the same obligation to the moral law as others. In their case this meant that they were obliged to serve their owners, in keeping with the teaching of Saint Peter, "Servants, obey your masters." As a man, then, the slave was no different from his master. But as long as slavery was upheld by the law, the slave was also legally bound to his owner by ties of mutual obligation—the master was required to respect the basic human and religious rights of the slave and provide for his modest spiritual and physical needs; the slave for his part was required to work humbly and obediently according to his lowly state in life.

The theologians had to agree that in the beginning no man was the master of others and that slavery was a human institution neither divinely ordained nor decreed by the natural order. In accordance with Catholic teaching, they could not attribute the system to any innate racial inferiority. They got around that difficulty by invoking the doctrine of evil: slavery was the product of human sinfulness. It should not be extended or encouraged. Nevertheless, once solidly established, as in the United States, it should probably be accepted as an unfortunate *fait accompli*. Efforts to extirpate it had to be judged by the new evils its abolition would create. If the results were war, the dislocation of the economy, political upheaval, and the pauperization of large numbers of people, including former slaves, the moral scales were tilted in the other direction: it was better to tolerate known evils than to court new ones.

The theologians' argument, coolly algebraic in the Scholastic fashion, took little account of the inner feelings and drives of the slaves themselves. But it was convincing to those who grew up with the system of thought it invoked and consoling to those who profited by the availability of slave labor.

Rome remained generally aloof from the American controversy, though in 1839 Pope Gregory XVI had flatly condemned the slave trade. The Pontiff adjured "all believers in Christ" thereafter not to "molest Indians, Negroes, or other men of this sort" or to "exercise that inhuman trade by which Negroes, as if they were not men but mere animals, are . . . bought, sold, and sometimes doomed to the most exhausting labors." The papal words, unequivocal though they were, were not applied to American domestic slavery. Even Bishop England held that the Pope's condemnation was limited to the enslavement of free men and the cruel treatment of those already enslaved. England favored the South, but he did not approve of slavery. Yet, following the logic of the theologians, he regarded its abolition as basically a sectional issue.

There were also social factors helping to mute the Catholic teaching on human dignity as the slavery question came to the fore. American Catholic opinion at the time was being formed in the slave-owning states, where the best-educated Catholics resided. These opinion molders, according to Orestes Brownson, the leading Catholic journalist of the time, were "intensely Southern in their sympathies" and "bitterly hostile to New England, or to Yankees." Brownson claimed that through them the Southern attitude was "diffused through the entire Catholic body even in the New England States themselves."

That may have been true, but Catholics in the North had their own reasons for remaining aloof from the abolitionists' cause. For one thing, abolition and anti-Catholicism were part of the same crusade for many; the antislavery movement was frequently led by the same persons who had fomented ill will and discrimination against Catholic immigrants. Again, the Democratic Party, which had become the national spokesman for the South, was also the favored party of the impoverished Catholics of the Northeast. These factors certainly counted in shaping the attitude of the Catholic masses. But the basic economic facts of life and the preoccupation of the Irish with their own problems were probably more important than either.

The Irish in the North were generally opposed to abolition. As William V. Shannon put it in *The American Irish*, "As the newest and least secure members of society [they] were the most rigid and least generous in extending their sympathy to a submerged minority like the Negroes whose circumstances they scarcely comprehended." The economic rivalry between white workingmen and their black neighbors in the cities of the North did not wholly explain the Irish feeling. The Irish may have been even more nettled by the idea that while their problems were being neglected by the powerful men in the Northern cities, the same leaders favored an all-out attack on injustices hundreds of miles away.

One prominent Irishman, Congressman Michael Walsh of

instigated

New York, was cheered in 1854 when he proclaimed in the House of Representatives: "The only difference between the Negro slave in the South and the wage slave of the North is that the one has a master without asking for him, and the other has to beg for the privilege of being a slave." When the greatly admired liberator, Daniel O'Connell, sent word to America urging the Irish overseas to support the cause of the abolitionists, his advice was deeply resented by the Irish-born leaders.

After Fort Sumter, the Irish rallied in great numbers to Lincoln's call for volunteers, but they made it clear that they were moved by a simple desire to keep the nation united. A popular jingle expressed their general attitude:

> *To the tenets of Douglas we tenderly cling,*
> *Warm hearts to the cause of our country we bring;*
> *To the flag we are pledged—all its foes we abhor—*
> *And we ain't for the "nigger" but we are for the war.*

In that spirit the Irish Catholics cheerfully went off to battle, and a number of "Irish" regiments fought bravely throughout the hostilities.

After the Emancipation Proclamation, however, there was widespread grumbling in the Irish community. Irish leaders charged that Lincoln had turned a war to save the Union into a war to save the black race. By this time the Irish—with more than a little justification—were feeling extremely sorry for themselves. A principal source of their grievance was that they were bearing more than their share of the burden. The losses in the Irish regiments were high, and many families had lost fathers and brothers on the battlefield. In 1863, resentments were intensified by the proclamation of a new draft law.

According to the law, a man whose name was picked for the draft, after paying three hundred dollars, could supply a substitute to serve in his place. Few Irishmen were able to put their hands on such a princely sum and they resented the *de facto* discrimination against them. In addition, in New York City, due to an official blunder in assigning quotas to different wards, a disproportionate number of Irishmen were picked for the draft. Celtic tempers flared when it was announced, on a Saturday in July 1863, that the majority of the new draftees would be Irish.

On the following Monday morning thousands of workingmen protested by staying away from work. Later in the day they began to cluster in angry groups on the East Side of the city. Their fury was also fired by resentment of the Negro workers who had been brought into New York a few weeks earlier to break a strike Irish leaders had called among dock workers. All the elements for an outburst of mob feeling were present on that hot summer day when the police—led by a man named John Kennedy—went out to break up the grumbling crowds who had gathered on the streets.

The crowd, easily ignited into action, turned on Kennedy. He and his outnumbered men soon retreated. Then began a shameful rampage directed against the black citizens of New York. It lasted four days. Negroes who ventured out on the streets were indiscriminately beaten by Irish mobs and several were hanged. An orphan asylum for Negro children was burned. Seen in even the kindliest light, "it was a classic example of the poor in their misery venting their fury on other poor who were even worse off," as Shannon put it.

John Hughes, the Archbishop of New York, finally succeeded in calming the mob when he addressed a great number of them in front of his home on the fourth day of the rioting. Taking their cue from the Archbishop, the priests of the city went out on the streets in an attempt to bring the Irish to their senses and restore order.

Later, *Harper's* magazine, a powerful voice of the Protestant establishment, generously pointed out that not only the rioters but some of the heroes in the disgraceful affair were Irish. *Harper's* cited members of the police force who held back the mob, a few Irishmen who braved popular disapproval by helping to rescue Negro orphans, and especially Archbishop Hughes and his clergy. ". . . the Roman Catholic priesthood to a man used their influence on the side of the law," the magazine stated. Nevertheless, the draft law riot remains the most disgraceful incident in American Catholic history.

The Civil War marked the end of large-scale discrimination against Catholics in America. For four years Catholic and non-Catholic got to know each other by living in the same barracks, and even more of the old prejudice was dissolved on the battlefields. After the war was over, the full-scale attacks on the Catholic faith which had been commonplace in the earlier decades came to an end. The service rendered to the wounded by nursing Daughters of Charity, Sisters of Mercy, and other nuns did not go unappreciated, and the favorable impression Catholic military chaplains had made on the troops, North and South, changed the impression many previously had of the Roman clergy. The "No Irish Need Apply" signs which had once been posted outside employment offices in Boston, Philadelphia, and New York gradually disappeared.

Through the American Protective Association and similar groups, anti-Catholicism remained a significant force in the nation for decades to come, but after 1865 it existed mainly in isolated pockets of rural and small-town bigotry or was transformed into the sort of genteel snobbism that kept Catholics ineligible for some social clubs, private schools and colleges, executive positions, and boards of directors. It no longer limited ordinary employment opportunities or led to street violence.

In the meantime, Catholics, the Irish particularly, were learning how to use political power. The peasants who had landed penniless and ignorant in New York or Boston a few decades earlier had become solidly urbanized. In the process they had developed a formidable base of power through ward politics, the control of city hall, and a strong voice in the Democratic Party. The now classical "Irish pol"—immortalized in Edwin O'Connor's fictional Skeffington—became a powerful figure in the nation, the protector of his people and their acknowledged leader. Through his office, baskets of food were distributed to the poor, jobs were found for the young, and Catholic interests gained potent support in state legislatures and the halls of Congress. In return, the recipients of the politician's largesse were expected to remain loyal to their benefactor's party, close their eyes to graft and corruption, and above all vote according to instruction in every election. Tammany became a power to reckon with in New York, and similar political machines were established in Boston and other cities.

There is an ironic twist in the fact that as America changed to an urban society the Roman Catholic Church, which was once considered even by such men as Thomas Jefferson to be the most hopelessly "un-American" institution in the land, became a force for the Americanization of millions of new citizens. After they arrived, the confused immigrants often found the parish church their only familiar landmark, the single public place where they really felt at home.

The American Catholic clergy, with some exceptions, took easily to the new country and transmitted their enthusiasm for its institutions to their people. The clergy naturally emphasized the theological foundations of American life, while playing down the distinctly Protestant character of the nation's religious tradition. Before long the new immigrant had no trouble in linking his Catholic beliefs to his patriotic loyalty. Protestant and agnostic preachers might thunder against the incompatibility of Catholicism and Americanism, but to those who learned about their adopted country in church halls or parish schools, devotion to the Church and love of country were seen as two sides of the same coin.

The priest was usually the best-educated person in the Catholic community. People turned to him not only for spiritual guidance but for direction about how to cope with the baffling social, economic, and political forces they were required to face. Serious anti-clericalism under such circumstances was practically nonexistent. The clergy collaborated with local politicians in meeting the immediate economic needs of their parishioners; they kept families together when no jobs were available, settled disputes, insisted on the importance of education for the young, and provided a forum for the airing of public issues. In city neighborhoods the Catholic parish was frequently a center of social life, political dialogue, and basic education in mastering the mysterious ways of life in the New World.

This dependence undoubtedly led to a less-than-healthy reliance on pastoral judgment and to undue clerical influence on civic affairs (the New York chancery office on Madison

Avenue is still known as "the powerhouse"), but it must also be credited with aiding millions to find their way into American society who might otherwise have been cut adrift. For those who were ignorant of city ways, the parish offered a school of urbanization. For those who found the mores and morals of their new home baffling, the parish established a link with a familiar system of ethics. To those ignorant of American history and tradition, the parish society or parish school frequently provided their only training in citizenship.

All this of course took place in isolation from the mainstream of American life. Inevitably the Catholic community more and more turned in upon itself, sometimes reaching levels of almost absurd sectarianism, as happened also to the Jews, the only other large non-Protestant element in the nation. In retrospect, however, it is hard to imagine what institution other than the Church could have met the need to Americanize so many millions in such a short time. If today Catholics are assimilated into American society, then much of the credit should go to the bishops and priests of the nineteenth century.

American Catholicism was thriving in the latter decades of the century, but elsewhere the future of the Church was in doubt. With Europe going through convulsions brought on by new political movements, rapid industrialization, and the rise of scientific inquiry, Catholic influence on the Continent was at a low ebb. Even more than is true today, the Church seemed out of touch with the times. It was widely regarded by the intelligentsia as an anachronism which had mysteriously survived the Reformation, the Enlightenment, the collapse of the old Catholic empires, and the rise of science. The Popes of the time, who seemed to be left-overs from the *ancien régime,* set themselves against everything modern and regularly issued sweeping anathemas from the Vatican condemning "progress," "liberalism," and almost every development in political thought, scientific advance, and theology as it came along.

It seemed to those who took such warnings seriously that the Church in Europe was forever wedded to medievalism. Catholics who still listened to their spiritual leaders were urged

*curses, denunciation

to struggle against the forces of modernity, in a (quixotic) spirit of decreed despair. Many, especially among the bourgeoisie, did just that. Millions of others, caught up in the spirit of the times or looking upon the ecclesiastical establishment as the private property of the upper classes, fell away. Some even turned passionately against the Church.

During the nineteenth century, as Pope Pius XI later confessed, the working classes in Europe were lost to the Church —a fact painfully recognized fifty years later when the priest-worker movement got under way in France.

The ideological and social struggles changing the face of Catholic Europe were not immediately felt in America, though even then the United States was widely regarded as being among the most up-to-date of nations. Yet, the American bishops were deeply concerned, for the papal encyclicals condemning "progress" and "modernity," and anathematizing the Continental versions of freedom of thought, speech, and assembly had not gone unnoted. Sharp criticisms of the Vatican's supposed antediluvian position appeared in the American press. In certain intellectual circles, as in Europe, "Rome" was more and more becoming a synonym for social and political reaction. This was certainly understandable, for when the papal condemnations were read literally, they appeared to be denouncing not only the spirit of the age but the most sacred of American institutions.

The Catholic clergy in the United States may have been privately embarrassed by such pronouncements as Pius IX's *Syllabus of Errors,* but in public they loyally came to the Pope's defense. Their argument, and the argument for generations of American Catholic apologists to come, was that the papal condemnation of free speech, freedom of conscience, and the Papacy's seemingly unalterable opposition to modernity did not apply to the United States, with its religious foundations, but were to be understood in the light of the pagan ideologies flourishing abroad. The papal denunciations of "liberalism," they insisted, had nothing to do with the Bill of Rights or the American system of government, since they were founded on altogether different, and to Catholics quite acceptable, premises.

This line of defense, however, was never very persuasive.

* idealistic to an impractical degree

Right up to the Second Vatican Council, the case against Catholicism as inescapably "un-American" was strengthened immeasurably by quotations that could be readily snatched from the *Syllabus* and similar papal pronouncements of the nineteenth century. They were unearthed again and again by polemicists exposing the "true nature" of Catholicism. Paul Blanshard, whose thickly documented books on Catholicism and American freedom became best sellers in the 1950s, was the last in a procession of publicists who relied heavily on them.

Interestingly enough, only the most church-centered Catholics had any knowledge of such compromising documents when they originally appeared. It never even dawned on ordinary parishioners that there could be a conflict in their twin loyalty to the Church and to the United States, and their pastors certainly gave them no reason to believe otherwise.

Al Smith, who was a youth in the 1890s, was typical. When he announced for the presidency in 1927, Smith was confronted with statements from papal encyclicals that appeared to rule out any loyally Catholic candidate, no matter who. This "evidence" of his own patent unsuitability for the White House took the New Yorker by surprise. Never in his life had he even heard of such things, he told the press, nor had any of his Catholic friends. John F. Kennedy, three decades later, was better informed but he made no serious attempt either to defend the statements or refute them.

In the 1860s, however, the statements were full of meaning not only in the Vatican, which was fighting a rearguard action against the new ideas coming into vogue, but among European intellectuals who, in dealing with the Church, felt they were at war to the death with medieval obscurantism and entrenched reaction.

The authority of the Pope, not only his temporal power but his claim to spiritual leadership as well, was being attacked on all sides—by the threatening armies of the Italian *risorgimento,* by intellectuals and reformers who wanted to extend the principles of the French Revolution throughout the Continent, by agnostic proponents of the new thought, and, within the Church, by an influential group of modernist theologians. The Pope was caricatured in the press as the enemy of science, social progress, and industrial development.* The Vatican was portrayed as the last bastion of outmoded superstition and arrogant privilege left in the modern world.

The American bishops, though many of them grumbled in private about reactionary prelates abroad (as they still do), remained effortlessly loyal to Rome. To a man they rallied around the Pope as the cold war between the Church and modernity escalated. But they were generally agreed that papal denunciations were not enough and that the Church had to do something to meet the challenges being hurled at it. Thus when Pius IX summoned an ecumenical council, to open at the Vatican in December 1869, most of the Americans responded enthusiastically. The council, they believed, would set down guidelines for a genuine confrontation with the new forces at large in society, and they felt that Americans would have more to contribute than others because of their experience with a nonrevolutionary democracy.

Soon after the meeting opened, however, it became clear that the major task set for the Council Fathers would be to approve the definition of a doctrine proclaiming that when a reigning pontiff speaks *ex cathedra* on matters of faith and morals, he is infallible. This was to be the Pope's defiant reply to his enemies. The doctrine had long been widely accepted in the Church, though it was not considered binding. With a few exceptions, the Americans already believed it. Yet, for reasons of their own, most of the forty-seven prelates from the United States who went to Rome were originally opposed to proclaiming it formally; they believed that such a proclamation would be "inopportune" in the climate of the time.

Any new definition of doctrine, especially a dogma affirming a papal prerogative, they argued, would set back the work of the Church in the United States by underscoring the very aspect of Catholicism Americans found most suspect—its ultimate dependence on foreign leadership. A few also feared that some Catholics, caught up in the spirit of Ameri-

* Ironically, by the 1960s, Christian teaching was being blamed for the ecological disasters resulting from the overexploitation of the earth.

ca's growing nationalism, might be led into schism if they were called upon to magnify even further the role of Rome. Yet, after the bishops' final vote approving the definition was taken, the Americans among them submitted, one by one, and steeled themselves for the inevitable attacks on papal power they would have to face after they returned home.

They returned sooner than expected. The Council was abruptly recessed when Rome was taken over by Italian unification forces in September 1870. Pius IX, who continued to lay claim to temporal powers—a position then bolstered by elaborate theological arguments—thereupon declared himself the "prisoner of the Vatican." But the Papal States ceased to exist and the popes were stripped of all secular authority until 1929, when the tiny Vatican City was granted independent sovereignty, by agreement with Benito Mussolini.

The sudden end of the First Vatican Council left no time for the bishops to formulate their own responsibility in governing the Church. Their role remained a disputed question for almost a century. One school of thought, the majority, believed that the bishops were basically legates of the Pope, exercising spiritual authority only in his name. The other, which was barely represented in the United States and never really took hold, accepted the "collegial" theory—the idea that the Sovereign Pontiff is the head of an episcopal body embracing all the bishops of the world, who are collectively responsible for the welfare of the whole Church.

In both accounts the Pope was the undisputed Chief Pastor. The question was whether his authority existed above and apart from the college of bishops or whether it was intimately linked to that of the entire hierarchy. The former view was held by most American Catholics until the Second Vatican Council, where the latter position triumphed. As Cardinal Spellman said in voicing his opposition to "collegiality" during the Council debate, complete papal power had long gone unchallenged in American seminaries. That may have been something of an exaggeration, but between the two councils the teaching certainly shaped the Catholic Church's deferential attitude toward not only the Pope but his bureaucratic arm, the Roman Curia.

During that period, no branch of Catholicism was more steadfast in its dependence upon the Vatican than the Church in the United States. (This may have had something to do with the outsize influence of the Irish. Catholic Ireland, in its defiance of British domination, had historically accented its ties to Rome to show its contempt for the Anglican claim that the Church of Ireland was the historic successor to the church established by Saint Patrick.) The Pope's authority—exercised in isolation from the bishops—was accepted by American Catholics as virtually unlimited, and the prestige of the Vatican, at least within the Church itself, reached a new peak. The American bishops turned to Rome for the solution to almost every important problem facing them. The most petty directives from Curial bureaus were obeyed as scrupulously and uncomplainingly as if they had been handed down from Mount Sinai.

Most of the clergy were as impeccably "papalist" as their bishops, and the clerical attitude of subservience to Rome was transmitted to the laity. Though it was all right to lambaste an Alexander VI (1431–1503) or his successor, Julius II, even the mildest criticism of a reigning, or even a recently deceased, pontiff was regarded as just short of treason. Certainly no such criticism appeared in the Catholic press and none was uttered in public by any Catholic who hoped to keep his credentials as a loyal son of the Church. In the same way, bishops themselves were largely immune from public criticism, though their foibles and failings were the topic of endless private conversations.

The result was that, whatever the subway rumblings, on the surface Catholicism in the United States was extraordinarily disciplined; the Church was run with military precision and dispatch. Everyone knew what was expected of him. Once decisions were made by the proper authority, they went virtually unchallenged. As long as the system worked, a bishop had no need to account to anyone this side of Rome, and the Pope's decisions were simply beyond further discussion. *Roma locuta est, causa finita est,* applied to the most trivial matters, became an unchallenged, even unchallengeable, proposition.

Actually papal infallibility had been carefully circumscribed by the wording of the dogma defining it, but for all practical purposes, after 1870 all Vatican teachings and policies were regarded as sacrosanct. There were always a few theologians who privately took issue with papal pronouncements—as became abundantly clear at the second Council—but even the most daring of them became so expert at interpreting and reinterpreting the Roman position that their public denials were usually camouflaged as fundamental assent to papal teaching.

The Second Vatican Council, restoring older notions of freedom, diversity, and pluralistic authority within the Church, changed all that. Once again, theological controversies raged, prelates and even the Pope were freely criticized, and there were constant demands on the bishops to justify their policies. After decades of juridical tidiness the transformation was so great that the turmoil seemed more like a revolution than the restoration of an older tradition. By the mid-1960s it appeared to many detached observers that the papal system was collapsing completely. This, however, was probably not true.

During the juridical century between the two councils, the Church in America ran so smoothly that American Catholicism came to look like a model of authoritarian efficiency. It was always something less than that, but there were very few open revolts, though many personal apostasies, and not one serious heresy arose—a record of orthodoxy American ecclesiastics took great pride in.

In the light of the record, it is ironic that one of the few latter-day heresies formally specified by the Church is still known as "Americanism." From the beginning the name was a source of embarrassment to the leaders of the Church in the United States. At the end of the last century they found the controversy that swirled around it even more upsetting.

"Americanism" was deemed serious enough to warrant a papal condemnation, which leading members of the American hierarchy did their best to stop or at least to keep from being publicized, but without success. However, Leo XIII, the Pope who issued the condemnation in January 1899, was careful not to make any specific charge against the American Church, its bishops, or any identifiable groups or individuals. In his letter to Cardinal Gibbons, who was the leader of the American hierarchy, Leo merely listed a series of theological propositions which were the subject of controversy in Europe, were widely attributed to a group of American priests, the Paulist Fathers, and were popularly known as "Americanism" in France and elsewhere. Somewhat tactlessly, the Pope himself used the word in his otherwise diplomatic warning.

The Paulists, founded in 1858 by Isaac Hecker, a convert from Brook Farm transcendentalism, had quickly become an intellectual force in the American Church. Their order had broken new ground in its attempts to win converts to the faith by preaching in the contemporary idiom, publishing a highly literate journal (*The Catholic World*), and writing and lecturing on secular topics. A number of the early members, attracted by Father Hecker's open attitude toward the modern world and the American spirit, were themselves converts who had received their early foundation in non-Catholic intellectual milieux.

The Paulists as a group were better educated than most American priests, more venturesome in exploring theological themes, and more daring in adopting new apostolic techniques for the changing times. For example, they were sometimes found preaching in Protestant churches, in a period when collaboration with non-Catholics was generally frowned upon by Rome. Though the community's purpose was frankly convert-making, the spirit Hecker bequeathed to his followers was consciously ecumenical and nonjudgmental, long before these attitudes gained favor in the universal Church.

A biography of the Paulist founder, published after his death, was the immediate cause of the charges made against the order. The book—a rather dull volume written by Walter Elliot (himself a Paulist priest) and with a preface by Archbishop John Ireland of Saint Paul—went unnoticed when it first appeared in the United States. Years later a French translation appeared in Paris, with a special introduction for

French readers by a progressive young abbé named Felix Klein. Klein, an enthusiast, hailed Hecker as a model for the priesthood throughout the world by reason of his democratic spirit and positive attitude toward modern culture. In doing so, the abbé implicitly criticized most of the clergy in his own country, who still identified the fortunes of the Church with the remnants of the *ancien régime*.

The original French charges against the Paulists, and by extension against the Church in the United States, were made in a lengthy, serialized critique of Hecker's theology published in a scholarly clerical publication. It was written by Charles Maignen, a French priest of the Society of the Brothers of Saint Vincent de Paul and a sworn opponent of the clergy who were urging the French Church to come to terms with the postrevolutionary situation.

Maignen's original objections seemed to be directed more against Abbé Klein's preface than against the book itself. But as the articles went on, his denunciations of Hecker's teachings escalated. Before the critical series was completed the Frenchman had elaborated a whole set of theological errors which he attributed not only to Hecker and the Paulists but to the large group of Paulist-admirers among the American clergy, who included some prominent members of the hierarchy.

The heresies, which were quickly summed up simply as "Americanism," included the following: the exaltation of the natural over the supernatural; the idea that action is superior to contemplation; the notion that the operations of the Holy Spirit on the individual transcend the need for the Sacraments and ecclesiastical authority; and the proposal that the Church should adjust or even radically change its basic teachings in order to accommodate modern science.

These were also among the propositions later condemned by Leo XIII. Perhaps more directly at the center of the controversy was the less abstract suggestion that a model of Catholicism for the modern age could be found in the New World—an idea that actually did have some support from priests and laymen in the United States who believed that the time had come for the Church to break with the static Latin traditions of the past and adapt to the dynamic tempo of the Anglo-Saxon world. For example, in a letter to Archbishop Ireland, Monsignor Denis O'Connell, who was then widely looked upon as a leading American Catholic spokesman, urged the prelate to "force upon the [Vatican] Curia by the great triumph of Americanism that great recognition of the English-speaking people that you know is needed."

O'Connell, an ardent supporter of the American conquest of Cuba, was caught up in the jingoism of the time. But, for all the glorification of America's "manifest destiny" which he and some other Catholic priests shared with many of their fellow citizens, there was a general outcry that "religious Americanism"—the theology Maignen had attributed to Hecker and his followers and which was later condemned by the Pope—was practically nonexistent in the United States. The Paulists, indignantly denying that their founder held such views, felt that he and they had been slandered. Many of them believed strongly that American political notions should be spread throughout the world, but "Americanism" as a theology was really a "phantom heresy." Neither the Paulists nor any other significant group of American priests or bishops were hesitant about endorsing Pope Leo's teaching, though some made it clear that they resented the publicity the papal condemnation had been given by the release of the text from Rome.*

The Notre Dame historian, Father McAvoy, summed up his definitive account of the controversy by noting that at the time it would perhaps have been too much to hope that the conservative Catholic leaders of Western Europe would accept with grace the "practical, rough, and democratic notions of American Catholicism," especially when it was put forth as the model for the whole Church. But though the "Americanism" controversy was something of a tempest in a teapot, the papal condemnation had certain lasting effects. Above all, it polarized American Catholics into the conservative and liberal wings which still exist. For many years, with the memory of the "phantom heresy" in mind, Catholic scholars were hesitant to speculate seriously about the theo-

---

* The "phantom heresy" actually did have a few American adherents, the evidence indicates, but hardly enough to justify Rome's reaction.

logical significance of the American experience, lest they too run the risk of being charged with heresy.

The debate about "Americanism" was only one among a number of controversies enlivening Catholic life at the end of the nineteenth century. Though they are now generally forgotten, some of these old battles were vigorous enough to divide American Catholics, including members of the hierarchy, into contesting factions.

Probably the most consequential was a profound difference of opinion about how acculturated the American Church should become. In time it was turned into a kind of Irish-German struggle, though partisans on both sides of the argument were found in both these communities. For example, Bishop Bernard McQuaid of Rochester, a doughty, outspoken Celt, once denounced Archbishop Ireland's integrationist policies from his cathedral pulpit. McQuaid believed that the Church should not go too far in adapting to the ideal of religious tolerance. His opposition to "Americanism" as it was then understood was shared by the predominantly Irish Jesuits. In general, however, the American Irish supported the "open," assimilationist policies of Cardinal Gibbons, Archbishop Ireland, the Paulists, and the Holy Cross Fathers of the University of Notre Dame. The German clergy in general leaned in the opposite direction, though some of them too were admirers of the Gibbons-Ireland policy.

By and large, the followers of Gibbons and Ireland held that the Church should take an active part in the nation's life and collaborate with non-Catholics whenever possible. For example, some of them participated in the Parliament of Religions held at the 1893 Chicago World's Fair, braving the charge that they were thereby reducing Catholicism to the status of one more religion among many.

Archbishop Ireland, the most vocal member of the hierarchy and the most outspokenly pro-American, constantly called upon Catholics to reconcile the Church and the new age. In keeping with his open-door policy, Ireland supported Gibbons when the latter successfully prevailed upon the Vatican to withhold a condemnation of the Knights of Labor, a "secret" organization that was a forerunner of the modern labor union. It was typical of both to do everything in their power not to cut off Catholics from their fellow workers by insisting that there was a crucial difference between the anti-Catholic "secret societies" abroad and some of their counterparts in America.

As Ireland and his friends envisioned it, the parish itself should be a kind of melting pot, bringing Catholics of all nationalities into a single "American" community. But the Germans—again, by and large—believed that the different national groups would make their greatest contribution to American life by maintaining their native culture, speaking their own language, worshiping in their own churches, attending their own schools, and observing their own religious customs and traditions. Doubtless, both groups were determined to be "good Americans," but the disagreement about how that end could be achieved ran deep.

The issue was complicated by the fact that the Irish by then were dominant in the hierarchy, while the Germans, who felt that they had a richer culture and a much more intellectual grasp of the faith, were convinced that they were being denied their proper share of influence in the American Church.

The argument between the two groups had simmered for years when it was brought to a boil by the emergence of what was later known as Cahenslyism. Peter Paul Cahensly, who gave the movement its name, was a devout layman who headed a group in Germany called the Saint Rafael Society. Members of the society were convinced that the Irish-led Church in America was not meeting the needs of German immigrants and were determined to do something about it. At a meeting held in Lucerne, Switzerland, in 1890, deciding to bring their case to the Holy See itself, they authorized Cahensly to draft a list of proposals for the authorities in Rome. Among other things, the Cahensly memorial urged that the American hierarchy be ordered to set up separate parishes in which the German language would be spoken; priests from abroad should be given equal rights with the native-born American clergy; missionary seminaries should be established in Europe to train priests for work among American immigrants; and finally the American hierarchy should be restructured so that every national group in the United States would be represented by bishops "of the same origin" who would "protect their interests."

When word of the Lucerne proposals leaked out, a number of Irishmen in the American hierarchy were indignant. Cahensly's criticism was quickly branded as officious interference in the affairs of the American Church. Ireland spoke contemptuously of "foreign intrigue" and wilful divisiveness by troublemaking outsiders. Gibbons agreed. Both prelates claimed that German Catholics were eminently satisfied with the leadership provided by their present bishops, but this turned out to be less than accurate. After the controversy erupted, German-American leaders rallied around the Cahensly banner and pressed for their own parishes and schools—and similar demands were soon made by the Poles, Lithuanians, Italians, and other groups.

Rome never acted formally on the Lucerne Memorial. However, as the years went on, more Germans and a few other non-Irishmen were brought into the American hierarchy, the number of ethnic parishes multiplied, and distinctively Polish, Italian, French, and other national enclaves continued to grow within American Catholicism. These groups had their own clergy, their own press, their own schools, and dozens of fraternal and service organizations, such as the Polish Roman Catholic Union and the Sons of Italy, whose interests were partially religious, partially cultural.

For years the "American" parish was called the "Irish" parish—an indication of the persistent domination of the Irish in mainstream Catholic life.

CHAPTER FOUR

MORE STATELY MANSIONS

The Church, which began with neither wealth nor power in the eighteenth century, became prosperous and powerful in the twentieth. By World War I, American Catholicism had entered a "triumphalist" phase and it continued until the shakeup following the Second Vatican Council. It was a period of tremendous expansion, extraordinary stability, and general optimism.

The brick-and-mortar bishops were in their heyday, and in the larger cities of America, Catholic affluence was almost flaunted. New parish churches made up in sheer opulence and size for what they lacked in artistic distinction; the rectories attached to them were all too often the most commodious homes in the neighborhoods they served; parish schools, private high schools and academies, seminaries, and colleges and universities mushroomed.

The religious orders of men and women grew spectacularly, and the American countryside was dotted with their spacious motherhouses and towering monasteries. Luxuriant houses of study for seminarians and young nuns were set down in sylvan isolation from the tawdry tenements where many of their students had grown up. New hospitals, orphanages, and homes for the aged were established by the hundreds, and old ones were enlarged and refurbished. In the exurbias of the nation, the lovely estates the old rich were giving up, due to the shortage of servants and increases in personal income taxes, were bought up and turned into convents, novitiates, and retreat houses for the laity.

New organizational techniques were developed enabling the clergy and religious to carry out their work with enviable efficiency. Many bishops, religious superiors, and even simple pastors gained reputations for their business acumen. Even in the most exalted financial circles, members of the hierarchy were respected as the administrators of vast holdings. The clergy were treated deferentially, sometimes fearfully, by local political establishments, the general press, and the movers of society.

Catholics still remained few and far between in the upper reaches of American life, but many of them were visibly coming up in the world. Though there were only a handful of millionaires in their number, the corporate wealth of the Church was no longer negligible. With the emergence of the lace-curtain Irish, the embourgeoisment of the Germans of the Middle West, and the growing prosperity of the Italians, the Church's financial picture was bright. Real estate and portfolio advisers became the most important of the bishops' lay counselors. There was little hesitancy about planning for an even rosier future. Administrators could count on steady growth when building plans were made or massive debts were contracted.

Of course this was not the pattern everywhere. In parts of the country where the Catholic population remained small or impoverished—notably in the South, the Southwest, and parts of the rural Midwest—the Church was necessarily modest in its expenditures. Even within the great citadels of Catholicism, in New York or Chicago for example, there were "poor parishes" whose priests and nuns shared the plainness of the parishioners' lives. For, while Catholicism as a whole was no longer poor, the American Church never actually abandoned the poor. Every urban slum had its parish church and usually a parochial school as well. But such was the mentality of the average Catholic that the priests assigned to the inner city were looked upon with a kind of admiring pity. When one of them was transferred to a "better" parish, the move was taken to be a promotion or a reward for time idealistically put in with the hidden poor.

It is extremely doubtful that respect for Catholic teaching kept pace with the increase of Catholic social prestige. But sheer power calls for some kind of recognition, and, with the Catholic population growing every year, Catholicism gained stature as a formidable political and social force, if not as a system of religious thought.

Politicians, concerned about the "Catholic vote," went out of their way to curry the Church's favor. Few of them outside the South were ready to oppose a measure that had strong hierarchical support. The general press added to the legend of Catholic solidarity by dealing gingerly with Church affairs, hushing up scandals, and going out of its way to avoid criticizing the aberrations of the clergy. For years the entertainment industry privately resented, all the while it publicly deferred to, mainline Catholic opinion of what was and was not censorable.

"Power tends to corrupt . . . ," a famous Roman Catholic thinker once said. The dictum applied to Lord Acton's

* deviations

coreligionists as much as to anyone else. Bishops, knowing that a mere nod of disapproval was enough to instill fear into ambitious politicians, timid journalists, or greedy movie magnates, sometimes took full advantage of the situation. Groups of politically motivated laymen wrapped their opinions in the mantle of Catholicism, with the hope of making them publicly invulnerable. Catholic politicians curried favor from their "own kind" by posing as defenders of the Faith, or as lonely soldiers of the Truth in the counsels of government.

All kinds of people tapped the source of American Catholicism's power and prestige, some for good causes, some for bad, some selfishly, some selflessly. The central fact was that, as the twentieth century progressed and American Catholics were numbered in the tens of millions, the power was there to tap; the prestige followed inevitably.

World War I brought the Catholics of America together as never before. For the first time they were united in a nationwide effort. Up to that time, the various dioceses had generally lived in isolation from one another, and the national groups within each were divided by customs, inherited prejudices, and even different languages. But in 1917, when the nation as never before rallied around the flag, the entire Catholic community was called upon to act in concert. With hundreds of thousands of young men under arms, it was clear that the duty to provide chaplains and religious services for them could not be handled on a diocesan level.

To meet the need, meetings of bishops, priests, and leading laymen from across the country were called, and the only truly national lay organization, the Knights of Columbus, enthusiastically plunged into war work.

The Knights, then a booming fraternity operating in the "lodge" spirit, set up U.S.O.-type facilities at home and in France which were open to servicemen of all faiths. The organization also supported auxiliary chaplains to supplement those who were commissioned as officers in the Army and Navy and, wherever feasible, set up makeshift chapels for servicemen. Their efforts were applauded throughout the nation.

Soon after war was declared, the clergy and leaders of the laity were mobilized under the leadership of a prominent Paulist, Father John J. Burke, as the National Catholic War Council. The N.C.W.C. began as an unofficial body but later gained the support of the American hierarchy and was authorized to act in the name of the bishops. Under its auspices, large sums of money were collected, enabling the Church to keep in touch with servicemen at home and overseas. The new organization also dealt directly with the Army and Navy in recruiting priests for the chaplains corps.

Before the United States actually entered the war, Catholic opinion had been divided. The Irish, with the dark memory of British rule still fresh in their minds, were generally less than enthusiastic about supporting a cause associated with England; the American Germans harbored enough sympathy for the Fatherland to hope that their sons would not be called upon to fight against kinfolk abroad. After America's entry, however, Catholics of all groups were swept up in the wave of patriotism that engulfed the nation.

For years thereafter, Catholic apologists boasted that throughout the hostilities there were proportionately more Catholics in the American fighting forces than either Protestants or Jews. Actually their statistics were open to question, but there is no doubt that the Catholic body did its full share to win the "war to end war"—a source of immense satisfaction to a community still eager to establish its patriotic credentials in a land where it had for so long been under a cloud of suspicion.

In America's later wars—especially during the Vietnam hostilities—thousands of Catholic conscientious objectors applied the standards of the Church's ancient just-war teaching to the situation at hand and concluded that it would be immoral for them to participate. But in 1917, patriotic loyalty was universally looked upon as the final value; it was taken for granted that once war had been declared, the Catholic citizen's obligation was simply to fall in line; responsibility for judging the justice of the cause rested solely with political authorities. This of course greatly simplified the moral problem connected with war. In any case—as the Church's spokesmen made abundantly clear later—the Catholic reputation for unquestioning patriotism was enhanced immeasurably in 1917–1918.

If, earlier, Catholics had looked on their religion and their patriotism as two sides of the same coin, after the war many began to feel that the Roman Catholic faith of itself put one's patriotic loyalty beyond question: to be a good Catholic meant *ipso facto* that one was a good American.

This rough formula was invoked during the McCarthy era in the 1950s when, as one Washington wag noted, the Harvard and Yale sons of the old Protestant aristocracy were regularly investigated for un-Americanism by certified products of Fordham and Notre Dame. The formula was also applied in reverse: the Catholic opponents of Joe McCarthy, many of his supporters felt, must certainly be deficient in religious orthodoxy or they would have joined his patriotic crusade.

The National Catholic War Council did not die with the Armistice. After some lively controversy about its tendency to centralize authority in the American Church, it was transformed into the National Catholic Welfare Conference and became a more or less official spokesman for the Catholic bishops of the United States.*

A number of conservative bishops through the years objected strongly to leftish positions put forth by N.C.W.C. bureaus and went out of their way to make clear that it was primarily a service organization with no authorization to speak for all the hierarchy; but, until the 1960s, the N.C.W.C. was as close to an official spokesman as could be found in a Church where every bishop was supreme in his own diocese.

The new N.C.W.C.'s most memorable statement, known as the Bishops' Program for Social Reconstruction, was issued in 1919, soon after the refounding of the organization. It was drawn up by John A. Ryan, a priest-professor at the Catholic University of America, who later became head of the Conference's Social Action Department and held the post until his death in 1945.

---

* In 1966, following the Vatican Council, the National Council of Catholic Bishops was formed and the N.C.W.C. was reorganized as the United States Catholic Conference.

In 1919 Father Ryan, a tireless scholar and the nation's foremost exponent of Catholic social thought, was undoubtedly ahead of his time and certainly far in advance of most of his coreligionists. For example, in the program he drew up for the bishops, he argued that women workers were entitled to receive equal pay for equal work—a cliché today but in 1919 a radical proposal; he also argued for minimum-wage laws, profit sharing for workers, free medical care and other welfare benefits for the poor, the abolition of child labor, public housing, and the establishment of graduated income and heavy inheritance taxes. He staunchly upheld the right to organize trade unions (which was being widely denied in 1919) and proposed that workers deal with employers through elected shop stewards.

Perhaps to Ryan's own surprise, the bishops, then as now a characteristically cautious body, accepted his draft, which they put forth as an updated application of *Rerum Novarum,* Pope Leo XIII's notable social encyclical of 1891. In the climate of the day it was a daring move, and no one was surprised when a spokesman for the National Association of Manufacturers charged that the hierarchy had clearly been led astray by a socialist propagandist. Later, when parts of the Bishops' Program were put into effect by the New Deal, Father (by then Monsignor) Ryan was both lavishly praised and blamed for helping to lay the theoretical groundwork for the Roosevelt administration.

The 1919 Program itself, along with *Rerum Novarum* and Pius XI's 1931 encyclical *Quadragesimo Anno,* became a kind of Magna Charta for the Catholic social actionists who moved on the scene in the turbulent thirties. But during the giddy twenties it was largely ignored, even by the bishops themselves. With the stock market climbing to dizzying new heights, not many Americans were interested in social reform. Even to Catholics, a donnish priest calling for a fundamental reconstruction of American society seemed hopelessly out of touch with the times. Middle-class Americans were blissfully content with the way things were going and saw no reason to rock the boat; as the nation's foremost wit, Will Rogers, said, even those who were not enjoying the new prosperity were excited by it.

Monsignor Ryan and other social reformers still continued to study, though, and when they had the chance, even to agitate for a serious social overhauling; but they and people like them were easily dismissed by the millions enjoying their first taste of affluence. A disproportionate number of Catholics, recently delivered from poverty, were among those millions. The official Church, liberated from its earlier minority status and preoccupied with building on what had already been accomplished, was more interested in celebrating its new-found respectability than in pushing any controversial reform program.

The biggest celebration of all—one that would have been inconceivable earlier—was carried out by the booming Archdiocese of Chicago, which sponsored an international Eucharistic Congress in the summer of 1926. Eucharistic Congresses —large gatherings of the faithful joined together to profess their faith in the Real Presence of Christ in the Eucharist— had long been known in Europe, but the Chicago Congress, the twenty-eighth in the Church's history, was the first to be held in the United States. It was scrupulously designed to be a purely religious event. No political discussions were permitted, nor were any civic affairs run in connection with it.

Catholic dignitaries from all over the world were invited to Chicago by its Archbishop, Cardinal George Mundelein, to take part in the great manifestation of faith he envisioned. Hundreds of highly placed ecclesiastics, including a dozen cardinals, responded, and the Pope sent an Italian cardinal to represent the Holy See. Tens of thousands of priests and nuns, and hundreds of thousands of lay Catholics showed up for the massive services, conducted in the city's newly built Soldiers Field and on the spacious grounds of the archdiocese's colonial-style seminary on the fashionable North Shore.

Before he reached Chicago, the papal legate, Cardinal Giovanni Bonzano, was ceremoniously received in New York by the city's Catholic mayor, and he then proceeded westward in a special train to Chicago, where he was formally welcomed not only by the clergy and hundreds of laymen, but by city officials, including the mayor, another Catholic.

The Congress had been a year in preparation, and Cath-

olic Chicago had talked of little else for months. For weeks
in advance, the papal flag, along with the stars and stripes,
was hung in living-room windows and attached to automobile
hub caps all over the city. Alerted that something big was
going to happen, newspapers and magazines sent dozens of
correspondents to Chicago.

On the days the Congress meetings were held, business in
the city came to a virtual standstill. There was a religious
hush everywhere, most of it attributable to the solemnity of
the occasion, but some could undoubtedly be traced to the
concern felt by many nervous non-Catholics that Roman Catholics had grown so numerous in the United States that a
display of such magnitude had become possible.

Aside from a furious summer storm on the last day, which
sent thousands scurrying from the seminary grounds, soaked
and miserable, and occasioned a monumental traffic jam, there
were no untoward incidents during the Congress. But Catholics, seeing so many of their coreligionists boldly proclaiming
their piety, felt a great surge of pride in their faith and a
tingling awareness of their new place in the American community.

Certainly the Eucharistic Congress, with its Roman panoply,
was an unfortunate prelude for the presidential candidacy, two
years later, of Alfred E. Smith, the Democratic Party's "happy
warrior."

Smith was a typical product of the American Catholicism
of the time—Irish, urban, undereducated, almost thoughtlessly
patriotic, quietly devout, proud of his religion, and wise in
the rough-and-tumble ways of politics. Born in 1873, he grew
up in New York's St. James Parish, a teeming Irish ghetto,
and reached the top via the Tammany route.

As a young man he served with some distinction in the
Albany legislature before he became governor and a power
in his party. After two unsuccessful tries, he finally reached
the height no other Catholic had yet achieved when he received the coveted presidential nomination in 1928.

From the beginning, Smith's religion was an issue in the
campaign, but so also were his big-city manners, his opposition
to Prohibition, his harsh New York accent, and his lack of

formal education, which in the Protestant heartland may have been even more crucial than his faith. In addition, as his friend Will Rogers once told him, with the nation enjoying unprecedented prosperity under the Republicans, a Democrat, no matter who, simply had "no issue" to run on.

Smith, however, did have his religion, which both helped and hurt him at the polls. Most American Catholics, coming from backgrounds very similar to his, identified with him in a way they could not with the elegant, Harvard-trained John F. Kennedy thirty-two years later. If in 1960 J.F.K. was the American Catholic idealized, A.E.S. in 1928 was almost a prototype of the parochially trained poor boy reaching the upper levels of American life. His coreligionists took immense pride in his accomplishment.

The identification soon made between Smith's success and the prestige of the American Catholic community was so pressing that the "religious issue" played a major part in the campaign from the beginning. Both the candidate's Catholic supporters and his non-Catholic opponents were constantly aware of it.

Smith later said that as a Catholic candidate he was the victim of the worst whispering campaign in American political history. While it cannot totally explain his defeat or Herbert Hoover's impressive victory, the statement was not greatly exaggerated. Governor Smith's candidacy once more unleashed the hidden demons of anti-Catholicism in America, to the dismay of many Catholics who had thought all that was finally behind them.

The Ku Klux Klan and other night riders took full advantage of the situation, and throughout the South, West, and Middle West used fright tactics and harassment to express their outrage that a Roman Catholic could come so close to the White House. Pamphlets and books reviving the ancient anti-Catholic canards and myths were distributed by the hundreds of thousands. The case of Maria Monk was unearthed and her creaky melodrama gained a second run on the bigotry circuit. Lurid personal charges against the candidate himself were coupled with hoary tales of immorality in the cloister and plotting in the Vatican to take over the United States.

All in all, it was a fairly obscene outburst for a nation

priding itself on its tolerance and devotion to religious liberty. Not only Catholics but liberal-minded Jews, Protestants, and nonbelievers were repelled by the viciousness of the attack, which acutely embarrassed the Quaker Herbert Hoover, who repudiated it during the campaign.

The experience, though it had its comic aspects, was a grim reminder, especially to young Catholics, that while they might think of themselves as paragons of patriotism, millions of their fellow citizens felt otherwise about them. Smith's defeat was taken as a painful declaration that Americans would simply not permit any son of the Church, no matter what his qualifications, to represent them before the world.

After the election, the Catholic community, disillusioned, retreated more deeply into its own ghettoized life. It did not really emerge from it until John F. Kennedy's success in 1960 finally seemed to remove the stigma of second-class citizenship once and for all.

American Catholic life in the thirties was marked by the burgeoning of social movements, leftist and rightist, reacting to the economic depression at home and the turbulent clash of ideologies abroad, which were echoed by their partisans in the United States.

In 1931 Pope Pius XI issued a new social encyclical, *Quadragesimo Anno,* which updated the teachings of Leo XIII's *Rerum Novarum.* Leo XIII had complained that his encyclical had been largely ignored; this time, with the unemployed numbering in the millions and the specter of hunger haunting the land, there was a tremendous response to papal leadership. The encyclicals and earlier writings of Catholic social thinkers, both European and American, were discussed by parish study groups and explicated from pulpits and lecture podiums, and in hundreds of classrooms.

A body of social-minded clerics, soon dubbed "labor priests," took the leadership in instructing workingmen in the principles of the encyclicals. These priests became the idols of many seminarians and other young Catholics tuned into the times by working side by side with union organizers, vigorously supporting strikes and boycotts, organizing labor schools, and otherwise popularizing the writings of John A.

Ryan, Raymond A. McGowan, Francis J. Haas, the prolific Benedictine writer Virgil Michel, and other clerical interpreters of the encyclicals.

The founder of the Catholic Youth Organization, Bishop Bernard J. Sheil of Chicago, was probably the most outspoken member of the hierarchy to take up the cause. Sheil, an indomitable activist, was among the least scholarly of bishops but he built up a lay staff of brilliant young people to direct the manifold activities of his C.Y.O.—which extended far beyond the Golden Gloves boxing competition for which the organization had already become famous.

Sheil's staff supplied him with fiery texts for numerous public appearances before business groups, striking workers, and concerned Protestant and Jewish organizations. The Bishop passionately denounced anti-Semitism and the encroachments of fascism at home and abroad; in ringing terms he called for slum renewal, the abolition of restrictive property covenants, and an end to segregation in all its forms. Using the press for all it was worth, he supported John L. Lewis's mine workers, Detroit's striking automobile workers, and the early attempts to organize the stockyards and steel workers in his own area.

Sheil was both bitterly denounced as an interloper and admiringly hailed as a prophet by his fellow Catholics. From the beginning he had the support of his Archbishop, Cardinal Mundelein, and enjoyed the personal friendship not only of Franklin Delano Roosevelt* but of leaders in the business community who admired the man and his work for youth more than they honored his liberal opinions.

Other "labor priests" were not as flamboyant as the publicity-conscious Sheil but were no less ardent in their support of organized labor. A number of them—in New York, Pittsburgh, Cleveland, Detroit, San Francisco, and other big cities—worked less publicly but even more closely with the young turks organizing the C.I.O. They did not always enjoy

---

* After Mundelein's death in 1939, Roosevelt played with the notion of urging the Pope to name Sheil Archbishop of Chicago but nothing came of the President's interest in the appointment. Sheil held the long-time-no-see record in the American hierarchy. He remained Auxiliary Bishop of Chicago until his retirement in the mid-sixties.

the confidence of their superiors and were looked upon as clerical rabble-rousers by a significant number of the laity; in spite of this criticism and some more or less good-humored ribbing from fellow clerics, however, they carried on and strengthened the already strong bond between the Church and the American working class.

Many Catholics, including some important bishops and other highly placed churchmen, took a somewhat dim view of any concrete involvement in the labor movement. The social ferment of the time, they were persuaded, was largely the result of communist agitation, and they were particularly put off by the violence that frequently accompanied labor strife and by such radical new tactics as the sit-down strike. With these apprehensions, they looked upon clerics tied to the unions' organizing efforts as muddleheaded dupes at best, and proclaimed on every possible occasion that the "labor priests" were acting strictly on their own, without official chancery-office endorsement.

Most of the clergy, getting this message, concluded that it was the better part of valor to confine themselves to their parishes. Others were sympathetic to the labor activists but avoided controversy by prudently limiting themselves to scholarly pronouncements and general statements about the wisdom of the papal encyclicals, not getting involved in actual cases.

The best-known priest of the time was the radio orator Charles E. Coughlin, a young pastor from Royal Oak, Michigan, who became a power to reckon with after his Sunday afternoon broadcasts began to reach a massive audience. Coughlin, an elocutionist of the old school, began his public career as a spokesman for the papal teachings but soon broadened his scope to domestic politics. At the height of his fame, his mellifluous voice poured into millions of American homes, Catholic and non-Catholic alike. After he won national attention unprecedented for a priest, Coughlin became a hero of the Catholic masses and was soon regarded as a formidable force in Washington, as any man would who could summon the 80,000 letters that arrived in Royal Oak every week. Neither the Administration nor Congress could long ignore him.

Early in his career he popularized the slogan "Roosevelt or Ruin!" Later, after he turned against the New Deal, it was bitterly transformed into "Roosevelt *and* Ruin!" The priest was a self-taught economist. His monetary theories on how to end the Depression were repudiated by such Catholic experts as John A. Ryan and Ryan's associates in Washington, by practically every university economics department in the nation, government practitioners, and all but a few eccentrics in the profession. However, he had a talent for leaving his untutored followers with the impression that the only explanation for those who opposed him was either their personal corruption and shameful involvement in the wicked system, or some hidden sympathy for communism; the more criticized he was, then, the more heated his popular support became.

As time went on, Coughlin became more strident. By 1936, his followers were organized into a grass-roots movement— the National Union for Social Justice, which put up its own candidate to oppose Roosevelt's second term, a lackluster North Dakota Republican congressman named Charles Lemke. Lemke was enthusiastically acclaimed in Coughlinite circles throughout the campaign, but in the end most of the priest's working-class followers shifted back to Roosevelt. On election day, the congressman was drowned in a great outpouring of support for the New Deal.

Later, Father Coughlin injected overt anti-Semitism into his broadcasts and revealed a hitherto unspoken admiration for finding an American counterpart to "Franco's way" of handling the problem of communism in the United States. Both his broadcasts and *Social Justice*, the organ of the movement, from that time forward concentrated on Jewish targets—Bernard Baruch and the popular radio entertainer Eddie Cantor, for example. Jewish religious teachings were distorted and such ancient legends as the forged Protocols of Zion were propagated shamelessly. After the war began in Europe, the movement's sympathy for Hitler and the Nazis became so evident that millions who had once looked on Coughlin as a demi-god turned away in disgust.

Eventually the priest's ecclesiastical superiors acted. A new Archbishop of Detroit, Edward Mooney, took advantage of a provision in Canon Law which permitted any bishop to censor the writing and public pronouncements of a priest in his diocese. Mooney appointed a committee of three diocesan priests to modify Coughlin's extremism. Coughlin responded by ostentatiously withdrawing from the staff of *Social Justice* and putting it under the control of his lay staff, over whom the Archbishop had no authority. The anti-Semitism issuing from Royal Oak only increased in volume.

Finally, Cardinal Mundelein, an early opponent of Hitler, went on the air and stated unequivocally that the radio priest "does not represent the doctrine or sentiments of the Church." Coughlin's anti-Semitic followers immediately charged that since any man with the Cardinal's name was probably a crypto-Jew, his condemnation was highly suspect and quite meaningless. This was a typical response. When Monsignor Ryan had publicly criticized Coughlin he was accused, not of being Jewish—here credulity would have been unbearably strained—but of being an instrument of mysterious Jewish forces set on communizing America.

In the late thirties, Coughlin gave his support to the Christian Front, a fascistic group of aimless New York bully-boys heavily concentrated in Catholic sections of Brooklyn, the Bronx, and Queens. The Christian Front had no serious program to offer but organized rifle clubs and quasi-military platoons—"against the day," as Coughlin put it, when they would be needed in America. The group, which had some support among older people in German and Irish sections of New York City, carried on anti-Jewish boycotts ("Buy Christian at Christmas!") and made vague threats of pogroms to come, at their public meetings. But they were so ineffective that probably a vast majority of Catholics, even in the New York area, never heard of them. Yet, their existence was deeply disturbing to the Jewish community and revived fearful memories of past persecutions at Christian hands.

A group of intellectuals, spearheaded by professors from Fordham, Georgetown, Notre Dame, and other Catholic universities, were so perturbed by the deterioration of Catholic-Jewish relations resulting from Christian Front activity that they organized a Committee on Human Rights, to combat anti-Semitism within the Church. Taking as their theme Pius XI's statement that "spiritually we are Semites," some of the outstanding leaders in the Church, lay and clerical, eagerly signed up; but the committee itself quickly became controversial because of its sponsors' obvious sympathy for American intervention in the war in Europe.

The nation at the time was still engaged in the furious isolationist-interventionist debate which was brought to an abrupt halt on December 7, 1941. Catholics, like every other group, were divided on the issues, but the heavier weight of Catholic opinion favored the isolationists. And the unhappy fact was that in many minds vigorous opposition to anti-Semitism at home was tied into support for intervention in the war abroad. By the same token, ardent isolationism was tied into anti-Semitism. This, however, was a vast oversimplification in both cases. For example, the radically pacifist *Catholic Worker* was as passionately opposed to intervention as it was to anti-Semitism.

The outburst of overt anti-Semitism among Catholics was brought to an early end after leaders of the Christian Front were arrested by F.B.I. agents in 1940, following a raid on their headquarters which had turned up a few homemade bombs and a small collection of rifles stolen from a nearby armory. Little was heard of them after that.

Not long after Pearl Harbor, Coughlin himself withdrew from public life to become a full-time pastor of the church in Royal Oak. Gradually he was generally forgotten, but to this day his name is revered by some of the now elderly adults of the thirties who once hung on his every word and the remnants of the youth crusade he once led. Such people never counted for more than a minority of American Catholics, even in their most powerful days, nor did they have any significant long-range influence on the Church; but, more than they deserved to, they made their literary mark as Catholic stereotypes in some of the novels, plays, and short stories which appeared later. Undoubtedly these stereotypes shaped a lasting image of the urban Catholic for many, many Americans who erroneously concluded from what they read later that the Coughlinite attitude toward life and politics completely dominated American Catholicism in the thirties.

The Catholic Worker, which was probably the most significant movement of the period, was at quite the other end of the spectrum. Founded by Dorothy Day and Peter Maurin in 1933, it never involved masses of people but only small groups, mostly young people, who were attracted by the radical monthly the movement published in New York. It was no more typical than the Coughlinite movement, probably less so; yet its indirect influence on the character of what Catholicism would become was incalculable.

The movement was neither planned nor organized. It grew up spontaneously among the readers of *The Catholic Worker,* a penny tabloid which was first distributed by its editors in a 1933 May Day parade in New York. Peter Maurin, a self-taught itinerant workingman who all his life lived in voluntary poverty and self-abnegation, had approached Dorothy Day with the idea of the paper a few months earlier. Maurin, who began life as a French peasant, was already in his sixties; Miss Day at the time was thirty-four.

Before her conversion to Catholicism in the late twenties, Dorothy Day, the rebellious daughter of a Hearst journalist, had worked on several Marxist publications, including the old *Masses* and the *Socialist Call,* and had moved in a free-wheeling bohemian environment, along with Eugene O'Neill, Rayna Prohme, John Reed, Mike Gold, Malcolm Cowley, Max Eastman, and other Greenwich Village intellectuals. Her religious conversion, if anything, only strengthened her social convictions and commitment to the cause of the poor. While she loved the Church passionately even before her baptism, she had nothing but contempt for the bourgeois Catholicism she found on all sides. Peter Maurin, seeking a collaborator to shake up the middle class, could not have chosen more wisely.

The first editorial office of their *Catholic Worker,* on the lower East Side of New York, became the movement's first house of hospitality after volunteers showed up to help the editors put Peter Maurin's program into action. Maurin, with his emphasis on evangelical simplicity, had insisted in the first issue of the paper that Christians should take personal responsibility for the poor and destitute and depend on Providence to supply the wherewithal. Dorothy Day, taking the Sermon on the Mount literally, agreed.

The two—an odd couple by any standard—went into the venture, then, with a wealth of faith and little else. Some money and a number of helpers turned up almost immediately. Maurin, who despised industrialism and all its works, also endorsed a back-to-the-land program and advocated the establishment of communal farms for young families, who would look after the old and impoverished. The New York group established its first farming commune in Easton, Pennsylvania, a few years later.

As the circulation of *The Catholic Worker* grew and the movement spread, its houses of hospitality and farms were multiplied by groups in other parts of the country. All of them lived from hand to mouth, and most were begun, without official ecclesiastical direction or support, by young lay persons who shared the life of the poor they served. Those who originally came to Worker houses for help frequently melted into the movement, and soon there was no distinction made between the volunteer staff and those who had first come seeking help.

By the late thirties there were about thirty-five such houses in the large cities of America, loosely affiliated with the New York house, and a half-dozen farms. Thousands of destitute men and women lined up outside Worker hostels every day of the week, in New York, Chicago, Detroit, Minneapolis, Milwaukee, Boston, Cleveland, San Francisco, and other cities; hundreds more lived in the houses and took over the day-by-day work of keeping the breadlines going. *The Catholic Worker*, sold by subscription for twenty-five cents a year (as it still is), was distributed on street corners and handed out to striking workers by college students. It reached a circulation of over 100,000—not truly a mass readership but one which included most of the opinion molders in the American Church, lay and clerical.

Peter Maurin, preaching the gospel of personal responsibility and voluntary poverty by word and example, traveled by bus from house to house and farm to farm until shortly before his death in 1949. He was almost universally revered as a latter-day Francis of Assisi. His pithy "easy essays," written in a kind of free-verse style, have been printed and reprinted year after year ever since in *The Catholic Worker*.

Miss Day constantly referred to him as the leader of the movement. This was more pious sentiment than accurate fact, however; from the beginning the undisputed leader was Dorothy
Day herself, probably the most influential lay person, man
or woman, in the history of American Catholicism.

Each of the C.W. houses and farms sponsored public
"round-table discussions," Peter Maurin's phrase for what
would later be called dialogues; but conversation about religion and the social order was ceaseless wherever Catholic
Worker people gathered. The C.W. centers were crowded not
only with the poor and unemployed seeking food, clothing,
and shelter, but with priests, nuns, seminarians, professors,
labor leaders, businessmen, college students, journalists, visiting foreigners, and even an occasional bishop, all heatedly
discussing the issues of the day as they served the breadline
or handed out the cast-off clothing the staff had collected.

C.W. groups joined picket lines and manned soup kitchens
at strike headquarters, side by side with communists, socialists,
and social activists of every hue. Others took to the streets
and distributed homemade leaflets advocating pacifism, racial
integration, and social change, to pedestrians who as often
as not were shocked to learn that such radical material was
published by a group calling itself Catholic.

Throughout the thirties the Catholic Worker remained the
most vital movement within the American Church and indirectly a catalyst for thousands of Catholics who were not directly touched by it. It reached not only the poor but thousands
of middle-class people who might otherwise have had no immediate contact with poverty or known anything about the
social thought of the Church. It radicalized the religious thinking of hundreds of young priests and nuns, collegians and
workers who would never have been attracted to any of the
secular movements, and it liberated countless others who might
otherwise have lived out their lives in the straitjacket of conventional anticommunism.

Inevitably, the movement was the object of bitter criticism,
as well as praise. Dorothy Day, today an awesomely dignified
lady in her seventies, is looked upon with a kind of reverence,
but in the early years she was the object of mean rumors,
shameless gossip, and outright calumny, which she bore, as

* the malicious uttering of false charge or misrepresentation
calculated to damage another's reputation

she did the adulation, with monumental poise. She has outlived many of her critics and outlasted them all in the constancy of her devotion to the poor.

The Catholic Worker did not disappear with the Depression thirties, though its influence became less obvious with the passage of time. Many of the early followers fell away when Pearl Harbor put the movement's pacifist tenets to the supreme test, but others came along to take their place, and the work was carried on without a break throughout the wartime forties, the complacent fifties, the action-packed sixties, and into the seventies. With its emphasis on personalism, pacifism, voluntary poverty, and disdain for political action or mass techniques, it is curiously contemporary and continues to attract the idealistic young. Its reputation as a genuinely Christian revolutionary force is more secure than ever.

Miss Day herself has mellowed with age but has lost none of her fiery indignation that injustices go on, wars continue, and most Christians are still content to let it happen. Through the years she has refused to rest on her laurels and has been in and out of jail as a political prisoner—now protesting air-raid drills as meaningless diversions from the threat of nuclear devastation, now opposing conscription, now the war in Vietnam; but she has lived long enough to see some of the C.W.'s earlier causes fully triumphant and has never given up hope for the future.

Over the years, Miss Day has shown equal disdain for conservative caution and radical cant, and, whatever the fashion of protest in vogue, has relied unfailingly on what she calls the "little way" of evangelical service, to influence the Church and the world. Without Dorothy Day, there would have been no Catholic Worker, but, with her, the simplicities of the Gospel have never been completely obscured within modern American Catholicism.

The manifold concerns of the Catholic Worker were taken up by a number of more specialized movements, organizations, and conventional associations. All were important in the development of "social Catholicism" in the years preceding World War II.

One of the most significant was the Friendship House movement, founded by the Baroness Catherine de Hueck, an emigrée White Russian. The Baroness opened her first settlement in Harlem in the mid-thirties and later set up branches in Chicago, Washington, and a few other places. The Friendship House workers sponsored interracial programs, crusaded against segregation, and brought blacks and whites together in their store-front centers on a level of day-by-day intimacy and equality hitherto unknown in the American Church. Like the Catholic Worker, the movement attracted young people from the middle class who were prepared to share the life and poverty of city slums as a witness to their faith. Among those who turned up in Harlem to join in the work was a recent convert fresh from Columbia University, Thomas Merton, who later gained international fame as a Trappist monk.

Catherine de Hueck, an imposing lady of great charm, and a rousing speaker as well, kept closer to mainline Catholicism than Dorothy Day and her Catholic Worker rebels. Throughout the thirties and into the forties, the Baroness crisscrossed the country on numerous speaking engagements, thundering against racism in parish halls and school auditoriums to audiences of conservative middle-class ladies, sedate nuns, high-school girls, collegians, and earnest seminarians who were stunned by her graphic portrayals of life in the Negro ghettos. She wrote dozens of articles for the popular Catholic press demanding an end to segregation and excoriating her fellow Catholics for maintaining segregated parishes, schools, religious orders, and lay associations. Through the "B" (as she was known), thousands of white Catholics were forced for the first time in their lives to face up to the racist attitudes dominant in the Church.

Closest of all to the ecclesiastical establishment was the liturgical movement spearheaded by Benedictine monks at Saint John's Abbey in Minnesota, and later joined by hundreds of other priests, religious, and laymen dedicated to promoting a richer understanding of worship and wider participation by the laity in religious services. The movement, which made no secret of its contempt for the sentimental and excessively "private" devotionalism found in most parishes and religious houses, was regarded with suspicion and not a little disdain

*to censure scathingly

by many of the clergy, who were disturbed by some of the liturgists' proposals—that priests offer Mass facing the people, for example, that the vernacular replace the traditional Latin, that groups of clergy concelebrate the Mass rather than each retiring to his own private altar, or even that a chewier bread be substituted for the standard white wafers which, according to the liturgists, obscured the fact that the Eucharist is above all to be eaten.

These and suggestions like them were widely looked upon as an affront to Catholic tradition and the product of minds seduced by a vapid search for novelty. Priests active in the movement—later good-naturedly dubbed "litniks"—found themselves on the receiving end of a great deal of criticism from their clerical confreres; in some places seminarians were forbidden by their superiors to subscribe to the liturgical publications; but the movement gained steadily, and before the Second Vatican Council, which authorized most of the changes it had advocated, attracted tens of thousands of followers. The national Liturgical Weeks, which the Benedictines first sponsored in 1940, ultimately became one of the largest annual conferences held in the American Church.

The liturgists were closely associated with the social-action movement. From the beginning they resisted the temptation to let their movement become an aesthetic diversion; again and again leaders of the movement, like Virgil Michel of Saint John's and H. A. Reinhold, an erudite priest exiled by the Nazis from his native Germany, pointed up the relationship between communal worship and such mundane matters as slum housing, racial segregation, and the issue of war and peace. In any accounting of liberal and conservative forces in the Church up to the Vatican Council, the liturgical movement would have to be scored as a significant plus for the liberals.

None of these movements, though they were well publicized in the more intellectual sections of the Catholic press, touched the life of the average American Catholic directly. Most American Catholics continued to go about their daily lives unaffected by the destitution of Skid Row or the misery of Harlem, knowing little about the papal social encyclicals, having few if any doubts about their own racial attitudes and behavior,

+ lacking liveliness.
** learned

appearing loyally for Mass on Sunday, supporting their parish drives, accepting listlessly their pastors' endless exhortations to remain chaste and faithful to their duties, and contentedly practicing a private piety that was cut off from social concern.

The 70,000 persons who, in the thirties and forties, lined up outside the Servite Church in Chicago every Friday for the Novena to Our Sorrowful Mother were undoubtedly more typical of the Catholic millions than the ardent supporters of the Catholic Worker or the elite devotees of the liturgical movement. While the "litniks" were eager to relate the worship of the Church to the broader needs of the time, the novenagoers were more likely to be found desperately praying for a boyfriend, a job, a salary increase, or the happy outcome of a private lawsuit.

But for all that, the seeds of change were being planted by the movements. In the long run, their leaders had far more influence on the future of the Church than the pillars of the Catholic establishment, who all too often made life difficult for the movement mavericks.

Catholic life in the United States came to something of a standstill during the wartime years of the early forties. With millions of men overseas and more than five thousand priests serving as military chaplains, everything else was subordinated to the national effort. Some of the movements which had been flourishing when the Japanese struck at Pearl Harbor were sustained by a mere handful of devotees; others disappeared altogether. With the economy booming for the first time in years, interest in the social question diminished almost to the vanishing point. The controversies that had so recently divided Catholics on such matters as isolation versus intervention were abruptly settled. With the U.S.S.R. the fighting ally of the United States and Nazi Germany its enemy, the issues involving communism and fascism were no longer looked upon as debatable. While the world beyond was torn by war and dissension, it was a period of extraordinary unity and calmness for the Church in the United States.

As had happened in the past, once the die was cast, American Catholics supported the war without question. There were only a few exceptions at both ends of the political spectrum.

The Catholic Worker's pacifism, which had been promulgated ceaselessly for almost a decade before Pearl Harbor, bore some slight fruit. There were at least enough Catholics registering as conscientious objectors to justify setting up a small C.O. camp for them. A very few, like the short-story writer J. F. Powers and the poet Robert Lowell (then a highly publicized convert), went to jail rather than comply with the draft law. Such men got little or no support and practically no notice from their fellow Catholics.

A handful of unreconstructed right wingers, emphasizing the dangers lurking in the American alliance with the Soviet Union, sniped at Roosevelt's policies throughout the war and took every opportunity to advocate a negotiated peace with Hitler. They operated as *ad hoc* committees or short-lived local associations, like the Patrick Henry Forum in Chicago, which blended anti-Semitism and anti-British sentiment with a kind of theological anticommunism and old-fashioned isolationism to produce a special American Catholic brand of homegrown fascism. But they too went generally unnoticed. At most, their activities amounted to a minor nuisance in a nation determined to gain unconditional surrender from its enemies.

After that surrender finally came in 1945, millions of Catholic servicemen and thousands of priest-chaplains returned home, profoundly affected by their experiences with death and destruction, sophisticated by their brush with foreign cultures, but remarkably unchanged in their loyalty to the faith, their acceptance of the Church's discipline, and continued readiness to live by its laws.

Church attendance increased after the war. Seminaries, which had lost students during the war years, were once again thriving. The novitiate classes of the religious communities grew so large that the more popular orders planned new facilities to take care of the influx of recruits.

One of the most remarkable developments was the interest of veterans in contemplative monasteries. The Trappist houses in America had always been small, as might have been expected of an order with an incredibly stern and unbending rule; but after the war, due in great part to the interest aroused by Thomas Merton's best-selling *Seven-Storey Mountain,* they received hundreds of novices. New houses were established in remote parts of the country and old ones were booming so that aspiring monks were required to set up makeshift dormitories in the corridors of Merton's own Gethsemane Abbey in Kentucky.

The Catholic colleges and universities were suddenly crowded with older students taking advantage of the G.I. Bill to get an education, most of them the first members of their families to enroll in an institution of higher learning. Each of these colleges required its students to take courses in traditional Catholic philosophy and theology. It can be said, then, that the new collegians, most of whom soon married and settled down, were the most theologically sophisticated generation of laymen in the history of the Church. Priests in parishes where they congregated were no longer able to count on the simple docility of Catholics in the past and had to face the fact that many laymen in the pew knew more about the teaching of Thomas Aquinas than the clerics in the pulpit.

In particular, the new-style layman had his own ideas on how religion should be taught to his children in the parochial school. This marked a distinct break with the past when the word of a priest or a teaching sister on matters of religion was taken as being simply beyond question. Some of the older clergy, unsettled by the theological sophistication of their young parishioners, spoke bitterly of rebelliousness and arrogance, and tended to be suspicious of the colleges which encouraged laymen to delve into what had long been professional preserves. Other priests, usually younger men, were stimulated by it and learned to work closely with the new breed of Catholic who seemed to take the intellectual side of the faith so seriously.

The postwar move was to the suburbs, away from the city environs where most of the traditions of American Catholicism had developed. So many thousands of young Catholics left the decaying city neighborhoods they grew up in for the promise of a home where their children would find trees and flowers and fresh air that by the 1950s suburban Catholicism had become a major force in the American Church. It was a new kind of Catholicism, not found anywhere else in the world— young, well educated, ambitious, uncertain in the new environment, experimental, child-centered, and unprecedentedly affluent.

New parishes were created overnight, and parochial schools were hastily built to take care of the postwar baby boom. Every September, anxious parishioners stood in line for hours waiting to get one of the coveted places for their children. An easy relationship, as close as that between a village curé and his flock, was frequently established between the young priests sent out to man the new parishes and their gray-flanneled parishioners. A sense of community, long since lost in the teeming urban parishes, was created.

The massive old churches in the inner city were still maintained, but many once-thriving Irish parishes, now set down in growing Negro ghettos, were sparsely attended and poorly kept up. The Catholic Church in the United States, which had so long taken its character from the urban environment, was changing perceptibly under the impact of the new suburban setting; parishes began to look more and more like their middle-class Protestant counterparts.

New movements replaced the social-minded organizations of the thirties, in significance and importance. Instead of gathering at a Catholic Worker House of Hospitality in the slums or a Friendship House in the black section of the city, the most concerned and committed of the suburban Catholics were now more likely to be gathered, with their curate, around the fireplace in a wall-to-wall carpeted living room. The preoccupations of the Catholics who set the tone for the American Church switched from such proletarian questions as the right to strike to the practicality of the rhythm method of birth control, the overcrowding of the local parochial school, or the constitutionality of bussing parochial-school children to school with their public-school playmates.

The new movements thriving in the Church put heavy stress on marriage and the family. Thousands of couples were enrolled in the Cana Conference movement, which emphasized husband-and-wife retreats; others joined the Christian Family Movement, which sponsored meetings and large conventions dealing with the difficulties facing couples trying to build Christian homes in the materialistic environment created by the new prosperity. The Serra Clubs, in which hundreds of business and professional men got together, encouraged vocations to the priesthood and religious life, using mass-media advertising techniques. Later, the *Cursillo* movement, an import from Latin America, gained surprising popularity among the suburbanites by using a sort of encounter-session shock technique to dramatize the need for personal conversion to Christian ideals.

For American Catholics as for the nation at large the most divisive force of the fifties was the crusade led by Senator Joseph R. McCarthy, a Catholic and Marquette University alumnus. McCarthy's demagogic charges of treason against the State Department and his know-nothing attack on civil liberties won significant support in Boston, New York, Chicago, Philadelphia, and other places where the Coughlinites had once been strong. Many felt the Senator was merely taking up where Father Coughlin had left off a decade or so earlier.

McCarthy was heroized in important sections of the diocesan press and more cautiously defended in others. He was cheered at Holy Name Society Communion breakfasts, and in some parochial schools the children added his name to those for whom they prayed regularly. In every poll on the Senator's popularity he did somewhat better with Catholics than with others, though he also counted a vast number of Middlewestern Protestants among his supporters. There was some basis, then, for the widespread suspicion among McCarthy's opponents that his fanatical anticommunism and hatred of liberalism stemmed from his religion.

McCarthy, though, was not as overwhelmingly popular among Catholics as was sometimes thought to be the case. In a Gallup Poll, taken in 1954 at the height of his power, 58 per cent of Catholics, as against 49 per cent of Protestants and 15 per cent of Jews gave him their support. Some of his most telling opposition came from his Catholic critics, who went after him just as passionately and often more effectively than his other opponents. Bishop Bernard J. Sheil, the Chicago liberal, made headlines when he contemptuously dismissed McCarthy as a "city slicker from Appleton" who was set on depriving Americans of their liberties. The two most influential Catholic weeklies, the lay-edited *Commonweal* and the Jesuit

America, frequently denounced the Senator and his crusade—*Commonweal* more vigorously than *America,* which did a certain amount of shilly-shallying on the issue. A few of the diocesan papers followed the same general line.

Most of the hierarchy kept silent on the question, looking upon it as primarily a political matter. However, Cardinal Spellman of New York, who, due to the massive publicity he received, was regarded by non-Catholics as the most authoritative spokesman for the Church, made no secret of his friendly feelings toward the Senator.

Whatever the true facts regarding the extent of Senator McCarthy's support among American Catholics, however, he represented to many, both within and without the Church, an almost perfect example of what was widely taken to be the authentic Catholic approach to the issues created by the Cold War.

It was a matter of pride to many Catholics of the time that even during the war they had not been caught up in the pro-Soviet enthusiasm which McCarthy freely attributed to the entire liberal community; they felt that Catholics and Catholics alone, because of the clarity of their own beliefs, understood the true nature of communism. At the same time, it was a matter of concern to many liberals that their Catholic fellow citizens seemed to be so caught up in ideological anti-communism that they would not hesitate to use the Church's influence to endanger freedom at home and reckless intervention abroad, in order to further the cause.

To the extent that such attitudes were important, McCarthyism really was something of a "Catholic" issue. But the growth of suburban Catholicism made a crucial difference, and only a few commentators gauging the depth of the Senator's support entered it into their equations. McCarthy's appeal was definitely limited among the new-style Catholics in the suburbs, many of whom had abandoned the Democratic Party to vote for the middle-of-the-road General Eisenhower in 1952 and would enthusiastically switch back again to support the moderate liberalism of John F. Kennedy in 1960. Such people were not likely to be found among the more zealous anti-McCarthyites, with whom they felt uncomfortable, but they were not prepared to go the whole way with McCarthy, either.

In the eight years between the two Presidents whom they did support wholeheartedly, Eisenhower and Kennedy, suburban Catholics grew increasingly numerous in the United States. It seemed that, with the tone being set by them, the Church could settle down to a steady course of peaceful growth, quiet deliberation, unending prosperity, and steady progress.

Certainly the note of Catholic optimism was loud and clear as plans were made for larger parish plants in the new middle-class settlements, for larger seminary and novitiate classes to come when the wartime babies reached maturity, and for a contented, ever more educated and affluent laity who might have intellectual needs different from their proletarian forebears but would be no less content to live according to the tried-and-true system of ecclesiastical authority that had become so impressive to outsiders that it was cited as a model of business efficiency by a management consultant organization in the late fifties.

When a seventy-six-year-old Italian cardinal was elected Sovereign Pontiff in 1958 and took the name John XXIII, it was generally understood that he would be an "interim" caretaker Pope and no real changes in the Church could be expected for a long time.

John XXIII, however, made it clear soon enough that he was not cut out to play the role assigned to him. He quickly broke precedents right and left and radically transformed the austere, unbending image of the Pope that had been studiously cultivated by most of his recent predecessors with the help of the Roman Curia. While Pius XII was remote and aloof, the roly-poly John was warm and outgoing, bringing everyone within the embrace of a fatherly concern. He was friendly to Christians and non-Christians, communists and capitalists alike. He received other religious leaders, Protestant, Orthodox, and Jewish, with respect and obvious affection and carefully minimized his theological differences with them, accenting instead what was shared in common. In a strikingly short time, the elderly Pope became a kind of father figure for the whole world, winning almost universal esteem. To his official power as Pope he added a personal prestige that was without precedent in the modern Church.

John of course knew that his reign would be brief. He

hoped, he said, to bring fresh air into the Church before he left this world, and he talked bravely of an *aggiornamento*—an updating that would renew the life of Catholicism the world over.

The Pope made no secret of his desire for change and even ordered an ecumenical council to bring it about, but no one in 1960 was prepared for what was coming.

CHAPTER FIVE

AGGIORNAMENTO—AND BEYOND

During the 1960s, Roman Catholicism throughout the world underwent more change than it had experienced in centuries, and nowhere was its impact more consequential than in the United States. When the fateful decade began, American Catholics were still exhilarated by the fresh air blowing through the Church as a result of Pope John's ecumenical spirit and openness to renewal. When it ended, the Church was throbbing with theological controversy, dissension, discontent, and in some circles a pessimism verging on despair.

Church attendance was down (even in the Catholic colleges only a minority of students went to Sunday Mass); bishops and priests were squabbling in public; several thousand priests had left the active ministry; even more nuns and brothers—perhaps as many as 20,000—had abandoned the religious life; dozens of seminaries and novitiates built in the fifties for the ever-larger classes confidently expected had to be shut down altogether or were maintained for much smaller groups of recruits; the number of children attending parochial schools, while still impressive, was diminished by over a million; the Catholic press had lost heavily in circulation and some of the oldest publications were closing shop; almost all the once-thriving lay associations and exciting movements of the past had fallen into decline. It was the most dramatic, critical ten years in American Catholic history.

The outstanding event of the decade had been the Ecumenical Council Pope John summoned, which met in Rome for four successive autumns beginning in 1962. The Council, as John had hoped, released religious energy and a zeal for reform that only a few had even suspected existed in the Church. When it was finally brought to a conclusion by his more cautious successor, Paul VI, in December 1965, most of the 2300 bishops who took part in it came home with the idea that Catholicism, purged of irrelevancies, anachronisms, and outmoded traditions, was on the brink of a second spring. But only five years later, many Catholics, not least of all in the United States, were convinced that the Council had also released unsuspected demons. Others, more hopeful, argued that the postconciliar disorders were inevitable and no more than a temporary setback on the difficult path to the renewal John had sought. In any case, all were agreed that a new era had begun; the Church had moved so far along the road to *aggiornamento* there could be no return to the tranquil past.

In the first years of the stormy decade, not only the Pope but another highly placed man named John was an immediate instrument of change. John F. Kennedy, the first Catholic in the White House, took little interest in ecclesiastical matters; he certainly never thought of himself as a Church reformer; but without intending to do so, he set a new tone for American Catholicism by exemplifying a nondefensive, coolly detached, urbane approach to the world. The Kennedy style established a fresh standard for millions of his coreligionists, who were extremely proud of him, impressed by his seemingly effortless loyalty to the Church and his easy assumption that the Catholic faith was in no way a strain on his character as an American fully at ease with the nation's traditions. At the very time when Pope John, by his pronouncements but more importantly by his public behavior, was turning ecumenism and the ecumenical attitude into a new reality on the religious scene, President Kennedy, almost inadvertently, was bringing an end to American Catholic sectarianism and withdrawal from the general culture.

As a candidate, Kennedy knew he had no choice but to face up to the "religious issue." He met it head-on, first by proving that he could win a primary in a non-Catholic state like West Virginia, and, after his nomination, by a successful televised appearance before the Ministerial Association of Greater Houston, which was shown all over the nation. "I do not accept the right of any ecclesiastical official to tell me what to do in the sphere of my public responsibility as an elected official," he told the Texas ministers. It was a kind of declaration of lay independence, easily misinterpreted as defiance. But Kennedy was not denying his Church or its authority to define the moral law; he was, rather, insisting on the layman's responsibility to make political decisions on the basis of his own conscientious judgments. The candidate's position was not only reassuring to his Protestant listeners but pleasing to fellow Catholics—and apparently acceptable to the bishops of the Church in America.

To no one's surprise, least of all his own, throughout his campaign Kennedy was on the receiving end of an attack from anti-Catholic forces comparable to that launched against Al Smith in 1928; he was also called upon to settle the doubts expressed by some responsible guardians of the Republic who were concerned about whether he would be able to fulfill his constitutional duty to maintain separation of Church and state and still remain a Catholic in good standing.

Kennedy responded to both groups—without rancor or defensiveness; but he shrewdly avoided getting tangled up in the theological underbrush in doing so. In response to queries about his independence, he simply invoked his past record as a wartime naval officer and member of Congress and said that, in his view, any President who could not in conscience live up to his oath would be morally obliged to resign the office. He did not anticipate any such conflict, he added; and there is no reason to believe that during his short presidency he faced any.

As with Al Smith, Kennedy's religion undoubtedly gained votes for him at the same time it cost him support he might otherwise have had. His victory over Richard M. Nixon was so narrow that the exact number of votes gained or lost might have been crucial, but it is impossible to say with any certainty whether his faith helped more than it hurt him: too many other factors were involved to isolate any one of them and say with finality that it alone had made the difference between victory and defeat.

In any case, President Kennedy's record in office was such that, less than five years after his death, during the historic Democratic primaries of 1968 when his brother Robert was running against Eugene McCarthy, another Catholic, the religion of the candidates was simply not an issue; nor was it a factor when Edmund Muskie, also a Catholic, ran for the vice-presidency on the Democratic ticket with Hubert Humphrey later the same year. By 1972, many in the Democratic Party felt that the Presidential ticket had to include a Catholic; that was taken into consideration when first the ill-fated Thomas Eagleton and later the Kennedy in-law, Sargent Shriver, were nominated for the Vice-Presidency.

John F. Kennedy never ceased to be aware that his behavior in office was being carefully watched for any signs of favoritism toward the Church. He was just as careful not to show any. Even his most severe critics found no cause for alarm, though some Catholics felt that had a non-Catholic sat in his place, the case for granting federal aid to parochial schools might have received a more sympathetic hearing in the White House than he gave it.

Probably more important than anything else Kennedy did or failed to do as the first Catholic President was the image he created as the quintessential man of his time, at home in the world of secular intellectuals and yet steadfastly, though never ostentatiously, loyal to the faith of his Irish fathers. The famous Kennedy style—his poise, sophistication, the modernity worn as casually as his London-tailored clothes—suggested more than any proclamation could that Catholics at long last were comfortably integrated into American society. It also meant a great deal to Catholics themselves, who stood a little taller because one of their own became an authentic folk hero during his lifetime and after his tragic death was quickly assigned to the company of American legends.

The American bishops arriving in Rome in 1962 were not prepared for the daringly new interpretations of Catholic teaching that came to the fore at the Vatican Council, nor were most of the priests who until that time had been accepted

*typical example or representative

as the leading lights of American Catholic theology. Before the Council, fresh theological thinking had been carried on in France, Germany, Belgium, and Holland, but in the United States most university departments of religious studies and the mainline theological publications were in safe traditional hands. Parish priests rarely veered from the catechism in their interpretation of doctrine.

Two of the three most influential theologians, Father Francis J. Connell, professor at the Catholic University of America, and Monsignor Joseph Clifford Fenton, editor of the *American Ecclesiastical Review,* looked on all doctrinal speculation as a danger to the faith and spent much of their time opposing suggestions that serious change in Catholic theological thinking was even possible.

The third and most distinguished of the trio was the elegant Jesuit scholar, John Courtney Murray of Woodstock College. On most doctrinal matters Murray was almost as conservative as the other two. However, he had specialized in Church-state relations, and ten years before the Council began he took a public stand in opposition to the troublesome "Catholic State" thesis. Murray's conclusion was that the American understanding of Church-state relations was not merely tolerable but most desirable, even from a strictly Catholic point of view. The position soon led him into bitter controversy with Monsignor Fenton, Father Connell, and other establishment theologians; it also made him suspect by the ultraconservative Vatican Holy Office, which quietly used its authority to silence him.

For some years prior to the Council, the Jesuit's ideas about religious liberty were looked upon as so dangerously unorthodox by Rome that he had been forbidden by his superiors to publish any more on the subject. Though he was far and away the most competent and best-known American Catholic theologian, he remained at Woodstock throughout the first session of the Council. The next year, after it became clear that the Council would chart new theological paths, the long-delayed invitation came. Murray went to Rome at the special bidding of no less a traditionalist than Cardinal Spellman, who appointed him a special theological adviser. It was understood from the beginning that he would concentrate his efforts on the question of religious liberty, which the Council could hardly avoid.

During the next three sessions, Father Murray probably had more influence on the Council than any other American. He was the chief architect of the historic declaration on religious freedom promulgated by Paul VI on December 7, 1965. That doctrine—a version of Murray's once-condemned thesis—marked a sharp break with the idea that the Roman Catholic Church had a right to claim special recognition from the state and that, ideally, non-Catholic religions, though they might be tolerated in the interest of civic peace, had no strict claim on civil rights. "This Vatican Council," the Pope said, "declares that the human person has a right to religious freedom. This freedom means that all men are to be immune from coercion on the part of individuals or of social groups and of human power, in such wise that no one is forced to act in a manner contrary to his own beliefs, whether privately or publicly, whether alone or in association with others, within due limits."

Because the new teaching on religious freedom—even Father Murray insisted on calling it a "development" rather than a reversal of the old thesis—was drafted by an American and strongly supported by the United States bishops and their theologians in Rome, it quickly became known as the "American" decree. Its formal acceptance by the Universal Church meant that the most serious doctrinal differences between Roman Catholic teaching and American political theory had been finally overcome.

A second issue dealt with by the Council, the Catholic attitude toward the Jewish people, also had unusual support from the American bishops. Immediately at stake was the question whether the Jews were particularly responsible for the death of Christ. The Americans found the idea repellent and theologically unsound. Such powerful leaders of the hierarchy as Cardinals Spellman of New York, Cushing of Boston, Shehan of Baltimore, Ritter of Saint Louis, and Meyer of Chicago fought valiantly, and successfully, to put the Church clearly on record as being in opposition to the ancient charge that the Jews were guilty of "deicide" and had been cut off from divine favor.

Both these questions—religious liberty and the spiritual equality of the Jews with the rest of mankind—struck most of the Americans at the Council as barely worth the attention they received. In the light of the American experience, the right to worship freely seemed utterly obvious, and the hoary canard against the Jewish people appeared to be patently absurd, unjust, and contrary to the Christian Gospels. However, there were bishops in Rome from less tolerant places who were still ready to argue for religious disabilities and the ancient anti-Jewish myths—and they did so shamelessly, in traditional theological language. It was necessary, then, for the Americans (along with European allies) to summon all the persuasiveness at their disposal to see to it that neither of the two issues was ignored, slighted, or watered down. This they did, not without opposition certainly, but with remarkable tenacity and good will.

On most of the other matters with which the Council was concerned, the Americans were divided between a liberal and a conservative faction. For example, some in the American hierarchy originally opposed switching the language of worship from Latin to the vernacular, among them the prestigious Cardinal-Archbishops of New York and Los Angeles, while others enthusiastically supported this and almost every other proposed liturgical change. On practically all the disputed theological issues there were similar divisions of opinion. As they learned more about the new theology, some of the bishops became ardent advocates of its basic thrust; others, faithful to the old-style seminary training, remained skeptical.

Among the Americans could be found prelates as ultra-conservative as Cardinal McIntyre of Los Angeles and as liberal as Archbishop Paul J. Hallinan of Atlanta; on the whole, however, the American bishops could be fairly characterized as moderate—neither as unbending as some of their brother-bishops from the tradition-laden Latin and Arabic countries nor as progressive as the hierarchies of Holland and most of the mission territories.

With the two "American" decrees safely passed and a clear go-signal for ecumenical efforts given by the highest authority, the bishops of the United States returned to their dioceses with a warm feeling of accomplishment, eager to implement the decrees of the Council, including those providing for a larger role for the laity, more democratic government of the Church, and an open, receptive attitude toward the world beyond the Church.

For a brief hour, in 1966, the spirit of Pope John's *aggiornamento*—a sense of spiritual renewal and reinvigoration—swept throughout the American Church. There seemed to be a general consensus that though the Council did not go as far in adjusting Catholicism to the needs of the times as the more progressive faction had wished, nonetheless it had moved a long way in the right direction. The bishops were optimistic. They had every reason to believe that Catholicism after the Council was notably more "American" in spirit and discipline than it had been under Pius XII. What, indeed, could be more American than religious liberty, ecumenical activity, a more democratic ecclesiastical structure, or a revised vernacular liturgy open to the participation of the laity?

To avoid the turmoil and division that historically had followed upon ecumenical councils, the Fathers of Vatican II had issued no anathemas, condemned no movements (not even communism), and avoided all dogmatic declarations. As Pope John had advised, the Council had been steadfastly pastoral in purpose and eminently positive in tone. It seemed, then, that this time the Church might be spared the dissension that had followed most of the earlier councils. But it was not to be. The optimism of the closing hours in Rome was soon dispelled as controversies escalated into revolts, tension between priests and bishops mounted, and the once-placid life of the cloister was disturbed by arguments over the meaning of the religious life in the postconciliar Church.

Some students of Catholicism hold that once the tightly run "system" was loosened up—even such a petty thing as lifting the ban on meat on Friday seemed shattering at the time—the whole edifice of law, custom, and religious practice that had supported Catholic stability since the Council of Trent was threatened. If *one* thing could be questioned, then anything could—and in time practically everything was. The idea that the Church could change—though it should have been obvious from ecclesiastical history that it frequently did just that over the long centuries—was such a startling discovery that it brought on an unendurable crisis of faith for many.

Other observers trace the upheaval to the new theology, which got a generous hearing at the Council. They point out that most Catholics never learned to distinguish between the dogmatic teachings of the Faith and the philosophical mode in which these teachings were presented. When the philosophy, the medieval style of thought, in which the teachings were presented was put aside in favor of a more modern way of thinking, it was as if everything were suddenly thrown up for grabs. In any case, there can be no doubt that for large numbers of Catholics the loss of the old certitudes about matters which really had nothing to do with Revelation ended up in a loss of faith, not only in the wisdom of the Church but in the basic doctrines on which it was founded.

Who was primarily to blame for the Catholic crisis, then, is still debatable—whether the bishops themselves because, reverting to type, they were too slow to implement the decrees of the Council, or the impatient priests, religious, and laymen who insisted on moving faster and further than either Pope John or the Council had ever intended. In any case, the first disturbances began not long after Vatican II was brought to a conclusion.

A period of liturgical experimentation had been granted and it quickly led to a highly conspicuous "underground Church." Groups of lay Catholics, unhappy with the spiritless Masses offered at their parish churches, took to meeting with rebellious priests for unauthorized Eucharistic liturgies in private homes, some of them verging on the bizarre. The prescribed rubrics were put aside and the liturgy was adapted to what the devotees of do-it-yourself reform took to be their own special psychological and spiritual needs. Mass was celebrated at coffee tables without the traditional vestments, with scant attention to the rubrical norms, and in bland defiance of canonical regulations.

The celebrant, no longer treated as a remote "holy man," was looked upon more as the presiding officer of an ecclesiastical assembly and discussion leader than as one set apart by his ordination. The Mass as festive Eucharistic meal was accented at the expense of the Mass as a representation of

Christ's Sacrifice; the emphasis was on palsiness and community at the cost of decorum and mystery.

Inevitably, such a flouting of ecclesiastical discipline, however satisfying to the participants, greatly disturbed Church authorities. Gradually, a barrier was set up between the temperamentally cautious hierarchy and the enthusiasts, priests and laymen, who were most eager for change and who shakily invoked the teachings of the Council when they instituted it even against the specific directions of local authorities.

More serious than defiant gestures of this kind were the controversies arising from the two big issues which the Council itself did not handle but had turned over to the Pope because they were looked upon as altogether too delicate for public discussion—birth control and clerical celibacy.

The Pontiff, Paul VI, had never made a secret of his position on priestly celibacy—he was for it unequivocally and, it appeared, unbudgeably. But for the first time in centuries the ancient discipline was openly questioned by large numbers of the clergy themselves. A new positive attitude toward sexuality and marriage, found not only among the younger Catholics but spelled out in several Council documents, inevitably posed the question of why priests, just because they were priests, should remain unmarried. Voluntary celibacy was still respected as an evangelical ideal but more and more of the younger clergy, and many of their elders as well, expressed their doubts in public about the wisdom of demanding celibacy of every man in Holy Orders. Poll after poll showed that growing numbers of priests and seminarians would marry if they were permitted to do so; even among those who said that they would remain single, the number advocating the clerics' natural right to marry was surprisingly high.

The Vatican Council had made it easier for priests who wished to marry to resign from the active ministry. Many immediately took advantage of the new permissiveness. With Catholic lay attitudes softening, the priest who wished to take a wife and was willing to give up his profession to do so was no longer stigmatized within the community. Most of them, after leaving the rectory, melted into the lay body, with a minimum of scandal. In a very short time, the ex-priests numbered in the hundreds, then in the thousands. Among them was a bishop—a promising young leader of the progressive wing of the American hierarchy, James P. Shannon, Auxiliary Bishop of Saint Paul, Minnesota, who married a middle-aged divorcee in a civil ceremony and immediately accepted an administrative post in a secular college. Others, including a number of prominent theologians, superiors of religious orders, and pastors, left around the same time.

In June 1971 a second bishop resigned from the active ministry. Bernard M. Kelly, the Auxiliary Bishop of Providence, Rhode Island, sent a letter to all the priests of the diocese giving his reasons. "The Church in which we grew up," he wrote, "was the Church shaped by the Council of Trent, a Church almost completely withdrawn from the world, living in a world of its own, impervious to the developments taking place around it. It was a Church that placed great stress on authority, sacred power, and the need for obedience. It was a pyramidal Church with emphasis on the prerogatives of the hierarchy. It was a Church that became increasingly irrelevant and unintelligible to me." The Vatican Council, he added, promised to bring the Church into the world but the American hierarchy six years later was still so wedded to the old ways that it was deliberately blocking the basic changes necessary. Kelly ended his letter, "I have come to the painful conclusion that the United States Bishops as a body are determined to preserve as far as possible the structure and forms of Trent. I see no hope for any future change in their attitude. Since discussion is impossible, I feel obliged in conscience to protest in the only way possible, by my resignation."

Not all the priests who departed did so because of the celibacy requirement. Others stated that the professional priesthood no longer made much sense to them. As priests, they said, they no longer knew what was required of them or what their role should be in a secularized society—a complaint also being voiced by many married Protestant clergymen. Feeling strangulated by a too-slow-to-change institutional apparatus, they simply gave up. A smaller number, generally more embittered, turned against the Church altogether and joined the millions of Americans who were alienated from institutional religion of all kinds. Some of them, like James Kavanaugh, author of a best-selling book, anguished in public; others walked away quietly.

Though the situation seemed critical, with so many leaving and so few coming into the priesthood, the authorities, from the Pope on down, remained firm about the traditional clerical discipline, including celibacy. Some relaxation in rules was established for the younger clergy, especially for those preparing for the priesthood, but not enough to meet the fundamental complaints of the dissenters. In one encyclical and in numerous public statements the Pope—who spoke poignantly of clerical defectors as his "crown of thorns"—continued to uphold clerical celibacy. The American bishops steadfastly followed his lead.

The most crucial controversy of the postconciliar period arose when Pope Paul issued a long-awaited statement on birth control in 1968. In *Humanae Vitae,* probably the most controversial encyclical ever issued by a modern Pontiff, Paul VI repeated the traditional ban against every form of contraception. "Every marital act," he wrote, "must remain open to the transmission of life."

The uproar that followed in the American Catholic community was wholly unprecedented. The papal statement, it was pointed out again and again, ignored the recommendations of a study commission which the Vatican itself had set up; it was also contrary to the position taken during the Council by several cardinals and to the opinion of the majority of contemporary Catholic theologians. The Pope, it soon became clear, had created a credibility gap between himself and millions of the faithful.

According to Catholic doctrine, the Pontiff is in no way bound by the theological views of others, one way or another. He was quite within his canonical rights then in adopting a position contrary to those of his cardinals, advisers, theologians, or members of the laity. Nevertheless, there was a widespread feeling that he had acted arbitrarily and unwisely. Almost immediately after publication of the encyclical, eighty-seven American theologians issued a public statement pointing out that the encyclical was not infallible and charging that Paul had betrayed "a narrow and positivistic notion of papal authority." A few priests spoke openly against the encyclical from their pulpits. Others kept a discreet public silence but privately advised Catholics to follow their own consciences in the matter if they thought the Pope was wrong. In Washington, D.C., a group of nineteen dissident priests—signers of a statement of conscience—were suspended by their Cardinal-Archbishop, Patrick O'Boyle, for refusing to support the papal teaching. Later some of the rebels were restored to good standing in the archdiocese; others among them dropped out of the active ministry altogether.

The controversy over the *Humanae Vitae,* which exploded throughout the world but nowhere more violently than in the United States, had implications transcending the immediate issue at stake—the control of population and the right to a full sex life within marriage along with the duty to exercise what a Vatican Council decree had described as "responsible parenthood." It also turned out to be a challenge to the Pope's prerogatives and a serious blow to papal prestige. After release of the encyclical, the crisis of authority in the Church was brought to a new intensity.

More and more Catholics announced freely that they no longer felt bound by everything the Pope, the bishops, or their pastors decreed. For the first time in American history priests refused to teach what the Pope had clearly defined as binding on the Catholic conscience. Millions of laymen dismissed the encyclical as simply wrongheaded and unrealistic. For thousands of them it marked the final breaking point. The new generation of Catholics, it seemed, would forgive almost anything but irrelevance and obscurantism, and Paul's encyclical was charged with promoting both.

The *Humanae Vitae* debacle marked a fundamental change in the character of American Catholicism. Reverential deference to the pronouncements of a reigning pontiff would probably never be the same again. Bishops and pastors would either convince people of the wisdom of their statements or they could expect no cooperation. Unquestioning obedience and unswerving loyalty to Rome, which had long been the dominant characteristics of the Catholic community, were now among the least valued of virtues. The individual conscience, in the new dispensation, was exalted with almost Protestant intensity.

After earlier ecumenical councils it took years before the particular theological *esprit* developed during a course of discussions and debates had become rooted in the minds of the laity, the ordinary religious, and the lower clergy. Perhaps because of higher literacy and vastly increased means of communication (Vatican II was the most exhaustively reported religious event in history), the venturesome spirit of the new conciliar theology caught on quickly in the American Church during the second half of the 1960s.

The propagation of its central themes was so dynamic that the Council was barely concluded when many of its decrees already seemed to be the product of a dead era. This was not really surprising, for many of these decrees represented a compromise between the old and new theologies—compromises politically necessary if the decrees were to be passed by a council divided between conservative and progressive forces. However, the result of the compromises was that the two large groups alienated in the postconciliar Church—conservatives, dismayed by the speed of change, and ardent advocates of *aggiornamento*, perturbed by the slowness of change—could appeal to the same set of documents in pleading their case.

In a certain sense, both groups were right. But if one thing was clear several years later it was that, from the beginning, the compromises were destined to be unsatisfactory to everyone. The old and new theologies could not be so easily blended as all that.

As it turned out, the new theologians gained the upper hand, especially among the opinion molders, while the guardians of what remained of the old theology were often found in the seats of power—in dioceses, parishes, and religious orders. A breakdown, then—the collapse of authority, the public squabbles, the defections and desertions—inevitably followed. Had the Council wholeheartedly adopted either one or the other of the competing theologies, the crisis might have been prevented, or at least it might have been minimized.

The new theology gave Catholicism a radically new face.

According to one of its central emphases, the Christian Church, though tragically divided into denominations and sects, is essentially one, with varying degrees of the fullness of Catholicity found in each of the separate bodies. Complete unity—between Catholic and Protestant, Protestant and Orthodox, Catholic and Orthodox—is yet to be fully realized in history, nor has it yet been given structural reality; but the words "schismatic" and "heretic," rarely heard after Vatican II, have already been robbed of so much substance that they have become practically meaningless.

In the meantime, efforts to signify the underlying motifs of the new theology are being given concrete expression not only in ecumenical dialogue but in joint worship and common theological enterprises. The religious exclusiveness once scrupulously practiced by Catholics now seems to be a thing of the past. Only a few appear eager these days to convert other Christians to Roman Catholicism, though there are unceasing efforts to convert diehards in the Church to the new idea of catholicity.

The notion that legalistic observance is the way to salvation has been almost completely exorcised. Many of the once-binding laws of the Church—Friday abstinence, Lenten fasts, and so on—have been formally repealed. Those that remain are taken much less seriously than they once were. Routinized religiosity has been replaced by attempts to achieve a personal confrontation with the divine, some of them patently gauche and naive but nonetheless genuine. The drastic falling off of the number of confessions heard, then, or the notable decline in Mass attendance, often do not necessarily indicate religious indifference or a lack of faith so much as a revolt against the highly structured and almost mechanistic observance of ecclesiastical rules and regulations characteristic of Catholicism in the past.

Almost all the verities of the old Catholicism now seem open to reinterpretation, not only by professional scholars and theologians but even by untutored men and women who have been at once shaken and emboldened by the questing spirit of the postconciliar Church, the tentative doctrinal pronouncements of the new-style clergy, and the changes they have personally experienced in the Church they were brought up to believe was forever immutable. The diminishing devout among the younger generation have a new conception of the Church. For most of them, it is no longer looked upon as the final authority whose every word is binding on the Catholic conscience but primarily as a manifestation of community, a "movement" of like-minded Christians intent on service to each other and to the world beyond the sanctuary. To the extent that the institutional Church, whatever its official pronouncements, fails to give actual witness to human brotherhood—especially when such failures are due to clerical or organizational rigidity—it is deemed mischievously irrelevant and unworthy of a Christian's loyalty.

Thousands upon thousands of the new young, convinced that failures of this kind are unavoidable in an institution as highly structured as the Roman Catholic Church, have turned away from it. The difference between them and the youthful apostates of earlier generations is that the fateful step is now usually taken without any feeling of guilt and in some cases with the conviction that to be a true follower of Christ one must sometimes put the institutional Church aside.

In something of the same spirit, thousands of men and women since the Vatican Council have left the cloister, with its conformity and strict rules and regulations, in order—as they themselves frequently put it—to live a more authentic religious life in the world based on service to others.

The Vatican Council did not give a great deal of attention to convent life, certainly nothing comparable to the effort that went into its debates on such matters as the relations between the Pope and his bishops, or the statement on freedom of religion. Still, the little said was enough to get a small-scale revolution under way among the almost 200,000 sisters then serving in the United States.

The Council had recommended that all religious, especially nuns, adapt their anachronistic habits to modern styling. Not long after the Council was completed, sisters began to appear in public dressed not only in modified religious garb but in straightforward secular clothing. The move was a small one but highly significant. It symbolized a change in attitude and a new understanding of the nun's role in the world.

More and more sisters, once they started to think about

* defectors

it, began to question the antiquated rules and canon laws that governed their lives in minute detail from morning until night; and from the convents of America there came a chorus of complaint that remote ecclesiastics, all men, were depriving religious women of the right to determine their own life styles and the kind of work they did, and were actually frustrating their efforts to live an authentic religious life.

Practically all the orders and congregations soon undertook self-study projects, with a view to rewriting rules and constitutions in the light of the new theology, rethinking the meaning of their commitments, and finding an interpretation of the traditional vows of poverty, chastity, and obedience which would be more realistic in the contemporary world.

In some communities it was decided that each nun could choose her own assignment and whenever possible the kind of work she preferred. The postconciliar religious women saw no reason why they should be limited to the teaching and nursing professions or to maintaining the institutions established by their orders. Some went into social work—the inner-city apostolate as they called it—and others took secular jobs as individuals in government offices, university counseling centers, and welfare departments. The long-unquestioned idea that sisters had no choice but to work as groups staffing Catholic institutions was finally gone.

Changes of this kind inevitably aroused controversy within the various religious communities as well as vigorous criticism from the outside. Some of the sisters, loyal to the old ways, felt that the innovators were actually destroying convent life and replacing it with possibly high-minded but still essentially secular social service. Convents in which basic decisions were reached democratically rather than handed down by an all-powerful superior, they charged, were simply turning away from the idea of consecrated obedience. The freedom of the new nuns to move about in society like other professional women seemed to convent conservatives to be seriously endangering the commitment to celibacy. And when sisters began to demand salaries commensurate with their work and were given the right to manage their own small personal expenditures without special permissions, it appeared to the guardians of conventual tradition that the virtue of poverty, too, was going by the boards—another casualty of the unchecked desire to conform to the modern world.

Many among the clergy and laity were equally disturbed by the turn religious life was taking. After years of expecting only unquestioning obedience and excessive decorum from the "good sisters," it was something of a shock to find nuns speaking out, sometimes quite critically, moving about freely, and taking an active part in secular affairs—including political campaigns, slum-renewal projects, and antiwar protests.

The first nuns on a picket line appeared even before the Vatican Council, when a group of Franciscans, still wearing their voluminous habits, protested against the racially segregationist policies of the Illinois Club for Catholic Women by marching up and down in front of a Loyola University building in Chicago where the club maintained its headquarters. The action was so unusual at the time that the nuns were photographed on front pages from coast to coast. Then, a few years later during the historic demonstration in Selma, Alabama, dozens of Catholic sisters answered the call of Martin Luther King for support and marched along with priests, ministers, and rabbis from across the nation. After that, the bars were down. Sisters took an active part in dozens of antiwar and antiracist demonstrations from one end of the country to another. In 1971 a small group of nuns and ex-nuns associated with the jailed pacifist priests, Philip and Daniel Berrigan, were named by a grand jury and charged with illegal revolutionary activity. It was a sign of how much Catholicism in the United States, and particularly its sisterhoods, had changed that the charges caused surprisingly little shock in the Catholic community.*

Such a probing of the real meaning of the nun's vocation was not carried out without serious consequences for the religious life itself. Some of the best-known religious in America —including the gifted Los Angeles artist, Corita Kent, and the dynamic president of Saint Louis's Webster College, Jacqueline Grennan—returned to lay life, as did dozens of the early advocates of change in the orders, who felt that the renewal they had worked for either did not come fast enough or, after

---

* Later they were found not guilty.

it did, that it was not as satisfying as they had thought it would be. A few of the more reform-minded communities, such as the Cincinnati-based Glenmary Sisters and the Immaculate Heart of Mary nuns of Los Angeles, faced showdowns with their bishops and then voted to pull out of the canonical structure governing religious life and carry on as independent lay communities.

All the sisterhoods lost significant members during the decade of crisis and the number of entering novices fell off drastically. Whatever the virtues of the new-style convent, it was clear that the life it offered no longer had a very wide appeal for the young. The orders, it soon became clear, were destined to get smaller and smaller as the older generation of nuns passed on, but most of them accepted that fact with equanimity.

However, more than the future of the orders themselves was at stake; the entire American Church would be profoundly affected by what was happening. The vast institutional apparatus the old-style nuns had created would have to be radically changed to meet the new realities. For example, the Church could no longer depend on an army of nuns, working for little more than subsistence pay, to staff the parochial school system which the sisters maintained from coast to coast. Without its schools the American Church might be better or worse off, but it would certainly be different.

The ferment in the convents was only among the most dramatic of the changes that transformed American Catholicism in the decade following the opening of the Second Vatican Council in 1962. Elsewhere, the *aggiornamento* Pope John XXIII had sought was accomplished beyond almost anyone's expectations—accomplished with a vengeance, some of the critics of the new Catholicism said, since it brought about what they regarded as the excesses of today and eliminated not only the bad features of yesterday but many of its virtues in the bargain. Others within the progressive party of the Church still insist that the present disturbances are due to the unwillingness of Pope Paul and most of the American hierarchy to free themselves from the dead hand of the past. With

*composure; evenness of mind esp under stress

a new generation of leaders, they are convinced the Church will thrive as never before.

In any case, an American Catholic miraculously returning from the grave, even a Catholic deceased as recently as 1960, would find startling changes that nothing in the pre-1960 Church could have prepared him for.

He would find not only that ex-priests, many of them now married to ex-nuns, are everywhere and are widely accepted by the larger Catholic community as prefiguring the clergy to come after the celibacy issue is finally settled. He would find that the birth-control question, which only ten years ago seriously bedeviled Catholic couples struggling to stay in the Church, has been practically resolved by a kind of benign neglect on the part of the clergy. He would find some of the avant-garde theologians now making a case for divorce and a few who are no longer as absolutistic as they once were about abortion. He would also find much less emphasis on sexual behavior than he remembered and much more on social justice and peace. He would hear demands that women be admitted to the priesthood and that bishops be democratically elected.

He would discover that the lines that once queued up outside confessional boxes on Saturday night have been reduced to a mere handful; that there are notably fewer people at Mass on Sunday; and that devotional novenas, like the public recitation of the rosary, have quietly disappeared—as have Latin in the liturgy, fish on Friday, the wearing of medals and scapulars, the gaining of indulgences, the Index of Forbidden Books, and the once powerful Legion of Decency. He would find, however, that something new had been added: a thriving Catholic Pentecostal movement, with "speaking in tongues," camp-meeting enthusiasm, and an intense awareness of the Spirit very much part of it.

If the man-come-back decided to drop in on Catholic churches he might still hear a few fiery sermons on purgatory or hell but many more on charity and the need to live in peace with one's neighbors—and perhaps some of the sermons would be delivered by visiting Protestant preachers. The emphasis on the evils of communism he would find strikingly diminished, but he would probably hear of Pope Paul's his-

* lined up in a line ** Roman Cath 9 day devotional

toric visit to the United Nations in 1965 and of the Pontiff's impassioned plea, *"jamais la guerre, jamais plus la guerre."* He would also learn of thousands of young Catholics, no longer worried about their patriotic credentials, offering the authorization of a Vatican Council document in pleading conscientious objection before draft boards. He might run across some of the hundreds of priests and nuns who are deeply involved in the war resistance movement.

Militant black and Chicano priests and nuns, he would discover, have formed their own pressure groups within the Church and are demanding an end to racism within its fold. Instead of an Irishman sitting in the Archbishop's House in Boston he would find a modest Portuguese prelate; in Brooklyn, the son of an Italian barber presides; and if he turned his eyes toward another old citadel of Irish dominance, Fordham University in the Bronx, he would find that Italian-American students outnumber all others.

He would hear little or nothing about the compatibility of Catholicism and American democracy because very few feel that it is still a serious problem. The Catholic community itself he would find sentimental about its ghettoized past but uneasy about its present and uncertain about its future. Catholics, he would discover, are more adjusted to life in the United States than they have ever been; they are less defensive, better educated, socially more secure, and strikingly more independent —independent of the clergy, of the claims of the dying ghetto culture, of ecclesiastical restrictions on their behavior, and of the thousand and one inhibitions that in his own day arose from being singular and "different" in a land first Protestant, later blandly secular.

Yet the visitor from the past might still conclude that something precious has been lost. The sometimes frantic search for relevance, it might strike him, may have led only to a more poignant irrelevance. The earnest pursuit of modernity may have only pointed up an essential anachronism in a nation ever more consecrated to the gods of secularity. Only the future can tell how it will all turn out.

Whatever that future, the visitor might be forced to conclude that Catholicism is ending its second centenary in the United States with a question mark.

Part Two

CHAPTER SIX

VARIETIES OF CATHOLICISM

American Catholics have always been different from their fellow citizens. In the beginning the outstanding thing about them was that they were not Protestants, in a nation where almost everyone else was, and this led to difficulties and misunderstandings. For example, most Americans assigned tremendous importance to the Scriptures, but Catholics put notoriously little emphasis on Bible reading and when they read the Good Book at all generally shunned the standard King James edition for a version of their own. In the Protestant-shaped religious climate of the time, this was looked upon as outrageously singular for a people who called themselves Christian. Again, Catholic religious services, particularly the Latin Mass and the use of private confession, seemed exotic if not downright superstitious to many Americans brought up on the straightforward liturgy of mainline Protestantism.

The deference Catholics gave to the Pope and his representatives (made even more perturbing after 1870 by the claim that in matters of faith and morals the Pontiff is infallible) struck their neighbors as a kind of intellectual enslavement unworthy of an American's proud independence of mind. Even such a small thing as the Friday abstinence law conspicuously set off Catholics. And there were numerous other signs—the blessed medals and scapulars they wore around their necks, the elaborate robes and baroque titles used by their bishops, the strange clothing affected by their nuns, the all-too-graphic religious images and prints found in their homes, the plaster statues of the Virgin Mary and the Saints cluttering up their houses of worship, their custom of tipping hats or making the Sign of the Cross every time they passed a church.

Later the sources of division rested more in the realm of behavior. Long after most Americans accepted birth control as desirable and planned parenthood as even a kind of patriotic duty, Catholic clerical spokesmen continued to denounce contraception as a heinous sin, and laymen took pride in their oversized families. Though they had their own mysterious marriage courts, which granted dubious "annulments" on grounds that only a Roman canonist could understand, Catholics adamantly refused to acknowledge the benefits of divorce or the right of even an innocent party to marry again after one had been granted. Later, their unyielding position on abortion became a serious source of tension.

More than anything else perhaps, the existence of parochial schools, segregating Catholics from others in early childhood, pointed up the apparent determination of members of the Church to go their own way in a nation which put more emphasis on conformity than it was always ready to acknowledge. In turn, the schools, which were designed to relate religion to every phase of life, strengthened a whole network of separatist institutions.

Almost from the earliest days American Catholicism has maintained its own press and publishing houses, fraternal organizations, hospitals and social-service agencies, professional and academic societies. Unlike their coreligionists on the Continent, they held off from establishing sectarian labor unions and political parties, but in almost every other area of life they produced counterparts of the dominant social structures —a Catholic poetry society, a Catholic sociological society, a Catholic war veterans association, Catholic Boy Scouts, a Catholic organization dedicated to the prevention of cruelty to animals, even a society for Catholic philatelists.

There have been Catholic debutante balls presided over by the Cardinal-Archbishops of New York and Los Angeles, Catholic bowling leagues, and Catholic travel agencies sponsoring vacation tours to the shrines at Lourdes and Fatima. There have been Catholic book clubs, a Catholic theatre guild, and from time to time Catholic cookbooks have been published featuring special dishes to mark the feast days of the

Church. Catholics have had their own *Nation* and *New Republic* (*Commonweal* and *America*), their own *Life* (*Jubilee*), their own *Reader's Digest* (the *Catholic Digest*), and even their own comic books.

At one time, an American Catholic who wished to do so could have enjoyed a fairly complete cultural life without venturing beyond the walls of his own religious community. Few did, however. Some managed to move in two cultural milieux, the general American and its special Catholic counterpart. But the arcane world of the Catholic subculture never actually reached more than a minority of the millions who made up the Church in the United States. Even when Catholicism appeared to be an extraordinarily cohesive force—as it no longer does—it was never really the social monolith many took it to be.

Actually, American Catholics have differed among themselves almost as much as they have from their neighbors. Liberals and conservatives, radicals and reactionaries, rich and poor, farmers and city dwellers, the highly educated and the illiterate, the devout and the lukewarm, earnest assimilationists and narrow tribalists have all found a place in the Church. Even within these subheadings, there have been significant differences. Polish workingmen of an earlier Pittsburgh, for example, would have been as baffled by the flagellant practices of the penitentes of the Southwest as their Protestant neighbors; the free and easy Sicilians of Chicago would have found the guilty puritanism of the Irish which James T. Farrell depicted in *Studs Lonigan* simply incomprehensible; the dutiful German farmers of Minnesota even today find the casual Catholicism of the Puerto Rican community something of a scandal.

Each of these groups, along with a dozen others, brought a particular national version of the many-faceted Catholic tradition to the United States, and each developed along its characteristic lines in the New World. Consequently many different Catholicisms have existed side by side since the first great wave of immigrants arrived on American shores. Some of them, tucked away in hidden corners of American life, were barely noticed, even by fellow Catholics.

* Decret, mysterious

The Irish created the central image and furnished most of the cultural stereotypes if only because they were the earliest to become Americanized, produced so many members of the hierarchy, the clergy, and religious orders, and were extremely vocal not only as Irishmen but precisely as Catholics. If one runs through the giants of American Catholicism, from the Carrolls to the Kennedys, Celtic names seem to predominate. Among the outstanding members of the hierarchy—England, Hughes, Ireland, Gibbons, O'Connell, Spellman, and Cushing come readily to mind—the Irish have produced more than any other group. Most of the major religious orders in the American Church—Jesuits, Dominicans, Augustinians, Christian Brothers, even the cloistered Trappists—have been strongly Irish, as have the largest sisterhoods.

Among the most active laymen, the number of Irishmen who made names for themselves as journalists, writers, and controversialists is striking—from Charles Carroll to William F. Buckley, Jr. And from the earliest days to the present, Irishmen have been prominent in almost every movement within American Catholicism, as leaders of right-wing and left-wing factions, as cautious conservatives and frisky rebels, rigid clericalists and free-wheeling liberals. They have varied widely, yet one way or another all of them have helped to establish the Irish interpretation of the Catholic tradition as the cultural standard.

The Catholicism of the Irish was generally observant to a fault and comparatively steady and untroubled. It lacked the intellectuality of the French and was neither as cynical about ecclesiastics nor as relaxed about the Faith as the Italian; it was not as absolutistic or mystical as the Spanish, as orderly as the German, or as nationalistic as the Polish. Unlike other brands of Catholicism, it put a central emphasis on strict obedience to ecclesiastical law and on sexual probity. One thesis offered in explanation for its preoccupation with sex is that during the years when the clergy of Ireland were forced to leave their own land for training in foreign seminaries, they picked up the spirit of Jansenism in France, brought it back home with them, and passed it on as true orthodoxy. This is perhaps too pat; but however one accounts for it, Irish Catholicism—and consequently the basic thrust of American Catholicism—was tinged with a puritanism not truly consistent with basic Catholic doctrine.

Another characteristic of Irish Catholicism has been its exaggerated reverence for the clergy. In the old Ireland the best-educated and most honored men of all were those called to the priesthood. The priest was almost always a trusted man of the people who remained close to them and served as a kind of protector during the years of their political subjugation. The priest in the old country was looked to for direction and leadership in all aspects of life because of his superior education, and this dependence was carried over in American Irish communities.

One result was that for many years the Church in America was habitually looked upon as an "other"—the bishops, priests, and religious, who were encouraged to man the Catholic institutions without any "interference." The laity were brought up to mind their own affairs and leave ecclesiastical matters to their clerical betters. Not until the Second Vatican Council did the phrase *"we* are the Church" become popular, for the first time since the early trustee controversy challenging the right of the clergy to run the Church as they saw fit.

Finally, Irish Catholicism—which was long under threat of extinction in the homeland and in the United States later became a target of powerful Protestant militancy—was marked by a touchiness and a defensive, at times even belligerent, determination to maintain itself in a world which it took to be hostile to just about everything it stood for. This spirit—the "siege mentality" as it came to be called—led to a suspicious attitude toward others and a predisposition toward exclusiveness that cut off Catholics from full participation in the cultural life of the nation. The postconciliar ecumenical movement changed all this, however. Present-day Catholics, maybe even especially the Irish among them, have become notably less sectarian in their approach to the world beyond the borders they once defiantly set up for themselves.

The strength of the Catholicism of the Irish has been its steadiness, realism, and practicality—qualities that do not readily produce mystics and contemplatives. But for a Church still finding its way in an alien cultural atmosphere, such characteristics may have been necessary for sheer survival. Aside from their early difficulties with the French-born bishops, Irish-American Catholics were remarkably stable in their loyalty. They rallied in support of their priests and the public positions taken by the hierarchy almost as a matter of habit. They were faithful about Mass attendance, exercised great care for even minor ecclesiastical regulations, and set an abnormally high standard of observance for other national groups in doing so. They contributed generously to the incessant building drives sponsored by the Church, only rarely questioning their wisdom, and wholeheartedly supported the vast Catholic educational system that grew up in the United States.

With few exceptions, Irish priests avoided theological speculation and held on tenaciously to the doctrines they were taught in the seminary, which they passed along to laity with extraordinary tidiness. As might have been expected, they did not produce many front-rank theologians, but they were excellent catechism teachers. Under their leadership, American Catholics became not only the most law-abiding but probably the best-instructed people in the entire Church.

The Irish were notoriously unconcerned about aesthetics—the churches they built in America are generally models of mediocre architecture—but their urge toward physical expansion was remarkable from the very beginning. The Irish-American hierarchy—brick-and-mortar bishops almost to a man—had their people behind them when they built churches, seminaries, schools, colleges, universities, hospitals, and orphanages by the hundred.

Though the Irish in the United States, like those who remained in the homeland, have never been free of nationalistic excess, their outstanding loyalty to Rome gave the American Church a cosmopolitan flavor it might otherwise have lacked. There have been practically no heresies or significant threats of schism among them. Whatever the Church asked for, whether speaking from Rome through the Pope or at home through their own bishops, they offered without complaint, including their sons to the priesthood and their daughters to the convent in impressive numbers.

The traditional Irish influence has waned as Catholics in the United States have become more self-consciously "American." But the formative role it played in creating the Catholicism of the New World remained critically important for many decades.

The Germans have been numerous ever since the waves of immigration in the late nineteenth century brought hundreds of thousands of them to the United States fleeing from militarism and the anti-Catholic policies of Bismarck's *Kulturkampf*. Though German Catholics settled everywhere in the new land, their strength was in the Middle West. They dominated in such dioceses as Saint Louis, Cincinnati, and Milwaukee, which produced a Catholicism more staid than that found in the Irish citadels of Boston, New York, Philadelphia, and other places on the Eastern Seaboard.

The Germans, who put heavy emphasis on the intellectual side of their religion, adapted readily to the American tradition of the parish school, where their treasured virtues of thoroughness, industry, and orderliness were studiously inculcated in the young. As early as 1837 German-American Catholics began to publish their own newspaper in Cincinnati, *Der Wahrheitsfreund*. The long-lived *Der Wanderer*—published in Saint Paul, Minnesota—and a dozen other publications were added later, in part to meet the challenge of Protestant missionary efforts and counteract American nativism but most of all to sustain German culture and tradition in the New World.

With their own parishes, schools, monasteries, foreign-language press, and vigorous societies of laymen, American Catholics of German descent lived in semi-isolation from mainstream Catholicism right up to the First World War. Their relations with the predominantly Irish hierarchy were not always smooth and occasionally broke out into open warfare, not only during the row over Cahenslyism but during the "Americanism" controversy, when a group of powerful German ecclesiastics charged that some of the Irish bishops were covering up certain heretical notions hidden in the effort to assimilate Catholicity to American pluralism.

In those early days, German Catholic leaders made no secret of the fact that they had little respect for Irish Catholicism, which they looked upon as arrogant, overbearing, shockingly pragmatic, and culturally inferior to their own. From time to time German bishops made it clear to Rome that they resented the Celtic dominance in America and predicted that the eagerness of the Irish leaders to acculturate the Church would eventually lead to a kind of doctrinal sell-out.

During World War I, when the nation turned bitterly and irrationally against all things Teutonic—a traumatic experience for Americans of German descent—the traditional nationalism among them cooled down somewhat; in time most of their earlier isolationism disappeared and there was a great deal of intermarriage with other Catholic groups, especially the Irish.* By the Second World War German Catholicism, with some exceptions, was comfortably integrated into the general life of the American Church.

German Catholicism in America has strong rural and monastic roots (Benedictine monks played a large part in its development). It has consequently tended to be somewhat more conservative than those versions of the Faith which were shaped at least in part by their reactions to the turmoil of the big cities. It has also been much less influenced by devotional fads than the Catholicism which set out to appeal to the urban masses with their sentimentality and hunger for novelty. When popular novenas (which published weekly scorecards on "prayers answered") were at their peak, the German parishes tended to put even stronger emphasis on the dignity, decorum, and inner meaning of the official liturgy; again, schools under the direction of German priests and religious were outstanding for their dedication to solid theological learning and respect for ecclesiastical tradition.

At first the German Catholics imported their clergy from the fatherland, but as time went on they were second only to the Irish in providing the Church in America with native-born priests and religious. The German clergy was never given the adulation that Irish clerics for so long took as their due,

---

* In this connection, it is interesting that a number of famous "Irish Catholics" are the product of an amalgam of the two traditions, among them Senator Eugene J. McCarthy (son of Anna Baden), William F. Buckley, Jr. (son of Aloise Steiner), and Fathers Daniel and Philip Berrigan (sons of Freda Fromhart).

but priests and monks were solidly respected in the German communities as men set apart; anticlericalism was never a serious problem among them.

A number of the outstanding bishops of the American Church were of German origin, among them Cardinals Mundelein and Meyer of Chicago and Archbishop Rummel of New Orleans. At least until recent years, dozens of American sisterhoods were almost exclusively German, and German-Americans outnumbered other members in some important congregations of priests and brothers, notably the Redemptorist, Capuchin, Marianist, and Precious Blood orders. The great American Benedictine foundations—Saint John's in Minnesota, Saint Meinrad's in Indiana, Saint Vincent's in Pennsylvania, and Mount Angel in Oregon, among others—were originally founded by German-speaking monks. They helped set the tone for German-American Catholicism, which, aside from its early tendency to be excessively nationalistic, has always been a steadying influence on the Church.

Up until the Civil War the number of Italians in the United States was negligible. The census of 1860 listed only 10,000, most of them middle-class merchants, artisans, and artists from the north of Italy. But between 1880 and 1924, when immigration was drastically curtailed, some five million more arrived in America, most of them from the impoverished South and only a few with even a primary education. In Italy they had been farm workers with no trade or profession to fall back upon. In the United States they clustered in the big cities—New York, Philadelphia, Boston, Chicago, and elsewhere—and were doomed to the back-breaking jobs with the poorest pay that the Irish were already moving beyond. Generally they were consigned to indescribably bad living conditions in urban slums.

With the exception of a small number of Waldensians who arrived earlier seeking religious freedom, the Italians were almost all Catholic, or at least nominally so. But under the pressures of slum living, some fell away from the Church completely; others, identifying their ancestral religion with the old country and Protestantism with the New World, joined Protestant denominations, believing it the "American" thing to do;

and still others, deeming themselves socialists and anticlericals, were set against all religion but particularly Catholicism.

Not until they fought their way out of poverty were the American Italians integrated into the life of the Church in America. In earlier days, almost all their priests were sent from abroad, and their Little Italies became like foreign villages set down in the metropolitan centers.

A special community of missionary priests and brothers, founded in 1877 by Bishop John-Baptist Scalabrini in Piacenza, was dedicated to working with the Italian emigrants in America. These religious, known as Scalabrinians, organized parishes in the larger Italian communities in the United States which kept the traditions of the homeland alive. Some of the well-established orders, including the Franciscans, Servites, and Salesians, also sent religious from Italy to take up the work, and a number of diocesan priests—many of them non-Italians—served other Italian-American parishes, which were almost always found in the run-down sections of town.

The most memorable of the missionaries was the extraordinary nun, Frances Xavier Cabrini, who in 1946 became the first American citizen to achieve sainthood. Mother Cabrini, a native of Lombardy, founded a community called the Missionary Sisters of the Sacred Heart, who worked as teachers and nurses in New York, Chicago, Seattle, and other places where Italian immigrants were numerous.

In all, the saintly foundress—a very practical lady of prodigious energy and zeal—established sixty-seven houses of her order in Europe, South America, and the United States, one for each year of her life. By the time of her death, in Chicago in 1917, there were 1500 nuns in the order, half of them working in the United States.

American-Italians, however, have never been proportionately represented among the clergy or in the religious orders. For one thing, it was a long time before they encouraged their young to go into the service of the Church. In southern Italy, having a priest or nun in the family was usually looked upon as a social asset; in the land of opportunity, as often as not, it was regarded as a step backward. Again, the anticlericalism the first immigrants brought with them from Italy remained a deterrent force for many years. Finally, if the truth be told, the clerical establishment itself did little to encourage religious vocations in the Italian-American community. Italian Catholics with their effusive devotion to unknown saints, their gaudy *festas*, sublime lack of concern about ecclesiastical regulations, and disdain for the censorious emphasis of Irish Catholicism were treated as people apart.

The piety of the Italo-Americans—which usually had little in common with the sophisticated Catholicism of Rome, Florence, or Milan but was more a reflection of the peasant faith of Sicily and the southern provinces—was characteristically explosive, sentimental, and frequently tinged with superstition. As such, it was something of an embarrassment to their more inhibited coreligionists, who were eager to conform as much as possible to American notions of sobriety and restraint in religious matters.

American Catholicism, however, was the loser. Had the Italians gained more influence in the Church in the United States, at least some of the less attractive aspects of the puritanical Irish version of the Faith might have been counterbalanced by Mediterranean wit, wisdom, and *joie de vivre*.

About one out of every eight American Catholics is of Polish extraction—a large, extraordinarily cohesive group which has jealously operated its own parishes, schools, and national societies within the larger diocesan structures. In the Great Lakes dioceses of Chicago, Buffalo, Detroit, Milwaukee, and throughout Pennsylvania parishes served by Polish priests and nuns, bastions of Polish culture, have maintained only minimal contact with their Catholic neighbors. To maintain this Catholicism-within-Catholicism, American Poles still support seventeen different sisterhoods and over twenty religious communities of men who, along with some two thousand diocesan priests, operate almost eight hundred parishes, six hundred schools, and more than two hundred charitable institutions.

There have always been Poles in the United States, beginning with the volunteers who served under George Washington in the Revolutionary Army. Millions more arrived in the wave of immigration that began in 1870. Still more were added after thousands of displaced persons arrived in the United States following World War II.

The first Polish immigrants in the eighteenth century, few in number, were easily integrated into American society, but the later arrivals had to cling together for support. They established their own enclaves in the cities and towns where they found jobs as factory hands and industrial workers. Wherever they settled, they set up national parishes and parochial schools where Polish was the language of instruction and the history of the homeland occupied an honored place in the curriculum.

Catholics in Poland have traditionally made a strong identification between their religion and the mother country. Other nations have had equally strong links between Church and state but probably nowhere else in the worldwide Church is there a more patriotic Catholicism or a more Catholic patriotism, a tradition which is almost as venerable as the thousand-year-old history of the nation. It was solidly implanted in America and has been sustained primarily by the national parishes which still exist wherever Poles are numerous.

As a matter of preference, then, the Poles have played no significant role in the general life of the Church in the United States, though there have been distinguished exceptions, including Cardinal John Krol of Philadelphia, now a leader of the hierarchy, and a number of other bishops and superiors of religious orders.

Polish nationalism was at the root of the only serious schism within American Catholicism—the Polish National Catholic Church, which had its genesis in Chicago in 1895 after Father Anton Koslowsky had clashed with diocesan authorities over the question of parochial administration. Koslowsky favored the trustee system of church ownership, though it had never gained a real foothold in Chicago. He won popular support for his stand against the Bishop's holding Church property in his own name, and many Poles followed him out of the Church after he organized an independent parish of his own. The rebellious priest was formally excommunicated not long thereafter. Later Koslowsky's supporters affiliated with other dissident groups in various parts of the country and declared their complete independence of Rome. Their Polish National Catholic Church eventually became associated with the schismatic Old Catholics of Europe. Father Koslowsky himself was consecrated a bishop—validly but illicitly in the eyes of the Vatican. He then procceded to organize a number of Polish national parishes in the United States and in the mother country itself.

Originally the new church differed only in that Polish was used in the liturgy rather than Latin and parochial property was owned by lay trustees. Later the new church approved some changes in doctrine which were regarded as heretical by the Roman authorities. As a result of this break with theological orthodoxy, the split became more serious than it had originally been when only schism and questions of discipline were at stake. By the 1970s there were four dioceses of the Polish National Church in the United States and more than fifty parishes in Poland.

The vast majority of American Poles, however, have remained utterly faithful to Rome and to the local bishops, while still living in self-chosen semi-isolation. In recent years, though, there has been a growing movement among younger Poles, as among other Eastern European groups, to break with the nationalistic character of their parishes and identify with a generally American Catholicism.

The other Eastern European Catholics followed the general pattern of the Poles in maintaining their distinctive religious cultures in the New World. The Slovaks, for example, established about three hundred parishes in the United States; the Lithuanians more than one hundred; the Hungarians several dozen. Even where these groups lived in the same city neighborhoods, as they still do in Chicago, they attended separate churches and schools and strove to hold on to their national identity by means of newspapers, magazines, cultural societies, social clubs, and youth organizations. Most of them also set up their own seminaries, monasteries, and religious orders. In a few cases they even established their own institutions of higher learning.

The Ruthenians, Ukrainians, Croats, and certain other Slavic groups are Eastern-rite Byzantine Catholics, in full communion with Rome but subject to a separate canonical discipline. They follow a liturgy almost identical with that prevailing in the Orthodox Church. Most of them now have their own bishops, though before the special hierarchies were set up they were subject to the local "Latin" bishop. A great deal of dissension resulted from the earlier practice. With ample reason, the Byzantines frequently complained that the "Latin" hierarchy was showing little sympathy for their distinctive religious traditions and age-old liturgical practices. The Vatican—in an effort not to sow "confusion" by the presence of a married Catholic clergy in the United States—merely exacerbated tensions when it decreed in 1928 that in America only single men could be ordained to the priesthood, even in churches where a married clergy had always been acceptable. As a result, thousands of Eastern-rite Catholics, put off by what they took to be papal contempt for their cultural and ecclesiastical heritage, converted to the Orthodox Church, while others established their own independent churches.

As time passed, even aside from these losses, the Byzantine Catholics steadily diminished in number. In all, less than a million American Catholics now belong to one or another of the Eastern, or Uniate, churches. Many, reaching adulthood, have transferred to the Latin rite, as a result of intermarriage or simply from a desire to be identified with the more "American" Catholicism of the overwhelming majority.

Frenchmen never came to America in great numbers. Even during the years of the great immigrations, less than a half-million left France for the United States. Most Americans of French background, then, descended from the Canadians who crossed the border into New England to become United States citizens.

Franco-Americans, as they used to call themselves, followed the usual pattern of setting up ethnic parishes, in their case as much out of a distaste for the Catholicism of the Irish as anything else. The French, who made no secret of their anti-Irish feelings, from the beginning resisted the efforts of the hierarchy to integrate them into local churches. Fiercely independent, they took a particularly dim view of the demanding American-Irish clergy and made it clear they would not work with them.

Because of their unwillingness to conform, the French were

long looked upon as something of a problem by the Church authorities of New England. Some of their leaders regarded every attempt to Americanize Catholicism as a shameful capitulation and scorned their coreligionists who were set on it, charging that they were motivated above all by a craven reaction to nativist mischief. In turn, the Irish made no secret of the fact that they resented the clannish ways of the French, whom they charged with strengthening the impression that Catholicism was a "foreign," divisive influence in American life.

In time, however, many of the French came around. Today, the younger generation, deliberately breaking with the cultural heritage their ancestors brought from Canada, no longer think of themselves as Frenchmen particularly but simply as Americans. French national parishes still remain but are gradually passing from the scene and the ethnic tensions of the past are slowly being forgotten.

New Orleans, a dominantly French city from the beginning, has provided the prime example of a Catholicism different in character and temperament from the Irish- or German-dominated Church found in most American cities. The tradition of the South mingled with a distinctly French interpretation of Catholic culture has given it a uniqueness that sets it off both from the rest of the Protestant South and the Catholic cities of the North.

Latin-Americans in the United States—mainly people of Mexican, Puerto Rican, and Cuban backgrounds—number in the millions. Mexican-Americans, in all about four million persons, form the largest body. One sector of this group, more properly called Hispanos, are the descendants of the Spanish colonists who originally settled the Southwest. Until fairly recent years they were almost exclusively engaged in stock raising or subsistence agriculture and lived in village societies, following folk customs handed down from father to son.

The Hispanos are characteristically devout, prayerful, and passionately Catholic, observing religious practices unknown elsewhere in the American Church. Largely isolated from their Anglo-American neighbors, they have gone their own way— a proud, impressively dignified people who have long been the victims of prejudice, economic exploitation, and racial snobbery. They have not only been cut off from the Anglo community but have suffered from the indifference of ecclesiastical authorities as well; over the years little effort was made to integrate them into the larger life of the Church. Barely represented among the clergy and shapers of lay opinion, they have never had a real voice in American Catholic life. Had they been better integrated, the Hispanos might not only have found powerful support in their search for justice but have enriched Catholicism with virtues of gentleness and sensitivity that no other group of American Catholics possesses in such abundance.

The larger group of Mexican-Americans emigrated in the twentieth century from Mexico itself. They too have suffered from discrimination and lack of education. Again, their fellow Catholics did little over the years to help alleviate the conditions under which they have been forced to live, though the bishops of the United States in 1945 organized a committee to give them special pastoral attention and twenty years later took effective action in opposing a labor-contract system which was exploiting them. In recent years, a group of militant Mexican-American (or Chicano) leaders have emerged, a few of them priests, who have not hesitated to demand full rights for their people, nor have they spared the mainstream Church in their scalding criticism of a society which has long made life intolerable for these poorest and least privileged of Americans.

Puerto Ricans and Cubans, the vast majority of whom are at least nominally Catholic, form the other large group of Latin Americans in the continental United States. The Puerto Ricans arrived in great numbers from the island after the Second World War. They settled in New York, Chicago, and other large cities—the last in the long line of ethnic groups subjected to hostility, prejudice, and segregation who found it difficult to adjust to the demands of urban living in an alien Anglo-Saxon culture.

In their case as well as in the case of the Cubans who poured into Miami fleeing the regimes of either General Batista or Fidel Castro during roughly the same years, no effort was made to set up special national parishes. With national parishes going out of style, the idea was to integrate them into existing structures. To meet their needs, many seminarians and younger members of the clergy, beginning in the 1950s, studied Spanish and attended special classes in the hope of sensitizing themselves to the cultural patterns of the newcomers.

Yet, due to ignorance of the true doctrines of the Faith, which was attributable above all to the paucity of priests on the islands, a great deal of bizarre superstition, confusingly mingled with Catholic practices, still has a strong hold on the people. It will take time to undo this, since most of them still have at best only a minimal contact with the institutional Church, and even those whom priests manage to reach find it hard to understand Catholicism in its efficient, straightforward American manifestation. Many have been won over by store-front missionaries whose peculiar "Protestant" version of Christianity—a mingling of evangelical fundamentalist fervor with corrupt Catholic devotionalism—is actually more congenial to their inherited ideas of religion than the highly structured, restrained worship available in the parish churches of New York, Chicago, or Miami.

The Negro Catholic in America has always been rare—at the present time there are somewhat more than 800,000, and even that small number represents a twofold increase since World War II.

The original black Catholics were slaves. After their emancipation many of them left to join Negro Protestant churches where they felt more at home than in the rigidly liturgical and Latinized Church they were born into. Between the two World Wars, the rate of conversions among them was steady but very small, despite the efforts of a few congregations of priests—particularly the Josephite Fathers and the Society of the Divine Word—who are pledged to work in black parishes, and such all-Negro sisterhoods as the Oblate Sisters of Providence, the Handmaids of Mary, and the Sisters of the Holy Family. Another group, the Sisters of the Blessed Sacrament, founded in 1891 by Katharine Drexel of the wealthy Philadelphia family, was dedicated to work among Negroes, but its members have always been largely white. The Blessed Sacrament nuns established Xavier University in New Orleans in 1925, the only Catholic institution of higher learning with a predominantly Negro student body.

Until the 1940s, Negroes, to put it mildly, were not encouraged to enter "white" seminaries or convents. The result is that today there are fewer than two hundred Negro priests in the American Church, almost half of them members of the Society of the Divine Word, an order which opened a special seminary for black candidates, in Bay Saint Louis, Mississippi, in 1920. (The seminary has since been integrated.) Two of the Bay Saint Louis graduates have been named bishops. One, Bishop Joseph Bowers, serves in Ghana; the other, Bishop Harold R. Perry, is Auxiliary of the Archdiocese of New Orleans, where a goodly percentage of the black Catholics of the South are concentrated.

American Catholics, it can hardly be denied, at all times in all places have shared the racial prejudices of their fellow citizens, though there is no justification for racism of any kind in the doctrine of the Church. Perhaps this failure more than anything else held back the development of a distinctly black Catholicism in the United States. For years the Negro Catholic churches of the South, following local laws and custom, were unabashedly segregated institutions. Even in the North, Catholics by and large conformed more readily to the mores of their surroundings than to the oft-repeated antiracist pronouncements of their popes. Black Catholics were made to feel uncomfortable in the general parishes and too often either attended their own segregated parish churches or none at all.

In recent years, however, there have been some improvements. Massive prejudice remains, but the leadership of the Church, clerical and lay, North and South, has been somewhat more courageous in speaking out against racism in the Church and, though there is still a long way to go, their work has been effective in desegregating Catholic institutions, which a quarter century ago were as exclusivist as any in the land. Such efforts, incidentally, have not gone unnoted in the black community. It is perhaps significant that a *Newsweek* poll in the mid-1960s showed that 58 per cent of "rank and file" Negroes felt that Catholic priests were "helpful in the struggle for civil rights," ranking them right behind the Supreme Court and the Kennedy administration and ahead of other white churchmen by 24 per cent.

But Catholic deeds still do not come anywhere near matching the Catholic creed in the matter of racial prejudice. At the end of the 1960s a (Catholic) Black Clergy Caucus was still able to charge that "the Catholic Church in the United States is primarily a white racist institution." The caucus based its conclusion on the small part black Catholics have played, and still play, in shaping American Catholicism.

Until very recently, Negro Catholics were required to conform to standard liturgical uses and white patterns of thought and behavior, while they were effectively cut off from Catholic cultural life by the patterns of social segregation. The result was that no distinctive black Catholicism was ever allowed to flourish in the United States. The Church thereby deprived itself of the particular contribution Negroes might have made in theological thinking, music, and art, for example. But with more liturgical freedom and variety provided for in the postconciliar Church and a steady if still slow breaking down of racist attitudes, American Catholicism as a whole may yet be enriched by the particular genius of its still pitifully few black members.

American Catholicism, an amalgam of all these traditions, customs, national temperaments, and even liturgies has been a kind of religious United Nations, on the surface monolithic but actually perhaps more varied than any other religious denomination in the nation. In addition to the major groupings there are smaller enclaves of Portuguese, Scandinavians (who have their own Saint Ansgar's Guild), American Indians, Eskimos, Chinese, Lebanese, and numerous others, each with its very special character. If it be true, then, that *"we* are the Church," Catholicism in the United States speaks, and has long spoken, with many different accents. Yet only a few voices have been actually heard beyond their own ethnic boundaries. There has been an identifiable Catholic ghetto culture in America, but by and large it has been representative of a privileged group—white, fairly assimilated, and, at least in recent decades, preponderantly middle class.

CHAPTER SEVEN

THE GHETTO CULTURE

What American Catholics themselves now good-naturedly refer to as their "ghetto culture" (which all seem to agree is dying) actually marked a departure from Archbishop Carroll's notion of a Church comfortably integrated into American life. The ghetto culture was not deliberately planned. It developed as an early defense measure, and as the years went on it matured into a whole set of institutions paralleling some of the basic structures of American life. In time it became the best organized and most powerful of the nation's subcultures—a source of both alienation and enrichment for those born within it and an object of bafflement or uneasiness for others.

Through the years, the Jewish community and various Protestant bodies also maintained their own press, social organizations, schools, and charitable organizations, but on a much smaller scale and with much less obvious effects. Catholics, America's largest minority group, long stood out, then, as conspicuously "separatist," not only because of the number and extent of their sectarian institutions—which began with the maternity ward and ended in the choice of gravesite—but even more because so many of their attitudes in so many areas of life seemed to be derived directly from the religious beliefs and social prejudices propagated within them. Until quite recently there appeared to be a "Catholic" position on just about everything under the sun, which leaders of the Church were usually eager to make abundantly clear.

At the beginning of the nineteenth century, the Catholic immigrants, even if they had wanted to, could not have afforded to set up their own hospitals, schools, orphanages, or asylums; they had no choice but to use the public institutions open to everyone. But that did not last for long, and for a good reason. In those days of unchallenged Protestant dominance, the nation's public institutions were nominally "nonsectarian," but "nonsectarian" meant only that they did not favor one branch of Protestantism over another. By and large, Catholicism was treated with the contempt which was thought due a "foreign" growth within the body politic.

The Protestant Orphan Society of New York, for example, was charged with the care of all the orphans of the city, but the children the Society educated—most of them Catholic— were systematically instructed in the tenets of Protestantism and the textbooks used were crudely anti-Catholic in tone. A similar situation in Philadelphia brought on bitter charges from Irish leaders that the publicly supported institutions of the city, including especially the schools, were being used to turn Catholic children against the faith of their parents.

To make the situation worse, many of the powerful social and benevolent fraternal organizations then mushrooming throughout America excluded Catholics from membership, the Irish in particular; and as often as not they used their life-or-death influence to deprive non-Protestants of job opportunities and other means of social advancement.

The Catholic immigrant leaders naturally resented discriminatory treatment of this kind. When they and their priests began to talk about the need for Catholics to set up their own institutions, whatever the sacrifices required, they had little difficulty in winning support. The response to such proposals, not unlike that given the advocates of Black Power more than a century later, was generally enthusiastic and, for a people who felt oppressed, psychologically liberating. In this way the movement toward Catholic separatism began as a reaction to discrimination. The ambition of the aristocratic Carrolls and others of the first American Catholics, it seemed clear, was unrealistic and had to be put aside in favor of a do-it-yourself Americanism.

Later, most of the original need for religious separatism ceased to exist, but the movement increased, carried along by its own momentum. For years it grew and grew, unquestioned. After a while only a few Catholics ventured to express any doubt about why the Church should conduct its own schools, for example. Moreover, as usually happened, once such establishments really got under way, they were undergirded by an elaborate theological and philosophical rationale, which loyal Catholics were hesitant to challenge; an attack on a separatist institution seemed tantamount to an assault on the Church itself.

Without its own press, the ghetto culture probably could never have survived. Uniting Catholics throughout the nation, it eventually reached millions of readers and it was complemented by a dozen or more publishing houses which eventually turned out hundreds of books every year that kept their readers proudly aware of the Church's glorious past, fortified them with "spiritual reading" and philosophical treatises for their unavoidable confrontations with the heresy-ridden present, and at the same time sustained their commitment to the culture of the ghetto.

Catholic educational institutions, finally ranging all the way from kindergartens to graduate schools, became the chief (and costliest) work of the Church in the United States. Catholic cemeteries, hospitals, orphanages, settlement houses, and homes for the aged came to number in the hundreds.

This massive apparatus engaged thousands of administrators and staff workers, most of them priests and members of religious orders but many lay men and women as well, all of whom were deeply involved in the internal life of the Church. The ghetto culture, then, enlisted the lives and talent of the most dedicated and church-centered Catholics to be found in America. Not surprisingly, it was impenitently "clerical" in spirit and for many decades was vigorously, sometimes aggressively, protective of the Church's ever-expanding institutional interests.

Catholics caught up in it even had a special language of their own, made up of catechetical catch phrases and snippets of scholastic terminology unfamiliar to others ("occasions of sin," "subjective guilt," "the apostolate," "temporal power," to name a few). They rallied around their own historic symbols of virtue and infamy (Mary, Queen of Scots, and Oliver Cromwell serve as classic examples), their own literary idols (for years, the brilliant British apologists, G. K. Chesterton and Hilaire Belloc), and their own universal genius (Saint Thomas Aquinas). Some sort of identification with Catholicism was very important to them in judging persons and causes; nuns made novenas for Notre Dame victories on the gridiron as if the very truth of Christianity were at stake, for example, and during the Spanish Civil War Francisco Franco was the beneficiary of schoolchildren's prayers. Practicing Catholics who made a name for themselves in the "non-Catholic" world (Fulton Sheen, Bing Crosby, Stan Musial, J. F. Powers, Loretta Young) were admired inordinately, and such prominent converts as Heywood Broun, Knute Rockne, and Clare Boothe Luce were counted as trophies.

The world of ghetto Catholicism had its own best-selling authors, prominent lecturers, and in-house controversialists who were known in ghetto circles from coast to coast. It was frequently divided by lively arguments over theological and philosophical issues which were barely comprehensible to persons outside the Church—such intramural disputes as whether Graham Greene's fictional Scobie was "saved," for example, or whether abortion was permissible in cases of ectopic pregnancy, or whether Catholic Action without a bishop's "mandate" was authentic. It dispensed highly sought-after sectarian awards and medals, maintained its own *Who's Who,* and cast up its own celebrities, who sometimes went altogether unnoticed elsewhere but were lionized within the walls.

The celebrity the ghetto culture offered was as open to the layman as to the cleric. Especially after World War II, mainly via the lay-edited press, it provided a means by which even critical laymen got a genuine hearing in the Catholic community. These gadflies sometimes became major movers of American Catholicism even though they went studiously unnoticed by the official Church establishment—no honorary degrees from the Catholic universities, no seats on policy-making boards, no invitations to the official meetings and gatherings of the approved organizations, yet an influential place in the ghetto itself.

Such a pattern was set early by the polemical Orestes Brownson, who was not born into the ghetto but came into it of his own volition. Brownson, a native of Vermont and a brilliant if somewhat sketchily educated alumnus of Brook Farm, joined the Church in 1844, after a roundabout journey from the Methodism in which he was brought up, through Presbyterianism, then Universalism, and finally agnosticism. Before he became a Catholic, he had already gained a solid reputation as a writer, editor, and advocate of radical social causes. But by his conversion he cut himself off from such old friends and associates as Ralph Waldo Emerson (who refused to talk to him again) and was content to settle down as an outspoken but always loyal critic of Catholic affairs.

As the editor of *Brownson's Quarterly,* he tore into the Jesuits, the hierarchy, and the leaders of the Irish immigrants, yet survived as a force within Catholicism that had to be reckoned with. His *Quarterly* was gone by the end of the Civil War, but during the two decades of its life, Brownson attracted a small body of faithful readers and admirers. Through them he exercised vast influence on the ghetto community.

Brownson argued that the Pope's claim to hold "indirect" political power was theologically defensible—an opinion widely assented to but at the time regarded by Catholic leaders as a troublesome thesis. He charged the Jesuits with pettifogging the moral issues involved in slavery. He criticized the bishops —who at first gave his *Quarterly* their endorsement but later peevishly withdrew it—for tolerating unrealistic and outmoded education in Catholic schools. And while he vigorously defended the Irish immigrants against their nativist enemies, he also denounced their tendency to isolate themselves from American society by withdrawing into their own nationalistic enclaves.

Brownson's religious orthodoxy was frequently called into question by the reigning powers, but he remained faithful to the Church until his death in 1876. Later he was remembered with reverence as a kind of prototype of the outspoken laymen in the ghetto.

There were other laymen in the Brownson mold during the nineteenth century, most of them now forgotten, but gradually the lay voice in the Church was muted to a whisper as the clergy took over the Church press. By the turn of the century, almost all American Catholic opinion was being shaped by clerically run papers and magazines which very rarely veered from the positions taken by the hierarchy. The diocesan papers were almost always edited by priests appointed by ecclesiastical superiors. These publications employed non-clerical writers as well; the lay journalists, however, were rarely allowed to forget that they were expected not to "undermine" official policies by criticism, the exposure of abuses in the Church, the airing of scandals, or even by venturing their own opinion on the theological issues that rose from time to time.

During the same years, many of the religious orders began to publish their own periodicals—in the main pietistic, moralistic journals dutifully reflecting the Catholic party line of the moment, though seldom with any measure of sophistication or finesse. Still, when the Catholic leadership went all out for a cause (the Franco side in the Spanish Civil War, for example, or the long crusade against Margaret Sanger and her birth-control movement) it knew it could rely on a sizable press to keep the drums rolling. The priestly character of the chief writers of course gave their opinions a special authority.

This was generally true of the more professional journals as well as of the publications edited by the hapless clerics who were assigned to the editor's chair by superiors with no understanding of the journalist's craft. After World War II, there was a decided improvement in all branches of the Catholic press, but earlier only a few publications were even passably professional in tone. Among them was the venerable *Catholic World,* the intellectual Paulist monthly which was founded by Isaac Hecker and was later edited by the feisty political conservative, Father James M. Gillis (1876–1958), and *Ave Maria,* a family weekly issuing from the Notre Dame campus. Both were established in 1865.

America, the leading weekly dedicated to social, political, and literary comment, was founded by the Jesuits in 1904. *America* never reached a mass circulation but it shaped opinions which were later passed on through more popular publications like *Our Sunday Visitor,* the Denver *Register,* and the ever-expanding chain of diocesan papers. It too was generally predictable until, in the 1950s, its editors broke with the reigning Catholic opinion by opposing the activities of Senator Joseph R. McCarthy. After that the review gradually became more open to nonconformist opinion, and for some time now it has revealed an editorial independence quite up to anything shown by most of the lay press.

America's lay counterpart, the weekly *Commonweal*, also published in New York, was established as an independent journal in 1924. It was designed to provide the Catholic community—which even then was becoming increasingly better educated—with sophisticated comment on the affairs of the day that would reflect a humanist tradition handed down from the Middle Ages. Carefully reasonable and "civilized," even in the heat of controversy, *Commonweal* quickly attracted contributors of some literary and intellectual standing and gained the respect of its peers in secular journalism. Though in time it attracted more non-Catholics to its subscription list than perhaps any Catholic periodical ever published in the United States, most of its faithful readers over the years have been laymen with a lively interest in the Church and ecclesiastical affairs who are seriously committed to relating their faith to life in the world.

Even the early *Commonweal* was not censored by anyone, and the review was immeasurably more urbane and literate than its contemporaries in the Church press. Only rarely, however, was it any more daring. It remained unfailingly deferential toward ecclesiastical authorities and for a long time its editors regarded theological speculation as being totally outside their competence. Its critical arrows, though frequently directed outward, were hardly ever dispatched in the direction of the Catholic community itself. As time went on, however, the magazine grew increasingly independent and bold. In the 1930s, it brought down a barrage of criticism upon its head—not only by branding the popular Father Charles E. Coughlin a demagogue but by refusing to endorse the Franco cause in Spain. In 1949 it gained even more disfavor by criticizing its own Archbishop, the formidable Cardinal Spellman, when he enlisted seminarians as scab gravediggers in order to break a strike of Catholic cemetery workers. In the view of many Catholics, it added insult to injury a couple of years later by running a harsh review of *The Foundling*, a now-forgotten novel written by the Cardinal, which was being treated seriously not only by Catholic reviewers but by a number of nervous critics in the secular media.

By that time, *Commonweal* really had little to lose. In the larger sector of the Catholic ghetto it had already become a symbol of tribal disloyalty. At the same time, it was accepted as a spokesman for a growing body of restless laymen of the new generation who seemed to be tempted to break out of the ghetto confines altogether but for some reason were still holding on. No one was really surprised in the 1950s when the magazine went after Joseph McCarthy, challenged the artistic judgment of the Catholic Legion of Decency, or charged that the anticommunist fervor then raging in the Catholic community was a threat to civil liberties and a danger to world peace.

Commonweal, predictably, was widely accused of being snobbish, muddleheaded, socially ambitious, theologically subversive, and downright un-American. It was blacklisted by many seminary rectors, kept under the counter by Catholic college librarians, denounced bitterly from pulpits, and excoriated mercilessly in some of the diocesan papers. It was unfortunate, a spokesman for the New York Chancery told the press in 1953, that *Commonweal* was even known as a Catholic publication, since it did not have the formal approval of the Church. Yet Cardinal Spellman could easily have put the review out of business by formally anathematizing it. He never did so, however, and despite all the attacks visited on it, the magazine managed to exercise an influence within the American Church which was all out of proportion to its small circulation.

A study of *Commonweal* editorials over the years would show that more often than not the unpopular positions it espoused were later quietly adopted by the wider Catholic community, including not only its stands on political and social issues but on one as churchy as the use of vernacular in the liturgy. Never quite in the ghetto but never wholly out of it either, *Commonweal* was for years the primary means through which the liberal lay mentality, as opposed to the conservative clerical outlook on life, made its presence felt within, and beyond, American Catholicism.

The *National Catholic Reporter,* a brightly edited tabloid published in Kansas City, built on the foundation *Commonweal* had laid. It first appeared during the Second Vatican Council as a national edition of the Kansas City diocesan paper, but its editors soon cut their ties with the officials of the diocese and went out on their own. Throughout the rest of the 1960s and into the seventies it has accurately reflected the turmoil, agonizing reappraisals, painful rethinking, uninhibited exploration of new theological themes, and preoccupation with clerical failings which have been characteristic of the postconciliar period.

Produced by talented graduates of the diocesan press, the *Reporter* has been aggressively "liberal" in tone and almost ostentatiously forthright in its coverage of Church affairs. It has not hesitated to criticize the Pope, the hierarchy, the clergy, the religious orders, and even its own earlier judgments.

Inevitably, with its relentless chronicle of clerical skullduggery, it was quickly accepted as a kind of high-minded exposé publication. But at the same time it provided solidly reasoned arguments against many of the old verities of the Catholic past and became a major force for change. It has run reams of copy on controversies involving birth control, clerical celibacy, and whichever old dogmatic position the avant-garde theologians might be reinterpreting at any given time. Though the paper has never quite succeeded in overcoming its original boob-shocker techniques, it generally deals with such matters seriously, managing to popularize advanced theological ideas that might otherwise go unnoted outside the circles of professional scholarship.

In a very short time, the *Catholic Reporter* gained a respectable circulation, displaced *Commonweal* as *the* daring Catholic publication, and made almost as much history as it recorded. Less rambunctious Catholics frequently denounce it, including the Bishop of Kansas City, who originally helped get it started; but many among the disaffected clergy and laity still managing to hold on to the ropes welcome it as the most authentic voice of postconciliar Catholicism—at least until such a time as they find themselves ready to put the Church, and the *Reporter* along with it, out of their lives completely.

The *Reporter,* founded by Robert Hoyt, a brilliant journalist later replaced by the paper's board of directors, is a genuine product of the Catholic ghetto. Though the terms of membership in that ghetto have changed radically, it remains the most authoritative chronicler of the Church's present ups and downs. The paper's preoccupations are still overwhelmingly ecclesiastical and clerical, and it still speaks a language that, even updated, communicates readily only to people with at least lingering ghetto loyalties. Though the contributors to its pages are often the most resolute undertakers of the old sectarian culture, it came along just in time to give the forces which originally produced that culture a fresh lease on life.

The ghetto culture during its long years of vigor was often at odds with powerful currents of American life. Until Pope John's regime, one of the important "hostile" forces was Protestantism, the rival Christian faith. Protestants themselves, they frequently made clear enough, had small regard for the Catholic tradition; Catholics in turn were taught to look upon Protestantism as the logical culmination of every schismatic and heretical movement which had ever gained a foothold in the Church Universal; they were systematically, if not realistically, prepared to deal with it as the tragic result of good men led astray by false doctrine. For example, long after such questions ceased to be generally discussed by Protestants themselves, young Catholics were instructed in how to counter the central tenets of classical Protestantism—not only the rejection of papal authority but the priesthood of all believers, the argument for consubstantiation (as opposed to transubstantiation), the absolute primacy of the Scriptures, and the doctrinal exaltation of faith over good works.

The theology passed on in the Catholic ghetto, then, was more often than not consciously anti-Protestant in content, determinedly defensive and apologetic in tone, and based on Ready Answers to questions which no one outside the walls was really asking. Protestants could be patently sincere, young Catholics learned, but they were also the "invincibly ignorant" victims of an erroneous system of theological thought. The conscientious Catholic for his part was solemnly obliged not to condone such errors by acting as if they were really of no serious consequence for either this life or the next. At the same time, the unfortunate heirs of Luther and the other Reformers were to be admired for their personal virtues, loved for their own sakes, and prayerfully encouraged to find their way back to Rome.

However, in their efforts to reach their Protestant neighbors, Catholics were not to make unworthy doctrinal compromises or give scandal by seeming to put their approval on the contemporary Protestant's unfortunate weakness for theological flabbiness. For example, except for funerals and weddings, the good Catholic would stay out of Protestant churches and under no circumstances would he participate in worship services conducted in them. Only Catholics duly certified as thoroughly qualified were permitted to read theological works written by Protestant authors; such books, being an exposition of heretical doctrines, were automatically proscribed by the Index of Forbidden Books. And some rigorists even went so far as to suggest that it would even be wrong to contribute to Protestant charities, since at least indirectly they promoted and strengthened the forces of heresy.

Priests were required to avoid all but the most innocuous and determinedly "social" interfaith meetings. They were usually turned down when they asked for permission to participate in public discussions with clergymen of other faiths, even when the questions under consideration were thoroughly secular in character. Under no circumstances was the impression to be left that Catholics put other religions on an equal footing with the True Faith. This became a guiding principle overriding every other consideration in Protestant-Catholic relations.

Though mixed marriages (nowadays tactfully called ecumenical marriages) were strongly discouraged, there was no objection to being personally close to Protestants; in fact bishops themselves frequently spoke of their ties of friendship with clergymen of other faiths. But theology was another matter altogether. It turned out then that, ironically, Catholics could join their fellow Christians for just about every kind of activity but prayer, worship, and theological discussion.

Catholics growing up in the ghettoized Church of the late nineteenth century and the first half of the twentieth accepted such restrictions as the price of their loyalty to the truth. They

rarely heard of the pioneering ecumenical spirit of earlier
American churchmen like Bishop England and the first generation of Paulists and accepted the extreme exclusiveness
later insisted upon as being as binding as the Ten Commandments themselves. It was quite a shock, then, when Pope John
XXIII, reaching out to men of all religions, actually encouraged ecumenical encounters and advocated joint prayer with
the "separated brethren."

During the Vatican Council the movement John encouraged progressed at a dizzying pace. John's successor, Paul VI,
led the way by presiding over a joint Protestant-Catholic service held in a Roman basilica during the Council. In the United
States, professional theologians, Protestant and Catholic,
promptly formed groups to discuss the doctrinal issues sep-
arating the two branches of Western Christianity, and hundreds of laymen of both persuasions met in each other's homes
for "living-room dialogues." There was no more talk about a
"return to Rome" being the only road to Christian unity.

As soon as the Council was over, a number of Catholic
priests were invited to join Protestant theological faculties and
Protestant (and Jewish) scholars were asked to teach in Catholic colleges and seminaries. On secular campuses, Protestant
and Catholic chaplains, responding to the new ecumenical
spirit, began to think of themselves as collaborators in a joint
Christian ministry, rather than as rivals. At the parochial level
there was unprecedented collaboration between neighboring
congregations. Interfaith religious services, once absolutely
verboten, became commonplace.

There has been almost a revolutionary change in Protestant-
Catholic relations since the death of Pope Pius XII. Because
of it, the Catholic ghetto will never be the same again. The
days when the issues of the Reformation were dealt with sim-
plistically as a contest between orthodoxy and heresy now
seem to belong to the past. Some of the old ecclesiastical laws
which made intermarriage between Protestant and Catholic
a humiliating experience for the Protestant and an embarrassment to the Catholic were dropped altogether. Catholic part-
ners these days are even being urged to attend the church of
their Protestant spouses on special occasions. And in 1972
the Vatican announced that, under certain circumstances,

Protestant believers may receive the Holy Communion in Catholic churches.

Today Protestantism is usually dealt with sympathetically in Catholic schools. The Catholics' share of blame for the tragedy of Christian disunity is freely acknowledged. Catholics are also encouraged to work for Christian renewal side by side with their Protestant brethren and to support every movement which promises to break down the old barriers between them. In fact, never in the past four hundred years have relations between the two branches of Western Christianity been more cooperative and cordial. The bruising anti-Catholicism which played such an important role in American Catholic history is also quietly passing from the Protestant scene, though there are still some holdouts whose distrust of "Rome" still seems to overrule every other consideration. Anti-Protestantism, similarly, is still found among a few Catholic diehards, but its persistence is attributed to a cultural lag.

Over the years Catholics and Jews in the United States shared a number of things in common. Both were largely urban peoples; in Protestant America both were religiously "different"; both sustained a vigorous subculture of their own; both had to overcome obstacles of widespread prejudice and discrimination in making their way; both finally reached a measure of social acceptance that would have astounded earlier generations.

Relations between the two groups nevertheless were not always smooth. Among Catholics there was a certain amount of crude anti-Semitism which was based on the usual stereotypes and was often made even more vicious because it was given the additional strength provided by an anti-Jewish reading of the Christian Gospels. Jewish autobiographical literature is full of bitter memories of city kids being pursued as "Christ killers" every time they ventured into a Catholic neighborhood. Both groups, to make things worse, often accepted the most appalling myths about the other's religious practices unquestioningly.

Catholics and Jews of course shared many of the same secular experiences as neighbors, members of the same political party, and fellow workers in the same plants and offices. Though many strong friendships developed between them as old prejudices disappeared under the pressure of familiarity, by and large there was practically no religious contact between the two groups. Neither normally visited the other's place of worship; both were lamentably ignorant about the other's religious beliefs—the basic teachings of both faiths were frequently crassly distorted in the textbooks used by the other.

Only in recent years has that situation begun to change. Though technically the ecumenical movement is concerned with Christian unity it also had a tremendous effect on bettering Catholic-Jewish relations. Theological and Biblical scholars of the two faiths are collaborating more and more. Catholics are now being invited to attend Jewish religious services. Temple groups play host to neighboring Catholic parishioners at lox-and-bagel breakfasts. Rabbis are called in to address Holy Name Society meetings, and bishops and priests are asked to speak to synagogue groups. Children of the two faiths are shown the houses of worship and have explained to them how much the two traditions have in common.

This movement has not totally exorcised the anti-Semitic spirit from the Catholic community, it must be sadly acknowledged, nor has it obliterated the last vestiges of age-old suspicion in the Jewish community; nevertheless, each year understanding and mutual respect between the two faiths seem to be growing.

An influence with which Catholicism found itself in frequent conflict over the years was the amorphous force represented by the liberal secular establishments, in which of course the more secular Jews played a prominent role. This antagonism led to Peter Viereck's oft-quoted mot in the 1950s that anti-Catholicism had become the anti-Semitism of the liberals. Viereck might also have added that frequently anti-liberalism was the anti-Catholicism of the Catholics.

The Catholic-liberal cold war that raged until Pope John XXIII was based on a clash of ultimate values and systems of thought which sometimes took on the character of a holy war, with each group valiantly defending its particular orthodoxy against what it took to be heretical assaults by the other. The bad blood between Catholics and liberals, however, was certainly as much the product of history as of differing ideology.

As heirs of the Enlightenment, the liberal intellectuals generally mistrusted all organized religion not only as an intellectual but as a political force. Because of the numbers under the influence of the churches, the liberals reasoned, religion was still capable of undermining the achievements of science, the struggle for democracy, and individual freedom of thought in the United States. Catholicism represented a particular danger, with its authoritarianism, Index of Forbidden Books, and hundreds of schools relentlessly indoctrinating students not only in an obscurantist theology but in the abstruse principles of Thomism, which the liberals regarded as a static "medieval" philosophy capable of producing little but political and social reaction. That the Catholic hierarchy could count on millions of unquestioning, obedient followers to back up its forays into public life made it especially fearsome.

Catholics, who were frequently enlisted in crusades for "decency" in the films and other causes that seemed to outsiders to infringe on their rights to see and read what they chose, offered few reassurances that the liberal nightmare would not come true. Over the years there were enough examples of the use of "Catholic power"—a phrase popularized by Paul Blanshard's best-seller—to unsettle any liberal dedicated to freedom of thought and expression who might be uncertain about the Church's ultimate aims.

Through Catholic pressure on the police and local mayors, for example, Margaret Sanger for many years had a difficult time getting her birth-control message across. In the early days, her meetings in Boston and elsewhere were raided; she and her first supporters found that they could not hire available halls or otherwise reach the public without constant harassment. Later, spurred on by bishops and priests, Catholics carried on successful "Vote God's way" crusades when attempts were made to repeal anti-birth-control laws in the New England states. These laws were originally put on the books by puritanical Protestant legislators, as Catholics delighted in reminding their opponents; nevertheless it was Catholic votes that kept them there, right up to the mid-1960s.

Again, there was the perennial influence of the Legion of Decency, which enlisted millions of Catholics who were solemnly pledged not to attend movies that did not get the Le-

*difficult to comprehend: recondite

gion's seal of approval. Hollywood dreaded the Legion's condemnation for economic reasons, but for a long time the
industry capitulated to Catholic demands in making, or even
remaking, pictures in order to win that approval. The liberals
took this as an outrageous example of Catholic pressure tactics. From its beginnings in the 1930s until its eclipse in the
early sixties, then, the activity of the Legion was a constant
source of tension.

To add fuel to the fire, there was also the strong Catholic
support for General Franco during the Spanish Civil War,
when, or so it seemed to the liberals, the forces of enlightenment, represented by the Loyalists, were engaged in a struggle
to the death with the forces of reaction and fascist oppression,
represented by Franco's rebels. Less than two decades later,
the strong support Catholics gave to Senator Joseph R. Mc-
Carthy appeared to be even more foreboding since it was
closer to home.

The opposition of American Catholics to the reform of
divorce laws, their adamant campaigns against legalized abortion, and the hierarchy's recurrent pressure for public support for the parochial schools, where such ideas were promulgated, were all taken to be serious threats to liberal values.
The fact that Catholics used such methods of "persuasion"
as boycotts, picket lines, demonstrations, and public rallies to
make their case—thereby threatening ambitious politicians and
nervous public administrators—was no more acceptable to the
liberals than the outbursts to come as a result of the Vietnam
war were to later conservatives.

Moreover, it was no secret that leading Catholic clergymen
wielded enormous behind-the-scenes influence in places where
members of the Church were numerous and that some of
them were not at all loath to use that influence in order to
prevent the kind of permissiveness they regarded as harmful
to the souls under their care, whether the issue was a change
in sex laws, the showing of an offensive movie, the publication
of a critical magazine article, or the delivery of a controversial lecture.

The liberals' case against Catholicism, in a word, was
founded on solid fact and easy to document.

The issue, however, was not seen in the same light at all

within the Catholic community. There the activities the liberals found so disturbing were generally viewed as a simple matter of using the political power democracy confers on all its citizens to fight for traditional American (not merely Catholic) values against the onslaught of a hostile secularist force which was set upon undermining the nation's religious character and was doing so with notable success, all in the name of a dubious "progress." The Catholic attitude toward the secular liberals in these struggles, ironically, was not too different from the earlier Protestant attitude toward the first Catholic immigrants: they were to be put down; to tolerate them and their outrageous principles in the name of the "freedom" they invoked would be to sacrifice the nation's finest traditions and character to a set of abstractions—"civil liberties," "free inquiry," "the marketplace of truth."

In the bread-and-butter world of wages and hours, labor contracts, social legislation, and the implementation of the welfare state—so the Catholic opponents of uppercase Liberalism reasoned—Catholicism was identifiably and unquestionably a truly "liberal" force in America. But when the word "liberal" was expanded to include ideological stances on such questions as sexual morality, religious (or antireligious) attitudes, the acceptance of Marxian and Freudian insights, progressive educational theory, or the reigning philosophical orthodoxy (whether Behaviorism, Pragmatism, or Existentialism) good Catholics would remain dogged traditionalists. One of the ironies of the situation, consequently, was that while Catholics and the secular liberals fought tooth and nail between party conventions, they often supported the same social programs and were frequently joined in uneasy alliances to get the same political candidates elected.

With the gradual dissolution of the Catholic ghetto, the breakdown of the earlier Catholic consensus on such matters as birth control and divorce, the weakening of clerical authority, and the exaltation of "dialogue" as the acceptable way to approach hostile forces, the antagonism between the Catholic and the liberal has been softened. Some of the once-despised liberal values have now been widely adopted by Catholics themselves. There is much greater respect in the Church for the views of others than there used to be and much less unanimity about the claims that can be made in the name of public morality. Even when Catholics and liberals still clash, as they sometimes do, the present Catholic ideal (not always practiced) is to be open to reasonable discussion and wait with the patience of the Lord for the acceptance of Grace.

As happened with the ancient contest with Protestantism, the long Catholic cold war against liberalism was unobtrusively brought to an end during the Second Vatican Council. If a winner were to be named, it would probably have to be liberalism. For with the nervous acceptance of modernity—which was *the* dominant change in Catholicism brought about by the Ecumenical Council and its turbulent aftermath—many of the issues that once bitterly divided the two groups simply do not seem as important as they once were taken to be.

Liberalism too has changed. Liberals are now beset by self-doubts of their own. They are being attacked by their own left-wing offspring and often enough are being bitterly charged with many of the failings they once freely hurled at their Catholic opponents: they are accused of obscuring realities with pious rhetoric, of impeding progress by a fanatical devotion to outmoded principles, and of looking wistfully toward the accomplishments of the past rather than toward the possibilities of the future.

The acceptance of modernity not only brought an end to the Catholic war against secular liberalism, it doomed the ghetto culture itself. That culture, though it was always deeply involved in the present, was rooted in a profound loyalty to the Catholic past and an almost pathetic nostalgia for another age. For example, Catholics living within it were preoccupied with literary revivals and renascences that would once again express the Catholic consensus in all its medieval glory. They talked bravely of Second Springs, of Returns to Tradition, and of the *Philosophia Perennis*. That Rome, casting a cold eye on the brutal present, saw everything *sub specie aeternitatis* was a source of immense pride and comfort. Even the radical *Catholic Worker* sponsored a back-to-the-land movement, vigorously denounced modern industrialism, and spoke glowingly of the peasant way of life. Other Catholics involved in the ghetto culture joined in the glorification of crafts over machinery and bravely propagated the distributive theories of G. K. Chesterton, Eric Gill, and the English Dominican writer, Father Vincent McNabb, as the answer to modern capitalism. At one point in the first years following World War II, a short-lived publication named *Integrity,* which was very much in vogue among Catholic intellectuals, actually advocated exorcism as the first cure to be tried in cases of mental disturbance, before any recourse to psychiatry was made. A return to the family farm was pushed by the leaders of the more sober Catholic Rural Life Movement long after subsistence farming ceased to be economically feasible. One of the liveliest controversies in *Commonweal* in the late 1940s was focused on the evils of industrialism and the virtues of the medieval guild system.

The intellectual Catholic in the ghetto culture—steeped in the world of Aquinas—was haunted by the integralist's dream of another *summa* of all knowledge even while he offered his pinch of incense to the gods of political pluralism. But with the Vatican Council, the spell was finally broken.

William Clancy, then a young lay editor of *Commonweal,* now a priest, wrote prophetically in 1953. First—perhaps unwittingly—he provided a rationale for the existence of the ghetto. "The American environment," he wrote, "is the heir, par excellence, of those dreams of material progress, human perfectibility, and earthly utopia which bemused the genius of Europe during most of the eighteenth and nineteenth centuries. It is a culture which, perhaps more than any in history, has sought to canonize the temporal. Having escaped the tragedies that awakened Europe from the Enlightenment's dream, America continues to enjoy that dream. In this sense, the most 'progressive' of countries is an anachronism in the modern world."

Catholics in the ghetto, Clancy suggested, were made too sophisticated by their Christian intuition to accept such a dream. But, quixotically, they nurtured a dream of their own. "There is, perhaps, deep in the Catholic memory, nostalgia for an older, a safer, a more certain temporal order. We may not, all of us, have grown used to the hazards of living within a pluralist culture," he acknowledged. "But as the nostalgia disappears, as we mature, it is to be hoped that our voice may be lowered, our demands grow less strident, and our own sense of vocation—in this time, in this place—may become more secure."

Secure peoples who have a choice do not deliberately live within ghetto walls.

CHAPTER EIGHT

THE SCHOOLS

The most remarkable thing about the Catholic educational establishment in the United States is that it ever came into existence. Today American Catholics are strongly middle-class, reasonably prosperous, and comparatively well-educated. But when the parochial school system got under way, most of them were members of the working class, poorer than other Americans, and barely literate. Their schools, unlike Catholic schools in Europe, Canada, and Latin America, had to be supported by voluntary contributions, without assistance from governmental sources or philanthropic foundations.

The only thing that made them feasible at all was the "living endowment" provided by teaching nuns and brothers, most of whom were themselves the sons and daughters of working-class parents. Even with this boon, extraordinary sacrifices have been required to keep the schools going, since Catholics also bear their full share of costs for public education. In fact, they have sometimes had to spend more on the public schools they did not use than on the schools that were actually educating their children.

Yet, even with these strikes against it, the parochial school system somehow managed to grow to massive proportions, expanding as the number of Catholics increased, until slightly more than half the primary-school children belonging to the Church were enrolled. By the mid-1960s parochial schools were educating 5,800,000 elementary and high-school pupils, or about one out of every seven American children. When to this number were added the several hundred thousand youths who were enrolled in more than three hundred Catholic colleges and universities, the total figure reached well over six million. In all, the Church maintained some twelve thousand educational institutions, ranging from kindergartens to medical schools.

Since 1966 the number has been decreasing rapidly, due to several factors. With the exodus from the cloister that followed in the wake of the Vatican Council, the number of religious available for teaching has fallen off drastically. To replace them with lay teachers who require normal pay is proving to be impossible. Again, with the breakdown of Catholic sectarian patterns, more and more young parents now see no reason to withdraw their children from the common public-school experience. In increasing numbers, they are no longer willing to make the financial sacrifice necessary to maintain a separate school system, especially at a time when the costs of education have skyrocketed. There is reason to believe, then, that in the days ahead the Catholic educational establishment will diminish dramatically.

The Church will doubtless continue to work in education, but the Catholic schools of the future will probably be more specialized; most of them may be designed for particular needs, complementing rather than replacing public education. The early goal of "every Catholic child in a Catholic school" —first proposed by the American bishops in 1884—was long ago quietly set aside as impractical; it no longer exists even as an ideal.

The tradition of parochial education is deeply rooted in American Catholic history, though it took a century or more before the first scattered schools run by devoted laywomen expanded into the parochial "system." Archbishop Carroll was so eager to set up schools that he attempted to persuade nuns of the Carmelite and Poor Clare orders to abandon their strict enclosure and take in pupils. These early attempts, though, were unsuccessful. The nuns, deciding to return to their Rule, soon gave up the attempt to do the work of the teaching orders.

The pattern which was to endure for so long was first set by Elizabeth Ann Bailey Seton, a genteel New York widow and saintly convert to Catholicism who, in 1809, founded a religious community in Emmitsburg, Maryland, which was later affiliated with the worldwide Daughters of Charity. Mother Seton's community flourished. Within a few years her nuns were found in classrooms attached to parishes in New York, Baltimore, Cincinnati, and elsewhere. Other women were inspired to follow their example. Communities of sisters originally founded in the United States, such as the Sisters of Loretto of Kentucky or the Dominicans of Sinsinawa, Wisconsin, also made teaching their primary work. After groups from abroad—the Sisters of Mercy from Ireland, for example, or Sisters of Saint Joseph from France—crossed the ocean to establish motherhouses in the New World, they took over the schools which one parish after another was setting up in order to protect Catholic children from the "Protestant" public schools. As the pioneering communities of teaching nuns grew, the schools multiplied. The nuns encouraged their students to enter the convent and each year the number of novices increased. The more schools, the more nuns, then; the more nuns, the more schools.

As the years passed, new orders from abroad sank roots in America and, no matter what their tradition in Europe had been, took up teaching in parochial schools. At the same time, the original American sisterhoods, growing more numerous, divided and subdivided into separate provinces; frequently, after the inevitable disputes that are found even in convents, entirely new orders were established by dissident groups of nuns. In places where sisters were scarce, new congregations were founded by pious girls working under the direction of pioneering bishops and priests. The cellular growth continued until there were over 150,000 nuns in more than two hundred separate orders throughout the United States, most of them dedicated to conducting parochial schools and academies. A smaller group of brothers—particularly the Brothers of the Christian Schools, the Marists, the Xaverians, and the Brothers of Holy Cross—also took up the work. Though they had to compete with the appeals made for seminary recruits, they attracted enough young American followers to expand beyond their founders' most sanguine hopes. The clerical orders specialized in high school and college training. Of this group the Jesuits were from the beginning, and still remain, the pacesetters. In Europe the Society of Jesus was traditionally engaged in providing an elitist education for the sons of the privileged. In the United States, Jesuit education at first remained rigorously classical but the priests themselves stayed close to the working class. In their colleges tens of thousands of working-class boys were first introduced to the mysteries of Latin and Greek and the world of classical culture. Later they moved into the professions, forming the nucleus of the middle-class Catholicism which was to come. The Fathers originally set up most of their schools in the inner city but moved to the suburbs as their graduates became more prosperous and were ready to send their own sons to the Jesuits for training.

Cardinal John Wright, a native Bostonian who is now the highest ranking American member of the Roman Curia, once adverted to this in an interview. "If one revisits the older sections of American cities," he told Donald McDonald of the Center for the Study of Democratic Institutions, "he finds an interesting illustration of what I mean. In almost all of them there is a great church of a religious order—the Gesu in Milwaukee, the Immaculate Conception in Boston, others of the Jesuits, for example, in New York, Philadelphia, Saint Louis, Baltimore—and invariably alongside of them there is the first college our people built in each of these cities. More often than not, the college itself has long since moved, but note well how early it was founded and that it was founded precisely in working-class areas."

The colleges Cardinal Wright referred to have developed into such institutions as Marquette, Saint Louis, Detroit, and John Carroll Universities, all still conducted by the Society of Jesus, along with Fordham, the Loyolas (Chicago, Los Angeles, and New Orleans), the University of San Francisco, Boston College, and a dozen other institutions of higher learning.

But the Jesuits have not monopolized the field. On a smaller scale, other groups of priests also established colleges and universities. Notre Dame owes its origins to an impoverished group of French Holy Cross Fathers who set up a small college in the Indiana wilderness in 1842. De Paul in Chicago and Saint John's in Brooklyn were established by Vincentians. Colleges and seminaries were attached to almost all the large American Benedictine monasteries. The Augustinians began Villanova University outside Philadelphia. The Holy Ghost Fathers opened Duquesne in Pittsburgh. The Premonstratensians established Saint Norbert's College near Green Bay, Wisconsin, and the Dominicans took over Providence College in Rhode Island. The Christian Brothers established Manhattan College in New York and Saint Mary's in California, and the University of Dayton owes its origins to the Marianists. The secular clergy also turned to education and still conduct such colleges as Saint Thomas in Saint Paul, Minnesota; Saint Ambrose in Davenport, Iowa; and Bellarmine in Louisville, Kentucky.

In the same manner, dozens of the academies and finishing schools run by nuns gradually developed into colleges for girls, many of them lamentably lacking in academic distinction but a few with excellent reputations, such as New York's Manhattanville, Washington's Trinity, and Saint Catherine's of Saint Paul, Minnesota.

The only educational institution supported by the entire Church in the United States is the Catholic University of America. It was founded by the nation's hierarchy in the 1880s. In its early days the university was the focus of stormy dispute among the bishops themselves, who were at the time openly divided on the issues raised during the "Americanism" and modernist controversies. Its first rector, Bishop John J. Keane, was ultimately forced to resign because of his strong assimilationist views. When the nineteenth-century controversies were at their peak, the German clergy, convinced that there was a conflict between the traditional Faith and the kind of American-oriented theology then favored by the university, pointedly withdrew their support. Later, in periods of economic depression, the university was threatened several times with serious financial troubles. But it survived these difficulties to become an important center of learning, especially for teaching sisters who needed certification and for the young men preparing for the priesthood.

Unfortunately, the Catholic University, as even its most ardent defenders will freely acknowledge, did not succeed in matching the glowing vision of its founders. It never achieved the eminence of a Harvard or a Yale, and even some of the other Catholic schools now outshine it, particularly Notre Dame and a few of the Jesuit institutions. But it is solidly rooted as a national university, one of the few Catholic establishments that belong to no one of the religious orders or individual American dioceses.

Catholic education has always been uneven. A great deal has depended on the standards maintained by the diocese where the school is located, the attitude of particular pastors (which ranged from indifference to careful concern), and even the level of competence reached by the particular religious community in charge. Some of the orders have long emphasized professional training for their nuns; others, at least until recent decades, were so carried away by zeal that they sent their sisters into the classroom with barely minimal preparation. The result has been that even in the same diocese scholastic standards have varied considerably.

The "system" has always been surprisingly decentralized. For example, a Notre Dame study released in the 1960s showed that only thirty-four of the nation's 2500 Catholic secondary schools were receiving more than half their income from a bishop's office. The others, like most of the 10,000 elementary schools then run by the Church, were supported by direct tuition charges. In almost all cases they had to be supplemented through special parish collections.

It has always been difficult, then, to make general statements about the Catholic schools that will apply across the board. The same of course is true of the nation's public schools, which are operated by tens of thousands of different boards of education with strikingly different notions about what a good school should be. In some American communities the parochial schools have fallen far short of the standards set by the local public schools; in others the parochial institutions have been superior.

The most authoritative recent comparisons were published in the Carnegie-sponsored Notre Dame survey, *Catholic Schools in Action,* released in 1966. Using standard tests, the investigators found that the I.Q.'s of Catholic elementary-school pupils averaged out to 110, a sign of superior academic learning potential. Eighty-four per cent achieved scores at or above national norms. Of the high-school students tested, about 17 per cent exceeded the national norms in academic achievement; more than 80 per cent were classified as reaching "total potential" in language arts, social science, mathematics, and science.

A complementary study released around the same time by the National Opinion Research Center of the University of Chicago (*The Education of American Catholics* by Andrew M. Greeley and Peter Rossi, Aldine Publishing Company, Chicago) concentrated on the relationship between religious education and adult religious behavior. Its authors concluded that Catholic education was more effective with youths who were brought up in a "devout" family and whose religious education extended all the way from first grade through college.

Greeley and Rossi found that collegians in Catholic schools were generally more "liberal" in their social and political attitudes than Catholic students attending public institutions. They were also less susceptible to anti-Semitic prejudice than college-educated Protestants—a conclusion sustained by a B'nai B'rith survey which was published about a year earlier. The graduates of Catholic colleges did somewhat better than other Catholic graduates in the professions, the authors found, and they were no more given to religious clannishness than Catholics who had received most or all of their education in secular schools.

The sociologists suggested explanations for each of these findings. For example, Catholic grade and high schools are able to dismiss obstreperous pupils and frequently do—an advantage denied public-school educators. Again, Catholic college students generally grow up in more prosperous homes than their Catholic contemporaries in public institutions and thereby get a head start in making their way in the world. The studies, then, did not prove much more than that the education offered in Catholic schools—at least by 1965—was not generally inferior to the education supplied in publicly supported institutions.

It was important, however, that evidence for this claim should have been produced, since, over the years, widely propagated charges were made that the Church's institutions fell far below acceptable scholastic standards. Most of these critiques, it seems, were based on flimsy impressions rather than empirical investigation. One of the most prominent and vocal critics of Catholic education in the 1950s, for example, admitted later that he had never set foot in a parochial classroom when he publicly branded them as dangerously "divisive" and academically inferior. Until the 1965 studies—actually the first time the parochial-school system was examined in its entirety—the hard facts were not available; critics as well as defenders of the parochial schools had little to go on but their suspicions and presuppositions.

It has long been clear that the very existence and extent of parochial schools in the United States has had a profound effect on the character of American Catholicism. Nowhere else in the world were so many Catholic children drilled in the catechism as thoroughly as in American parochial schools; nowhere did the notion of Catholicism as embodying a tidy system of rules and regulations covering practically every aspect of life gain a stronger hold on the faithful. As a result, the schools were widely charged with failing to develop the "inquiring mind." At least originally, the charge was justified. Catholic education, with characteristic Catholic certitude, was founded on the idea that the main purpose of the school was to transmit the truth in the Church's possession. Teachers made no particular effort to stimulate an individual search for it on the part of their students—why seek for what was so readily available? Even at the higher levels, the confidence with which religious teachers expounded theological dogma was frequently transferred to philosophy, political theory, and even the interpretation of history. But with the influence of laymen in Catholic education and the emergence of a new-style teaching clergy all this has changed. Professors in the better Catholic schools who have had experience elsewhere now testify that they have as much freedom in the Catholic institutions as anywhere else in academia.

For many years, however, the influence of laymen in parochial education was practically nil. As a result, the Catholic schools strongly reflected the "clerical culture" that was so important in the lives of the priests and religious who dedicated their lives to keeping them going. And for many years it was this culture, transmitted through the schools, which gave American Catholicism its basic identity. If there is such a thing as a distinct lay spirituality, it was slighted in favor of the conventual view of the world and of the Church itself which so many cloistered teachers innocently passed on to their students as *the* Christian ideal. This meant that for generations Catholics in the United States, unduly dependent on the judgment of priests and religious, cultivated an almost monastic view of the virtues of chastity and obedience to ecclesiastical superiors, and put tremendous emphasis on such matters of discipline as meatless Fridays and attendance at Mass on Sundays. Such rules and regulations, cut and dried as they were, were taken much more seriously, for example, than the less precise instructions given in matters concerning social justice and race relations or the issues involving war and peace.

The schools, it must be said, instilled enormous pride in the Catholic intellectual tradition. Teachers tried earnestly to acquaint their students with every aspect of that tradition. Psychologically, the very existence of the schools, then, was probably liberating for a people who might otherwise have come to feel culturally inferior in a confidently "Protestant" nation. But by no means was the defensive posture wholly beneficial. For example, theology was taught as a series of ineluctable syllogisms rather than a delve into mystery, and the "siege mentality" the schools inculcated was often carried over to life outside the classroom. Their graduates, as a result, took extraordinary satisfaction in being skilled in defending Catholic beliefs on rational, logical grounds, and frequently showed at best only good-natured tolerance toward what they took to be the vaguely rooted, vaguely held religious opinions of the majority of their fellow citizens. Should a question arise which even the long years of catechetical drilling did not equip them to handle, there was the comforting feeling that somewhere, nonetheless, there must be a reply tucked away in the Church's treasury; the search for answers was only a matter of locating a properly educated priest, who would have it at his fingertips.

Until the upheaval following the Vatican Council, American Catholics, due above all to their extraordinary investment in parochial education, remained unimpressed by the charges made against the Church and were remarkably loyal to its teachings even when they did not actually succeed in observing them. The general feeling was that if the Church taught something, it must certainly be true, though it might be almost superhumanly difficult to live up to.

Take the long-standing Catholic opposition to birth control. The Church's unyielding condemnation of contraception was rooted in an interpretation of Natural Law doctrine that, until the Vatican Council, went practically unchallenged within American Catholicism. The fact that Catholics accepted the doctrine, however, did not necessarily mean that they always honored it in practice, or even that they really understood the abstruse philosophy on which it was based. This was generally recognized throughout the Catholic community, especially by priests who had the evidence supplied by experience in the confessional.

From time to time the popular women's magazines triumphantly published polls showing that millions of Catholic couples were limiting their families by contraceptive means because they found the Church's teaching impractical or a threat to their marital happiness. It was clear that the writers, in presenting such evidence, felt that they had scored significantly in the battle for planned parenthood. But in Catholic circles exposures of this kind really proved nothing other than that there were sinners in the Church, which had never been much of a secret to anyone. It didn't change the argument. Human frailty was quite forgivable. Truth, however, was a divine abstraction which man denied at his own peril. That was why the Church did not excommunicate ordinary sinners, though it was hard on those who disputed its doctrinal authority. To deny a central teaching meant that one was no longer truly a Catholic and had excommunicated oneself, at least until such a time as one again saw the light.

Religious education in the Catholic schools was carried on in this spirit until the fateful 1960s. Teachers and professors were imperturbably sure about what the Church taught; their duty, consequently, was to transmit it as the truth—unchangeable and eternal—to their students, an obligation they could fulfill with supreme confidence as long as the teaching was clear and unambiguous, as it certainly was at that time in the case of birth control.

At the higher reaches of education, the principles of Aristotelianism-Thomism were implanted with almost equal assurance, above all because Leo XIII and his successors had endorsed this particular philosophy as supremely compatible with Christian teaching. No one held that any philosophy, even the purest Thomism, was the product of divine revelation, but the claims made for the *philosophia perennis* fell just short of that. Students were relentlessly instructed in the philosophy of Saint Thomas, and in the classroom short shrift was given to most of his ancient critics and contemporary opponents.

As a result, the teaching of philosophy, not even to mention theology, was carried on in a cock-of-the-walk spirit which was later roundly criticized at the Vatican Council. Students were expected to leave school convinced not that they had been exposed to one important philosophical system among many but that, with their knowledge of the *Summa*, they had been given an insight into the Truth itself.

Because they were carried on in this spirit, the Catholic schools turned out graduates who were generally not only secure in their belief and extremely proud of their ancient cultural heritage but confident that they were prepared to face the intellectual confusion reigning in the heresy-ridden modern world. More often than not, they later desired the same kind of education for their own children.

Much of this was changed only by the Ecumenical Council, but the winds of modernity were blowing through the Catholic educational system somewhat earlier, due to the increasing number of teaching religious who had received their own professional training on non-Catholic campuses and in the course of it had been influenced by the skeptical spirit of secular education. Interestingly enough, though, the greatest impetus for change came from the ecclesiastical authorities themselves during their historic meeting in Rome. Clericalism, legalism, and triumphalism—all marks of the Church that had developed since the Reformation—were vigorously condemned one day in Saint Peter's Basilica, by a Council Father, as a great danger to the Christian spirit. Surprisingly very few of his fellow bishops ventured to contradict him. The effects of that particular intervention were soon felt throughout the Church and its schools, not least of all in the United States.

The legalistic spirit which had characterized American Catholicism for so long was dissipated rapidly after certain laws —like the once-sacrosanct Friday abstinence—were abolished, soon after the bishops returned home. Ecclesiastical law, it quickly became evident, would never again be taken quite so seriously. In no time the younger clergy, thoroughly caught up in the new spirit, were repudiating every manifestation of the old clericalism, often to the dismay of older priests and many of the laity. And any expression of the Catholic triumphalism which had been so dramatically pointed out, ironically enough in the imperial setting of Saint Peter's, was seen as not merely out of key with the new theology but downright ridiculous for a Church which, by its own public admission, was steadily losing its influence throughout the world.

The parochial school system adjusted almost overnight to these changes in Catholic thinking. Compulsory religious services, for example, were clearly out of place in a Church whose leaders had so recently repudiated legalism as a threat to Christian values. Priests and religious logically could no longer pontificate as near-infallible mentors in a Church set against clericalist pretension. Any indication that Catholics were the sole guardians of the Truth, whether found in theology or philosophy, simply fell away in the sudden reaction against triumphalism. The Council's more or less open acceptance of philosophical and theological pluralism meant that the dominance of Thomism as the beginning and end of philosophical wisdom was finally at an end. The notion that everything the Church had ever taught authoritatively was forever true could no longer be held comfortably after it became clear that the Council had actually reversed several long-unquestioned papal positions.

Whatever the prospects for the American Catholic schools, it is now evident that the kind of religious education they offer and their effect on the American Catholic community will be different in the future, if only because the Church they serve has changed so radically. The spirit that long gave them their special character no longer exists in Catholicism, and it is still too early to say what will replace it.

The changes in the schools are already striking. The traditional reliance on strict discipline and catechetical rote learning which used to set them apart are now a thing of the past. An emphasis on free inquiry, discussion, and dialogue characterize most Catholic high-school and college campuses today. Academic freedom, now highly valued, is vigorously defended in the institutions of higher learning. "Interference," even by ecclesiastical authorities, is being stoutly resisted.

Even the ownership of many institutions has changed hands. Colleges and universities which were once the property, lock, stock, and barrel, of the orders that founded them no longer depend on the decisions of remote religious superiors but have been turned over to lay boards of directors. Members of the orders are no longer assigned to college faculties by their superiors but are accepted on their professional merits by the lay boards. Lay members of the faculty, who now outnumber the religious ten to one or more, are no longer kept in the subordinate positions that once were their lot. More and more of them serve as department chairmen, deans, and chief administrators.

Some see in these trends a move toward the total secularization of Catholic institutions of higher learning, following the pattern set by the once-Protestant Ivy League colleges. Others feel that the Catholic colleges and universities will keep their distinctiveness but operate according to a new understanding of what a commitment to Catholicism really means. In any case, a recurrent, still unresolved argument being carried on in practically all the colleges and universities is focused on such questions as: What is a Catholic college, anyway? How does it differ from a secular school? What can it teach, or refuse to teach, that makes it different from any other institution of higher learning?

Among the changes in Catholic education, those involving the training of seminarians are among the most striking. In days gone by, future priests were educated in isolated seminaries and monasteries, segregated from other students their age, and cut off from normal contact with the world, under a regimen of spartan discipline. Many of the dioceses maintained their own seminaries, staffed almost exclusively by local clerics. In almost all cases, they were found in remote rural areas, far from the turbulent cities where the majority of their students were destined to serve as parish curates. Even the aspirant for the secular priesthood lived the life of a monk until he was finally ordained, rarely visiting home and cut off from lay company even on his vacations, which were spent with fellow seminarians in camps hidden in the woods.

In recent years, there has been a move to put the candidate for the priesthood more in touch with life by bringing him into the world he will later serve. Seminary students are no longer restricted in their movements or protected from exposure to arguments against the Faith. They are allowed to read what they wish, attend public lectures, move about freely in society, and participate in social-action projects among the poor and depressed. In most places, seminarians are now able to take part in antiwar protests or antiracist demonstrations if they have a mind to; they may come and go without special permission when they are not in class; some assist priests on parish assignments during their free time in order to gain practical experience in the work of the ministry. Others attend college classes along with lay students in ordinary universities or study theology with Protestant divinity students in ecumenical centers; and most pick out their own classes instead of conforming rigidly to a course of studies laid down by authorities in Rome.

Seminaries in the countryside have been shut down and moved to urban centers in order to take advantage of the cultural and social-action opportunities found in a city environment. In several places, a number of religious orders have combined their seminary programs and no longer run separate institutions for a handful of students. In Berkeley, California, Jesuits, Dominicans, Franciscans, and others have pooled their intellectual resources and study together; in Chicago, the Catholic Theological Union was established in 1968 in an old hotel near the University of Chicago campus by members of the Passionist, Franciscan, and Servite orders, who were later joined by the Augustinians, Divine Word Fathers, and several other communities of priests intent on broadening the educational opportunities of their young members. This new-style priestly training, keyed in to general American education, represents a radical break with the old ideal of the priest as the remote Man of God who should be isolated from others in his young manhood, protected as much as possible from alien ideas and the lure of the world, and steeled by years of monastic discipline and withdrawal until finally he is ready to take his place as a certified, if totally inexperienced, leader of the community.

Would Catholicism in the United States have fared as well had it not set up its own educational system in the nineteenth century? When the schools were first established, a small minority of the bishops privately argued that they were really unnecessary and might even hurt the Christian cause by isolating Catholics from other Americans and thereby limiting the influence of the Church on American life. Most of the hierarchy, however, felt that without parochial schools the faith of the immigrants' children could be lost altogether, not only because of Protestant militancy but because unless the Church provided an education which integrated religion with life there would be no way to resist the inroads of anti-Catholicism in a nation where Catholics were still besieged. The opinion of the majority easily triumphed, but the argument has never really ceased. Even when the schools were thriving beyond all expectations, there were Catholics who continued to believe that establishing parochial schools had been a bad idea from the beginning because they ate up a disproportionate amount of the Church's resources in money and manpower. In recent years, though the schools still have enthusiastic supporters, the same charges have been increasing in volume.

Father Greeley and some other authorities on American Catholicism seem to have concluded that the early pessimists were wrong in concluding that the Church's survival ever depended on its schools, but they are also persuaded that the bishops were not necessarily mistaken when they insisted that Catholic children be educated in them.

They are probably right. There is little reason now to believe that the Church in the United States would have withered without its schools; but over the years, for better or worse, they contributed more than anything else to the special character of American Catholic life.

The very existence of the parochial school system, however, has been the source of serious disagreement between Catholics and other Americans. The public school has long occupied a unique place in the American myth—as the great leveler, the shaper of democratic attitudes, the basic unifying force in a nation made up of many different racial, religious, and social elements. That Catholics held off from putting their full seal of approval on the experiment and set up a rival system has been baffling to some of their fellow citizens. When, in the heat of controversy, Catholic spokesmen have even allowed themselves to speak harshly of public education as "godless," feelings have been exacerbated.

Though at least every second Catholic child in the nation has always been educated in the public schools, the impression that Catholics have merely tolerated public education and would even abolish it if that were possible has not been totally ungrounded. A widely publicized statement by a Jesuit polemicist of the 1930s strongly reinforced the impression. "Our first duty to the public school," Father Paul J. Blakely wrote in a pamphlet which was cited for many years, "is not to pay taxes for its maintenance."

The damaging quotation was used triumphantly by the professional critics of the Church, but at no time was the sentiment it expressed really accepted by a significant number of American Catholics. Yet the fact that the Church went to such expense to maintain its own institutions indicated beyond doubt that Catholics did not find the public schools satisfactory. The dissatisfaction went all the way back to the beginnings of public education in America.

More recent Catholic arguments against the public-school system have been focused on the charge that they were allowed to become citadels of secularism and religious indifference. The original argument against them, however, was that for all intents and purposes they were really Protestant—and overtly anti-Catholic—religious establishments supported by public funds. Bible reading was obligatory in all the early

* made more violent, bitter or severe

public schools, and the only version of the Bible allowed was the Protestant King James edition; religious instruction was given by Protestant ministers, many of them openly hostile to Catholicism. Priests were not even allowed to instruct their own communicants among the pupils. Textbooks frequently portrayed Catholicism in an unfavorable light and, at least in Catholic eyes, maliciously distorted the doctrines of the Church and held its teachings up to public ridicule.

While Catholics were still few in number and politically powerless, nothing could really be done about the situation; but with the growth of Irish immigration in the nineteenth century, resentments were brought to the boiling point, particularly in New York City where in the mid-eighties the Archbishop, John Hughes, launched a campaign to oust the trustees of the Public School Society, after branding them anti-Catholic bigots.

Earlier there had been controversies in New York and Boston among various Protestant groups over charges that one or another denomination was being favored in the schools. But under the influence of the distinguished educational reformer, Horace Mann, "nonsectarianism" had triumphed by the 1840s. Yet even Mann, a free-thinking Unitarian, had stopped short of full secularization. In his final report as secretary of the Massachusetts Board of Education, in 1848, he denied flatly that he had ever attempted to exclude religious instruction from the schools. "Our system earnestly inculcates all Christian morals; it founds its morals on the basis of religion; it welcomes the religion of the Bible; and in receiving the Bible, it allows it to do what it is allowed to do in no other system, to speak for itself."

Protestants by and large were content with the "nonsectarian" solution. Strangely, it was Catholics, whose descendants would later complain about the "godless" schools, who were the strongest force for the complete secularization of public education—though what Archbishop Hughes actually sought was either the right to bring priests into the public schools to teach religion to Catholic pupils or some kind of public support for parochial schools. Hughes got neither of his demands, even with Catholics of the city rallying around him, carrying on public protests, and arguing his case in the courts.

The "secularization" solution of course turned out to be as unacceptable to the Catholics of the nineteenth century as the continuation of the Protestant character of the schools would have been. However, since neither side would compromise both sides lost. According to Leo Pfeffer, author of *Church, State, and Freedom* (Beacon Press, 1953), "American Protestantism—whether because of its devotion to the principle of separation of church and state (as many Protestants say) or because of its antagonism to Catholicism (as many Catholics believe)—would not yield . . . and preferred to see even Protestant religion taken out of the schools."

The original school controversy was extremely bitter. Archbishop Hughes, a pugnaciously anti-Protestant prelate, took an aggressive stance throughout. His bellicosity certainly did nothing to allay fears that Catholics were intent either on "taking over" public education or actually destroying it.

Of all the churchmen of the period, Hughes was the most unbending in his response to Protestant militancy. He consistently showed his contempt for Protestant culture and frequently spoke ominously of the Catholic Church's intentions to win everyone back to the True Faith—after which, his audiences concluded, Church and state in America would work hand in glove. It was ironic, then, that it was Hughes—the arch foe of religious indifferentism—who helped bring about the secularization of the schools. Moreover, the Archbishop's truculence played into the hands of anti-Catholic leaders by providing them with a basis for their argument that it was Catholics who were primarily responsible for the removal of the Bible from the classroom.

In the meantime parish priests throughout the country were throwing all their efforts into establishing schools. At the Third Plenary Council of Baltimore in 1884 the Bishops of the United States finally decreed that "near each church, where it does not exist, a parochial school is to be erected within two years." Already there were in the United States 2500 schools, attended by half a million young Catholics.

The Plenary Council's goal of a school for every parish

* n fierceness

was never fully reached. But over the next eighty years the Church came remarkably close to achieving it. As the number of Catholics grew, the parochial school system expanded without any significant interruption until the recent reverses.

Until the Second Vatican Council, these schools, more than any force, strengthened Catholic determination to hold the line against religious indifference, to resist the breakdown of the old Christian culture, and to counteract the force of modernity. In the age of ecumenism, acceptance of the contemporary world and the notion of the "servant Church," however, they have a new task set before them. The big question facing Catholic educators at this point is to determine precisely what that new challenge is and whether a separatist school system is really a way to meet it.

CHAPTER NINE

THE CLERGY

Almost all of the really significant decisions affecting American Catholicism throughout its history were made by the clergy and religious. Until very recent years laymen had little to say within the Church and were rarely consulted before action was taken. It is not surprising, then, that the standard historical accounts of the Church's experience in the United States are focused on clerical activities—the comings and goings of priests and bishops, the differences of opinion among them, the pronouncements issuing from episcopal meetings, the decisions reached during synods and councils, the establishment of new dioceses, the disciplinary measures taken to put an end to abuses, and so on.

The religious orders were an important influence, but even they came into the picture as devoted assistants carrying out policies set by the higher clergy. The laity, however, were definitely in the background; only a few of them are even mentioned by name, and even these few had little direct influence on the fortunes of the Church. For better or worse,

American Catholic history has been shaped by men of the cloth.

Most important of all of course were the bishops, who enjoyed almost unlimited power in their own dioceses; their authority throughout most of American Catholic history was rarely even questioned. The Bishop of a particular diocese had the last word on practically everything affecting the Church in that place. His priests were bound to him by the promises at ordination; rebels among them were few and far between. The religious who worked with him were subject to his rule in all matters impinging on the welfare of the diocese. They too were noted for their readiness to go along without challenging Chancery office decisions. The laity, though they were technically freer to act, were extremely slow to move on their own initiative and were almost always quick to give full public support to the Bishop's policies.

Actually, probably no group of Americans had at its disposal power quite as absolute as that enjoyed by the Catholic hierarchy within its own sphere of authority. Small wonder, then, that Catholics used to joke among themselves that, after the day of his consecration, no bishop for the rest of his life would ever again eat a bad meal or hear the whole truth. The bishops—set apart from other priests by elaborate clothing and feudal forms of address—were awesome figures in their public appearances and usually remained majestically remote at other times as well. In the light of their enormous prestige within the Catholic community it is surprising how few of them were remembered as individuals after they passed on. In his exhaustive, detailed history of the Church in the United States, Father McAvoy lists the names of only thirty-five American bishops in his index, and most of these come into the narrative incidentally.

Aside from John Carroll, the founder of the American hierarchy, probably the best remembered are Cardinal James Gibbons of Baltimore and Archbishop John Ireland of Saint Paul, who were contemporaries and frequent comrades in arms in the controversies that enlivened the nineteenth century. Cardinals Francis J. Spellman of New York and Richard J. Cushing of Boston, both colorful figures recently deceased, may be joined to that small company as time passes.

James Gibbons (1834–1921) was an extremely popular prelate. During his years as Archbishop of Baltimore—from 1877 until his death—he was generally recognized not only as the undisputed leader of Catholicism but as one of the nation's leading churchmen. Theodore Roosevelt went even further when he described Gibbons as the most respected and useful citizen of the United States, bar none. It was a measure of the Cardinal's personal prestige, and perhaps of the growing respectability of Catholicism as well, that the guests who came to Baltimore to celebrate the twenty-fifth anniversary of his elevation to the College of Cardinals in 1911 were described as the most distinguished gathering of Americans ever assembled to honor a private citizen.

As Archbishop of the oldest see and the nation's second Cardinal (John McCloskey of New York was the first), Cardinal Gibbons was generally accepted as the spokesman for the hierarchy, though there were bishops—notably the autocratic Archbishop Michael Corrigan of New York and his brusque Suffragan, Bernard McQuaid of Rochester—who disagreed with Gibbons' liberal views and openly resented his influence in the Vatican.

Throughout his career, the Archbishop of Baltimore used his prestige to sell the idea of the United States as the land of the free and home of the brave, and to strengthen the nation's cause, whatever it might be at any given time. On the occasion of his being named a cardinal, he delivered a widely reported sermon in a Roman Church exalting the American system of Church-state separation as not only tolerable but eminently favorable to the preaching of the Gospel. Later he not only persuaded Vatican authorities to withhold the formal condemnation of the Knights of Labor, but got them to cancel a public denunciation of Henry George's controversial single-tax theories.

The single-tax movement, which had won the allegiance of many American Catholics, had provoked a bitter controversy within the Church in the eighties that led to the excommunication of Father Edward McGlynn, a stormy New York pastor and one of the foremost single-taxers in the nation. Gibbons was not personally sympathetic to the Georgist cause. But he was thoroughly sold on the American idea of free speech and the free exchange of opinion, and he used his influence in Rome to uphold them as much as possible.

Such actions made him a favorite in working-class circles. His interests also ran to the life of the mind. He played a central role in the founding of the Catholic University of America and later served as its first chancellor. During the conservative attacks on the university in its early days he repeatedly came to its defense.

Gibbons once described the United States Constitution as "the most noble document ever written by the hand of man." The citizen's first duty, he stated on another occasion, was to come to his country's aid whenever called upon to do so. The same spirit of indiscriminate acceptance of whatever the authorities in Washington finally decided upon accounted for the support he gave to the war against Spain. Before the actual declaration of war he had made it clear that he would regard such an adventure as "unrighteous," but in the course of the hostilities he issued a somewhat different statement: "Catholics in the United States have but one sentiment. Whatever may have been their opinions as to the expediency of the war, now that it is on they are united in upholding the government." Later, when the United States entered the First World War, the Cardinal, all too predictably, again urged his fellow Catholics to give their full support to the cause. As was true of other prelates, once the fateful step was taken, the moral complexities of war simply did not bother him greatly; patriotism was all-important. Whatever "mistakes"—ill will was really unthinkable—that might have been made in the name of America were the responsibility not of the individual citizen, who was called upon to obey orders, but of the political authorities who had issued them.

Gibbons' unequivocal Americanism was known throughout the United States, and his reputation probably did more to counteract antagonism to Catholics than any other factor until John F. Kennedy came along. The Cardinal was so far above suspicion himself that it was impossible, as his friend President Roosevelt once told an anti-Catholic propagandist, to believe that the people he represented could present any real threat to American institutions.

The Cardinal is remembered as the author of *The Faith*

of Our Fathers, the most widely circulated volume of religious
apologetics ever published in the United States, and also for
his quiet skill in dealing with the thorny internal problems
the Church had to deal with because of the American hierarchy's differences over cultural assimilation. But his lasting
fame is due above all to the pride he took in the United States.
During his years of priestly service—which stretched from his
days as a volunteer chaplain in the Civil War up to the beginning of the Jazz Age—he was accepted as a symbol and spokesman not only for American Catholicism but for the nation
itself—the most Catholic of Americans and at the same time
the most American of Catholics.

Gibbons was an authentic product of nineteenth-century
Americanism—more than a little jingoistic, utterly sold on the
notion of the nation's "manifest destiny," and imbued with
the idea that in the United States the *novus ordo seclorum*
that the Pilgrims established was truly opening up a new page
in the history of mankind. He was convinced that even the
Church had a great deal to learn from the experiment with
political freedom being made in the New World. He might
have been overly cautious about taking a stand at times but
he always acted in the belief that nothing essential in Catholicism would be lost if the Church put less trust in *Romanità*
and adapted its ancient ways to the new order.

For more than forty years, at a crucial period in the history
of the American Church, the Cardinal's leadership, though
frequently challenged, remained basically secure. Had another
man, say a member of the "Roman" faction in the hierarchy,
held the same position, American Catholicism would probably
have taken a different turn. With Gibbons at the helm, the
special character of the United States as a democratic, religiously pluralistic nation, was never really lost sight of; at
least the genuine integralists in the Church never gained
control.

Gibbons' friend and close associate, John Ireland, was
brought to the United States from his native Kilkenny in 1849,
at the age of eleven. After a stay in Chicago, the Ireland
family finally settled in the Minnesota Territory. Soon thereafter young John made up his mind to be a priest. He was

sent to a small French seminary where he picked up a measure
of Continental sophistication at that time rare among the Irish-
American clergy, as well as a life-long devotion to everything
Gallic.

Ireland, who was ordained a priest of the Saint Paul diocese
in 1861, was quickly recognized as a young man of promise.
As early as 1875 he was appointed Coadjutor Bishop of his
home diocese and a decade later its Ordinary. He became
the first Archbishop of Saint Paul after the diocese was up-
graded four years later. Throughout most of his career he
was in the thick of one battle or another, beginning with his
combat experiences as a very young chaplain in the Civil War.
Later he was at the center of the heated controversies over
the question of "Americanism" and the extent to which Catholics should become assimilated to the going culture.

A more fiery and opinionated partisan of the "Americanist"
wing of the hierarchy than the gentle, tactful Gibbons, Ireland frequently exasperated his conservative brother-bishops
by his abrasive remarks and unconventional behavior. He was
particularly anathema to the German bishops because of his
explosive reaction to the idea that a German-American Church
should be set up in the United States. The followers of Peter
Paul Cahensly, he once wrote in a letter to Gibbons, were
really attempting to "foreignize our country in the name of
religion" and had to be stopped.

Statements like this did not endear him to members of the
clergy who were sincerely set on holding to their ethnic identity. Some of them felt that to agree to the thoroughly "Americanized" Church the Archbishop of Saint Paul envisioned
would in effect be to accept the domination of the Irish as
a permanent norm. Others, themselves Irish, were more than
a little suspicious of his unqualified endorsement of the optimism that characterized *fin de siècle* America. John Ireland
urged the Church to see in the "ambitions of the nineteenth
century" what he called, in characteristically florid prose, "the
fervid ebullitions of her own noble sentiments"; this in contrast to dozens of warnings issuing from American pulpits
and from the Vatican against the spirit of the age, which the
popes themselves said was leading to skepticism, irreverence,

and rebelliousness, and would in the end result in the complete destruction of Christian culture.

But if Ireland was anathema to the "Roman" party in the hierarchy, he was a hero to the Americanists and was held up as a model of the progressive prelate by Catholics who were urging the Church to come to terms with modernity. He was almost as well known in Europe as in America, and every year dozens of foreign visitors traveled to Minnesota to meet him.

The Archbishop of Saint Paul throughout his life was deeply involved in politics, ecclesiastical and civil, and he did not care who knew it. He made no secret of his devotion to the Republican Party and did everything in his power to break the hold the Democrats had on the Catholic community. He believed that political activity on the part of every American was the price of citizenship and did not exempt even bishops from the general obligation, though he also insisted on every clergyman's right to support the party of his own choice. Catholics in Minnesota were quite aware of their Archbishop's partisan sentiments, since he did not hesitate to support Republican candidates on the stump, but they felt no obligation to follow his lead in political matters.

His partisan activities, however, were not taken with such equanimity elsewhere. In 1894, he stirred up a storm by campaigning in New York City for the Republican platform. This was too much for the New York chancery office, especially since its efforts to get the G.O.P. to follow the example of the Democrats and condemn the anti-Catholic American Protective Association had proved to be unsuccessful. Bishop McQuaid was so aroused by Ireland's open politicking that he denounced him by name from the pulpit as an ecclesiastical interloper—an unusual breach of episcopal courtesy. McQuaid was later required to justify himself to the Vatican. He did so with a long letter of complaint. In it he charged that the meddling Saint Paul prelate had caused so much grief to Archbishop Corrigan that Corrigan's health had been seriously impaired.

In addition to his zeal to Americanize the Church, Archbishop Ireland devoted a great deal of his boundless energy to two causes of a more secular character. From his earliest days in the priesthood he was a firm supporter of the temperance movement; later he ardently promoted the establishment of small Catholic colonies in Minnesota. However, he was not very successful in either effort.

The Germans in his flock, who were quite aware of the virtue of moderation and generally practiced it better than the Archbishop's own countrymen, resented his wholesale condemnation of anything short of total abstinence; they contemptuously brushed aside his claim that anyone engaged in the liquor or brewery business was involved in a sinful enterprise. He actually had more luck with the hard-drinking Irish, though many of them also charged that his enthusiasm for temperance was altogether too intemperate. Despite the Archbishop's lack of success with his own people, however, his antiliquor crusade was taken by many of his abstemious Protestant neighbors to be a sure sign of his own moral rectitude and concern for good citizenship, and in general he was treated kindly by the secular press.

The enthusiasm for the establishment of Catholic colonies in what Ireland was wont to refer to as "my prairies" was closely connected with the temperance crusade. The Archbishop admitted that he felt the Irish could not be expected to pass up the lure of the bottle unless they were removed from the temptations offered by the big city. This was not his only reason for bringing immigrants to Minnesota to form their own colonies but it was certainly a primary one. People in the East who went hopefully to hear his talks on the colonization program came back complaining that what they heard was nothing more than a disguised temperance lecture. In any case the colonization scheme did not work out.

Nor did Ireland's controversial "compromise" school plan—an attempt to gain public support for what were actually parochial schools taught by Catholic sisters—work out. In 1891, in Faribault and Stillwater, two towns within the Archdiocese of Saint Paul, agreements were made by the local Catholic pastors to turn the parochial schools into public schools by putting them under the authority of the public school board, at the same time keeping the same teachers and pupils who had been in attendance before the transfer was made. There were, then, two public schools in each of the towns—the regular school and the "Catholic" school, both supported by public funds. The only real change made by the agreement was that religious instruction would be given by the nuns to their Catholic pupils after the normal school hours.

It was no surprise when the plan was denounced throughout the United States. Critics saw in it not only a brazen attempt on the part of a bishop to get tax monies for parochial education but a clear denial of the First Amendment. After the arrangement was publicized, "John Irelandism" became shorthand for a supposed hierarchical plot to dip into tax funds for the support of the Church; the Archbishop of Saint Paul was caricatured in every anti-Catholic paper in the land as a scheming prelate out to subvert one of the nation's most sacred traditions. Even some of his admirers took issue with his contention that the agreement was unobjectionable on constitutional grounds.

What really was surprising, however, was the amount of criticism Ireland was subjected to within the Catholic community itself. Shortly before the Faribault-Stillwater experiment, he had disturbed a number of his confreres in the hierarchy by lavishly praising the public schools in a speech to the National Educational Association. In fact, he went so far as to say that he wished that the Catholic schools did not exist—a particularly galling remark to make at a time when the hierarchy was doing everything in its power to sell Catholics on expanding the parochial system.

To be sure, in his N.E.A. speech Ireland had also insisted that the Church's schools would remain necessary as long as religious instruction was not found in the public school curriculum. But because this qualification was obscured in the reports in the Catholic press, word got around that the irrepressible Minnesotan was opposed to the Church's running its own schools. In the light of this impression, his experiment was taken to be a first step toward the elimination of parochial schools.

Ireland was accused of granting the state, rather than parents, supreme rights in education—a position which had already been repudiated by the Holy See in official documents. Though he had the support of the prestigious Cardinal Gibbons, formal complaints against him were made by some of his clerical opponents. The charges were taken seriously in Rome, but in time word came back that the Archbishop of Saint Paul, though he might have been characteristically imprudent, had actually remained within the bounds of orthodoxy in his speech. There was nothing improper, either, at least from a Catholic point of view, in the arrangements between the pastors of Faribault and Stillwater and the school boards in their towns.

In the meantime, however, the Archbishop's reputation as a maverick spread and the Church-state issues raised on the distant plains of Minnesota received a surprising amount of attention in Europe. The ensuing controversy, all out of proportion to the actual case, was carried on—in typical clerical style—through abstract treatises on parental rights and scholarly exchanges justifying the Church's interest in education. By the time it finally died, Ireland's experiment—which had been brought to a halt after only two years—was just a memory.

Archbishop Ireland never ceased to be the center of such controversies. Always somewhat larger than life, he was bound to stand out in a hierarchical body of prudent, "safe" churchmen. It was not simply his gift for rolling grandiloquence, which exactly fit the oratorical style of the period, nor even his constant readiness to stand up and be counted that set him apart from his fellow bishops. Everything about him seemed to be outsized—his zest for life, his sublime certainty that his own opinions were simply beyond debate, his readiness to do battle for his beliefs, his enthusiasms, virtues, even his faults.

His contemporaries recognized Ireland's extraordinary personal stature—even his sworn "enemies" in the hierarchy. Either in spite of or because of it, however, he died without getting the Red Hat he sought for many years. Though several attempts were made by powerful friends in the hierarchy to get him named to the College of Cardinals, none succeeded. This was the great disappointment of Ireland's life. It was an indication of the many-sided nature of this most democratic of American prelates—and perhaps also symbolic of American Catholicism as a whole—that while he worked incessantly to be more American than the native-born, he never lost the desire to cap his career by also becoming a Prince of the Church.

Francis J. Spellman (1889–1967) was also in the tradition of the volubly patriotic prelate. But by the time he came into his own America had changed greatly, and many of his "pro-American" statements and actions over the years were widely dismissed as obscurantist and politically reactionary.

Cardinal Spellman, the son of a small-town Massachusetts grocer, was never as beloved as Gibbons or as candid a politician as Ireland but he actually reached a higher pinnacle of power than either of them. As a force within both the Church and the state, he dominated American Catholicism for more than a generation. Though technically his authority was neither more nor less than that of any other Ordinary, his influence was so great during the reign of Pius XII that he came to be thought of as a kind of American Pope.

Spellman did not begin his studies for the priesthood until after his graduation from Fordham College, which he entered upon finishing the public high school in his native Whitman, Massachusetts, in 1907. For theological training, he was sent to the North American College in Rome, which had been established forty-eight years earlier by the American hierarchy. In Rome he attended classes at the international Urban College of Propaganda. There, fortuitously, among his teachers were several young Italian priests who were soon destined to reach high positions in the Vatican.

The young Spellman took easily to the curial style of ecclesiastical Rome. Though he always remained unmistakably American in character—unlike some other Rome-trained American clerics who became more Italian than the Italians as time went on—he received his first lessons in how to survive in the ecclesiastical jungle during his years as a seminarian and proved to be a very adept pupil. By the time of his ordination in 1916, he spoke Italian fluently and, as he himself said cryptically on the occasion of his first Mass in Whitman, he had learned some other things he could never have picked up at home.

Back in Boston, with a spanking new doctorate in Sacred Theology, the young priest was assigned to a very humble post on the staff of the *Pilot,* the archdiocesan newspaper. His particular job was to go out to a different church every Sunday and sell parishioners on the need for a Catholic press, particularly the *Pilot.* He did this dutifully for the next four and a half years, restless but resigned to the will of his superior, the autocratic Cardinal William O'Connell, who was never particularly fond of him. In his free time he studied Spanish and translated two volumes of devotional books written by one of his old Propaganda University professors, Monsignor (later Cardinal) Francesco Borgongini-Duca, who was already rising in the Vatican Secretariat of State. Then for a brief time he was assigned to the very minor position of an administrative assistant in the Boston chancery office.

By 1925 Father Spellman was back in Rome, this time shepherding a group of Bostonians on a Holy Year pilgrimage. He saw a great deal of Monsignor Borgongini-Duca during this second stay and impressed the Roman with his intimate knowledge of the city and understanding of how the Church there operated. By the time he was ready to return to Boston he had an invitation from Pius XI himself to come back as soon as possible in order to become the director of a playground for Roman children which was being financed by the American Knights of Columbus. The titular head of the program was none other than Monsignor Borgongini-Duca; as his representative Spellman would be attached to the Vatican Secretariat of State.

The energetic young priest soon found he would have time on his hands as a playground director, and at his own request was put to work in the Vatican translating official documents into English. Later when Pius XI made a historic radio broadcast to the entire world, Spellman was chosen to give the English-language interpretation of the Pontiff's words. In 1929, negotiations were being conducted between the Vatican and Benito Mussolini to solve the "Roman question" and the young American was called upon for advice. Somewhat to his own surprise, a number of his suggestions were accepted.

During the period of his assignment to the Vatican, Spellman met Cardinal Eugenio Pacelli, later Pope Pius XII. The two quickly struck up a friendship which had tremendous consequences for American Catholicism over the next three decades. Soon after their first meeting in Berlin—Pacelli was rounding out an assignment as Papal Nuncio at the time— the future Pope was named Vatican Secretary of State. Spellman in short order became one of his closest confidants, a genial traveling companion, and a kind of a chaplain-assistant. Though the relationship between them was never formalized, the Bostonian's future in the Church was assured.

When he finally returned home it was with a mitre, but with the comparatively modest assignment of Auxiliary to the Cardinal-Archbishop of his home diocese. In addition, the youthful bishop was appointed pastor of the church at Newton Center, where he gained the parochial experience every Ordinary needs, and his administrative talents were developed.

When Cardinal Pacelli visited the United States in 1936, Spellman again became his traveling companion. Among other high places, the two prelates visited the home of Franklin Delano Roosevelt at Hyde Park. Throughout the rest of the President's life he and Spellman remained close friends. "My favorite bishop," Roosevelt once called him. After Pacelli's visit, the President made a point of keeping in touch with the pastor of Newton Center. Though Spellman was then on the lowest rung of the hierarchy, he quickly became a quiet go-between for the White House and the Vatican.

In 1939, Cardinal Pacelli was elected Pope. One of his first acts was to appoint Spellman Archbishop of New York, neither the oldest nor the largest American diocese but, after Gibbons' death, unquestionably the most prestigious and quite the richest. No consistories were held in the Vatican during the war, so it was not until 1946 that he received the Red Hat.

During the war, with President Roosevelt's blessing, Spellman visited practically all the battlefronts in his role as Military Vicar for Catholics in the Armed Forces. His fame spread throughout the world as an outspoken American patriot whose influence at the Vatican was probably greater than that of any other foreign prelate. It was also widely believed that his diplomatic gifts were being put to use by the reigning Pontiff, though the Vatican remained scrupulously "neutral" throughout the hostilities and none of this was made public. His personal prestige shot up accordingly. The close relationship to the Pope was well known, and Spellman was treated deferentially by the Allied leaders with whom he came in contact.

A friendly, engaging man, often quite witty, he soon numbered among his friends many of the great figures of the world. At home, it was taken for granted that he towered above every other Catholic bishop because of his special ties to the Pope. As an articulate opponent of Nazism and an ardent supporter of the war, he was admired throughout the nation for his patriotic services and the personal attention he gave to American fighting men, Catholic and non-Catholic alike. Nor did his friendship with the Roosevelt family go unnoted. Not since the days of Cardinal Gibbons had a Catholic prelate achieved such personal popularity.

In the years following the war, however, Cardinal Spellman, now firmly established as primate in all but name, became highly controversial. Within the Church, his power had grown so great that it was generally believed he had more to say than anyone else about appointing new bishops and setting policies. It was well known too that he took a dim view of the progressive forces within the American Church and that he was using his power to hold back reforms. Though he said little in public, he made no secret of his lack of sympathy for lay initiative, the liturgical revival, the early ecumenical movement, and the "social Catholicism" being promulgated by some of the most articulate young priests and laymen in the land. This inevitably created a gap between him and those who were actually molding the Catholicism that was to come. At the same time, his frank exercise of the extraordinary power he had accrued over the years was heartily resented. Nor was he simply the bête noire of the liberal faction. For quite different reasons, many of the bishops and other leading clergy privately shared the liberals' antagonism toward him.

Spellman as Cardinal actually represented the embodiment of the Catholicism he was born into—preoccupied with hierarchical privilege, pietistic and fundamentalist in his understanding of the Faith, profoundly suspicious both of the impact of secular modernity and of intellectual developments within the Church, unbudgeably conservative in his attitude toward liturgical change, puritanical in his approach to the arts, unhesitant about using political power to get his way at home but yet ready at all times to defer to "Rome" without murmur. Prayerful, paternalistic, hard-working, personally very charitable, business-minded, and seemingly impervious to the stirrings of change in the Church, he might have escaped criticism in an earlier era, but it was his fate to preside over a church in transition and he was just not able to read the signs of the time.

For some of these same reasons he also became a controversial figure in the world at large. In the 1950s, though he remained a favorite of the political conservatives, American liberals were deeply suspicious of his simplistic anticommunism. As the Cold War escalated, so did his rhetoric, and more and more people began to suspect that beneath the bland clerical countenance there was the soul of a fanatic. No one was ever quite sure how much influence he had on decisions taken in Washington, but there was a widespread suspicion that it might be downright sinister. At the same time he was portrayed in the communist press throughout the world as a warmonger, a willing agent of American imperialism, and a compliant servant of vested financial interests. The Cardinal took pride in the communists' attacks; the liberals he pointedly ignored.

His highly publicized forays into the censorship of movies suggested to others that the Boston Irish puritanism he betrayed in his public statements was not just a personal characteristic but a danger for America itself because in the last analysis he was a man with real power who would give no quarter to any concern for civil liberties. The same impression was greatly reinforced after his sympathy for Senator Joseph R. McCarthy became generally known. Many Protestants and Jews, disturbed particularly by his repeated demands for federal aid to parochial schools, were persuaded that he was equally indifferent to the principle of Church-state separation.

Feelings toward the Cardinal reached a high point in 1949 after he became involved in a public dispute with Eleanor Roosevelt over the school-aid issue. Mrs. Roosevelt had opposed such aid in several of her syndicated columns, arguing that it would amount to the establishment of religion. After the columns came to the Cardinal's notice he was provoked into sending her a testy reply in defense of his own position. He ended a highly emotional letter by saying dramatically, "I shall not again publicly acknowledge you. For whatever you may say in the future, your record of anti-Catholicism stands for all to see—a record which you yourself wrote on the pages of history which cannot be recalled—documents of discrimination unworthy of an American mother!" Mrs. Roosevelt, as was to be expected, flatly denied the anti-Catholic charge but she added reprovingly at the end of her response, "I shall, of course, continue to stand for things in our government which I think are right. I assure you that I have no sense of being 'an unworthy American mother.' The final judgment, my dear Cardinal Spellman, of the unworthiness of all human beings is in the hands of God."

The exchange between the two celebrities turned out to be a sensation. Both parties were both lavishly praised and denounced in the press; and Democratic politicians, eager not to offend either one or the other, felt they were caught in a hopeless bind. That Mrs. Roosevelt had many enemies as well as strong admirers was well known, but as a result of the controversy the latent antagonism toward the Cardinal was also brought out into the open, and he drew down upon himself a cascade of hostility.

Some months later, the Cardinal, carrying a small peace offering (a delicate lace handkerchief), called upon Mrs. Roosevelt, unannounced, at her rural Hyde Park home. Presumably a reconciliation of sorts was effected. The former First Lady gave no detailed account of their conversation, however, though the visit was duly noted in her sly chit-chatty newspaper column. "We had a pleasant chat and I hope the country air proved as much a tonic for [the Cardinal] as it always does for me," she commented blandly.

With the death of Pius XII in 1958, the Cardinal's influence gradually diminished. He had no great voice at the Second Vatican Council after it became evident that the American bishops, confronting abstruse theological issues, were looking elsewhere for leadership—specifically to the shy, intellectual Cardinal Albert Meyer of Chicago, who died while the Council was in session. Spellman received a great deal of public attention once more, however, toward the end of the Council when, as Archbishop of New York, he hosted Pope Paul during the Pontiff's short visit to the United Nations in the fall of 1965. But with the changes in the Church, to which the Cardinal in his latter years adjusted with remarkable grace (unlike his strong-willed protégé on the West Coast, Cardinal McIntyre of Los Angeles), Spellman finally seemed to recognize that a new day had dawned and the power and the glory were now behind him.

He tried to resign as Archbishop of New York after the Council, but the Pope asked him to stay on, which he did until his death two years later. He was succeeded by the youngest of his own Auxiliaries, Bishop Terence Cooke—a modest, bland, middle-of-the-road prelate who only a few years earlier would have seemed to be among the most unlikely of priests to be chosen to succeed the strong-willed man who presided over American Catholicism for so many years.

Richard J. Cushing (1895–1970), a fellow Bostonian, was cut from very different cloth, though as young priests he and Spellman were close friends and associates. Like most Irish-American clerics of his generation, Cushing was born into a poor working-class family. "I brought nothing with me to the priesthood and I will leave nothing when I go," he said frequently. And he kept his word. After more than a quarter century as head of one of the world's richest archdioceses, he left nothing but his books and a few sets of ecclesiastical vestments, which he bequeathed to missionary bishops.

Cushing ran a tight ship in Boston but he never sought the kind of wider ecclesiastical power that Spellman exercised. Yet, he made a tremendous impression on the Church in the United States and was revered in his home town as a kind of tough-talking saint.

A graduate of Boston College, he first considered being a Jesuit but finally decided on the diocesan clergy and went off to the local seminary. He began his career in the priesthood as Boston director of the Society for the Propagation of the Faith—an organization which supports missionaries throughout the world. He was highly successful in this and developed a talent for fund raising which served him well throughout his life. Later as Archbishop of Boston—in that Irish city a position second in influence to none—he raised millions of dollars for churches, schools, orphanages, homes for the aged, institutions for retarded children, and foreign missions.

He never lost his interest in the missions. In the 1950s he established the Society of Saint James, a group of priests who volunteer to spend several years in Latin America during their younger years before returning to take their place as pastors in the home diocese. After his retirement, he used to say, he wanted to spend the rest of his life on one of their missions as a simple pastor. But by the time he reached retirement age he was racked with illness.

Cushing was finally made Cardinal by John XXIII in 1958 after fourteen years as Archbishop of Boston. No matter what official eminence he achieved, he remained the same blunt-spoken, down-to-earth churchman, with no intellectual or social pretensions of any kind. Yet, he was as much at ease with the rich and powerful as he was with the poor and powerless, who always had first call on his attention.

It was typical of him that he answered his own phone, danced merrily with octogenarians during his regular visits to the old people's homes in the archdiocese, and tried on funny hats at social affairs in an effort to cut down on the solemnity attached to his presence.

The Cardinal broke all kinds of rules. He was anything but circumspect in his speech and put small emphasis on either prudence or consistency during his public appearances. Sometimes he astounded audiences by saying what they definitely did not come to hear. Speaking to a gathering of zealous liturgical reformers, he once upset everyone by glorifying the virtues of the traditional liturgy they were earnestly set on changing. Presiding at the reception of novices in a cloistered contemplative convent, he took the opportunity to praise the active life exemplified by nuns who worked in the slums of the city. Priests who came to him with problems of faith as often as not were told to get back to the work of helping other people and stop worrying about such recondite matters. He was quick to belittle his own intellectual accomplishments but saw no reason to be overly deferential toward theologians or scholars. During the Vatican Council, he announced that he was leaving Rome because he could not understand the

Latin spoken in the conciliar sessions—a refreshing admission coming from a member of the College of Cardinals; besides, he added, he had more pressing things to do in Boston than sit around in Rome listening to speeches that would put him to sleep even if he did know the language.

Cushing's interest was centered primarily on people and their problems rather than on either ideas or books. Frequently he did not bother to distinguish men from the causes they represented, which caused no end of confusion about his real views and gained for him the reputation of being completely erratic.

His public statements and pastoral letters were generally conventionally liberal in tone, and his personal friendship with the Kennedy family was well known. It was baffling, then, when he was suddenly publicized from coast to coast during the Kennedy administration for endorsing the aims of the John Birch Society, the right-wing extremist group which was dead set against the President and his New Frontier. The Cardinal later explained that Robert Welch, the founder of the society, was an old and trusted friend of his and he was sure Welch's motives must be sincere.

Cushing's relationship to the Kennedys brought him to national attention, since he usually presided at their well-publicized weddings, baptisms, and funerals. It was he who officiated when John and Jacqueline were married in Newport, Rhode Island. Less than ten years later, he was at President Kennedy's side at the Inauguration, and a few years after that the Cardinal consigned the remains of "dear Jack" (as he impulsively added to the formal prayers) to his grave. After the Bay of Pigs fiasco, when the President set out to raise a vast sum to be used for the ransom of the captives taken by Fidel Castro, Cushing got on the phone and quickly produced the money. He was always ready when the Kennedys called on him for help. Yet he never used his closeness to the President to gain any favors for himself or preferential treatment in the White House. As he told his friends, he made a point of keeping out of "Jack's affairs" and he expected Jack to stay out of his.

Cardinal Cushing, in any bloodless accounting, would probably not be counted among the greatest of American bishops.

His record as builder and administrator was impressive but not really unmatched; his publications—depending on the particular "ghost" he employed—range from the thoughtful to the shockingly irresponsible; he was respected by most of his peers in the hierarchy but none of them really looked to him for leadership. In the long run, what may assure him a permanent place in American Catholic history was his unmistakable humanity, extraordinary care about people, and utter absence of side.

He was indestructibly American in his emphasis on the practical over the speculative, in his cavalier attitude toward forms and traditions, and perhaps even in his indifference toward intellectual consistency. None of these characteristics of course normally counts for much on the scale of values by which prelates are judged in Rome. Yet, somehow the Cardinal of Boston, with only a few setbacks, held his own there, too, apparently without trying very hard. He and Pope John met late in life but they struck it off immediately; Cushing liked to believe they were two of a kind. Neither an elegant nor a particularly eloquent man, even in the center of Catholicism where the ecclesiastical style is so very different, he was generally recognized as a diamond in the rough—a genuine product of the best that American Catholicism had to offer.

It was perhaps a measure of Cushing's human appeal that, in the summer of 1963, when all the Cardinals marched into the Vatican Palace for the election of the Pope who would succeed John XXIII, the Bostonian received the loudest applause of all from the sophisticated, always dryly cynical Italians who were watching the procession. His special quality, like that of the dead Pope, attracted all kinds of people, Protestants, Jews, and unbelievers alike—and much was forgiven him because he loved much. Boston, which appreciated him most of all, is not likely to allow history to forget him.

There were undoubtedly many other outstanding men among the two thousand or so American Catholic priests who have been appointed to the episcopacy since John Carroll. There was, for example, John Keane (1839–1918), the fifth Bishop of Richmond, Virginia, and later the first rector of the Catholic University, which he served for nine years before being ousted because of his liberal attitudes. Keane later became Archbishop of Dubuque, Iowa, after an unhappy tour of duty in the Roman Curia, where he simply did not fit in. He was a contemporary of Archbishop Ireland and shared the Minnesotan's ardor for American institutions.

More than once he was quietly called to task for his unequivocal endorsement of religious tolerance. At a time when the "error has no rights" attitude toward other faiths was the official view of the Vatican and had a strong hold on the "Roman" faction in the American hierarchy, Keane did not hesitate to address his Protestant neighbors, "Brothers, though you do not serve God in our way, serve Him the best you know how in your own way." Again, he once said that he never visited the old countries of Europe without thanking God that he was an American. Such statements did not make the Archbishop particularly popular abroad or enhance his standing with the integralists among his fellow bishops at home, but they went a long way toward "Americanizing" the Church in the United States.

Another prelate of the same generation, John Lancaster Spalding, Bishop of Peoria, Illinois, was the most intellectual member of the hierarchy of his day and probably the most thoughtful advocate of the assimilationists' cause. His influence was drastically limited, however, because of his personal moodiness and temperamental inability to work as a member of a team. An elegant writer and poet, he was a man of fierce intellectual independence, habitually critical not only of his opponents but of his allies as well. For instance, he caustically dismissed Ireland's position on parochial schools and ridiculed the Saint Paul prelate for being unduly concerned about advancing himself in the hierarchy. Spalding thought that Keane, another of his allies, allowed himself to be used as a doormat by the Roman authorities out of a mistaken sense of humble obedience, and he said as much.

Though he was one of the earliest advocates of establishing a national university, it was typical of Spalding that he was unwilling to accept the position of rector of the Catholic University when it was offered to him. He also turned down several offers to take over more important sees and sulked in

Peoria for long periods, remaining loftily above the fray when his leadership was clearly needed.

A scion of an old Maryland Catholic family, Spalding was a third-generation American—a rarity in the hierarchy of the nineteenth century. It is clear now that he was a man ahead of his time in his thinking, probably altogether too advanced for his fellow ecclesiastics, who were not ready to entertain such opinions as his view that women had as much right as men to be educated and should receive exactly the same kind of education, or to face up to the implications of his statement that "Aristotle is a great mind, but his learning is crude and his ideas of Nature are grotesque; Saint Thomas is a powerful intellect, but his point of view in all that concerns natural knowledge has long since vanished from sight."

Spalding's life, on balance, unhappily represents an almost classic example of promise unfulfilled. In Andrew Greeley's words ". . . his career was obviously a tragic one, tragic not only for himself personally but also for the American Church."

Men as intellectually gifted as the brooding Bishop of Peoria are hard to come upon in any organization. Certainly in the long line of American bishops there were few who even approached him. Most of them have been churchmen of mediocre intellectual attainments, picked for their organizing talents, administrative abilities, and financial acumen—qualities, whatever else might be said of them, which were needed to support the ever-expanding clerical bureaucracy that kept the Church running on an even keel for so long.

Some who were consecrated bishops, it will surprise no one, were careerists who on their way up avoided saying or doing anything out of the ordinary in order not to offend anyone in a position to push their fortunes along. Others were chosen from humble, hard-working pastors who never sought honors but had shown that they were trustworthy administrators ready for larger responsibilities. An extraordinarily high percentage were alumni of the North American College in Rome—the "nursery of bishops"—men well schooled in the ideal of the bishop as a cleric distinguished not for his originality but for his readiness to obey as well as to command, to hold tenaciously to orthodox positions, and scrupulously observe ecclesiastical tradition. Few were chosen from the ranks of the religious orders, at least after the diocesan priesthood in the United States was firmly established.

But if the American hierarchy, by and large, has been neither a notably independent-minded nor intellectually elite group, it has been an intelligent body of cautious men who knew the rules of effective Church leadership and carefully observed them. Their brick-and-mortar accomplishments are obvious enough, and the cohesiveness of the American Catholic community throughout most of its history stood as a tribute to their leadership.

Whenever that leadership has faltered, as it has in recent years, the explanations must be sought in the fact that the kind of priests chosen to be bishops have usually been too bound up with the ecclesiastical "system" to see beyond it; their weakness has been that they automatically resisted change until it was upon them; typical of bureaucrats everywhere, they put too little emphasis on ideas, especially new ideas, and habitually lost sight of the trite dictum that nothing on earth can stop an idea whose time has come.

For instance, while the bishops encouraged schools and every manner of educational experience over the years, their main interest was in conserving tradition rather than expanding it, so that D. W. Brogan, the British observer, could write in the 1940s that "in no Western society is the intellectual prestige of Catholicism lower than in the country where, in such respects as wealth, numbers, and strength of organization, it is so powerful." In the years since Brogan handed down this judgment, the intellectual prestige of American Catholicism has risen; but it may also be significant that the change generally took place without the cooperation of the bishops, and, indeed, often in spite of them.

It would seem now that a renewed Catholicism will require a new kind of American bishop—a man more in tune with the times, more roundly educated, less narrowly clerical in his outlook, closer to his priests, more open to change and innovation, more personally persuasive and less dependent on sheer authority. In all probability such bishops will actually be forthcoming to meet the future needs of the Church. It is only fair to say, however, that they will be successful only if, in their own way, they can match the accomplishments of the perhaps colorless but hard-working churchmen who succeeded in rooting in the New World the now thoroughly indigenous Catholicism they will inherit.

American Catholic priests, on the whole, have always administered their parishes efficiently if somewhat unimaginatively, performed their duties studiously, and have been compensated by the assurance that they were the custodians of a vibrant religious tradition, assigned by ordination, if not by temperament, to be community leaders. There were always some saints and a few scoundrels among them, but most were ordinary Christians who felt that they had been called to lead extraordinary lives in order to fulfill their vocations.

The priest has been highly respected in the Catholic community, where much has been asked of him—perhaps altogether too much for run-of-the-mill men picked from run-of-the-mill families. He has been expected to be an exemplar of virtue, a custodian of Christian wisdom, an infallible guide to proper conduct, a wise counselor, and an uncomplaining servant of his people. While some priests, overburdened by the demands made upon them, clearly failed in one or more of these assignments, a remarkably high percentage succeeded as pastors. In doing so, they only raised the impossibly high expectations of the Catholic laity, who have always tended to take their clergy for granted.

It was not until very recently that any sound study was made of the American clergy. Until then, priests were looked upon almost as a race apart, without the needs of ordinary men for human companionship, compassion, and understanding. The most recent psychological studies, however, show that the foremost problem of American Catholic priests today is loneliness, a painful awareness of being set apart from their fellow men, and a poignant sense of being constitutionally incapable of fulfilling the high expectations of the laity. These findings may also have been true, more or less, of the hundreds of thousands of priests who lived and died in the service of the American Church over the past two hundred years, but in a less candid age their personal difficulties went unrecorded and unstudied.

Very few of them are even remembered by name, and among these only a handful were simple shepherds living out the ideals of the seminary in a busy city parish or forgotten rural mission. The remembered ones were more likely to have done specialized work, like Father Flanagan of Boys Town, Father Daniel Lord, the youth worker, or Father James Gillis, the editor and columnist. Still, the Church depended upon obscure "parish men" to keep its massive apparatus going and do the humble daily chores that produced in the United States a Catholicism second to none.

If such priests frequently lacked a certain vision, it was perhaps because, like most men, they rarely succeeded in seeing beyond their own times or in cutting themselves off from the pride and prejudice of the community that gave them their identity. It was at once the weakness and the strength of the American priesthood that it remained united to the people it served and all too accurately reflected the community's limitations and sometimes misplaced ambitions, which in turn were not merely the product of the age-old Catholic tradition but of America itself, with all its hopes, dreams, myths, superstitions, prejudices, and presuppositions. Nowhere else in the Church have the clergy been closer to their people than in the United States. Where they have failed, the failure perhaps was due in large part to the fact that they were too close and provided too clear a reflection of a people who were not only faithfully Catholic but uncritically American.

The diocesan clergy have always been at the heart of Catholic life—in the parishes. But the religious orders, which soon flourished in the United States, also played a major role. Almost all the great orders of Europe sooner or later sunk new roots in America—Benedictines, Franciscans, Dominicans, Augustinians, Carmelites, Jesuits, and so on. And many of the less prestigious groups got a new lease on life after they managed to establish themselves in the New World.

In the beginning, the "order priests," as they are called, were barely distinguishable from the secular clergy. They operated parishes or met the pastoral challenges of the day as itinerant missionaries, without any overriding concern for monastic observance. The Trappists, for example, were committed by rule to a life of contemplation and withdrawal, but they did not hesitate to turn to teaching when that was a pressing need of the times. Benedictine monks and Franciscan and Dominican friars who had joined their orders expecting to live out their lives in monasteries came to America and frequently spent the rest of their days as parish priests or as lonely missionaries cut off from community life.

But as time went on and native-born priests became less scarce, the various orders were able to establish genuine houses in their separate traditions, and an authentic religious life— as varied as the orders themselves—was finally possible. The monks, friars, clerks regular, and canons attached to them became distinct and identifiable.

The largest and most influential of all were the Jesuits, the group to which Archbishop Carroll and his first associates originally belonged. American Jesuits—ultimately the largest branch of that cosmopolitan order—have been primarily educators, but they have also served as pastors, diocesan administrators, editors and writers, retreat masters, convent chaplains, missionaries, seminary directors, and a dozen other specialists.

The Jesuits have long been famous for their scholarliness, urbanity, and worldly sophistication; many American members of the order, however, have been simple men, no more intellectually distinguished than the average diocesan priest. Still, the Society's total impact on American Catholicism has been unmatched, mainly because Jesuits have dominated so much of the intellectual life of the Church and through their schools have been responsible for the education of so many of the laity. The influence of the Society has been so pervasive that it might not be going too far to say that, for better or worse, the Church in the United States has been "Jesuitized." Jesuit notions of spirituality have been propagated, not always consciously, by the secular clergy and members of other orders. Until quite recently, the historic Jesuit emphasis on reason and syllogism has determined the stance of Catholic apologists. The highly structured Jesuit notion of classical education was soon adopted by practically all Catholic institutions of higher learning. The Counter-Reformation spirit of the Society, a heritage from its tumultuous beginnings, shaped the American Catholic response to Protestantism right up to the Second Vatican Council.

For all this, the individualism encouraged by the Society also made it possible for practically every movement within the Church to include among its leaders a certain number of Jesuits. There were Catholic Worker Jesuits, Coughlinite Jesuits, conservative and liberal Jesuits, pacifist and cold-warrior Jesuits. It is a sign of the freedom of action presently found in the order that the right-wing spokesman, Daniel Lyons, and the radical poet, Daniel Berrigan, both put S.J. after their names. Somewhere in between is Robert Drinan, S.J., who in 1970 became the second Catholic priest to serve in the Congress.

Ignatius Loyola, the soldierly founder of the Society, lived in a religious and political society markedly different from that prevailing in the United States. But it is clear, after two hundred years of Jesuit adaptation to life in America, that the genius of his idea transcended the limitations of his own time and place.

No order has had as much influence as the Jesuits, but others have added their particular spirit to the amalgam of traditions that helped shape American Catholicism. The Benedictine monks—long the favorites of the Catholic intelligentsia —contributed a certain poise, with their emphasis on the long view of history. Benedictines provided a link with the early medieval past and in their unhurried way challenged the hectic activism of America by emphasizing liturgical observance, modest self-subsistence, and patristic scholarship.

The Franciscans, by the time they got to the United States, were already far removed from the days when they were literally wandering friars, gently rebuking their fellow Christians by the poverty and austerity of their lives. American Franciscan houses in time became as secure and comfort-ridden as those of any other order. But as Thomas Merton once noted, something of the playful spirit of the Poverello has always mysteriously persisted among his friars. Because of it, the genuine Franciscan witness was never wholly absent in the American Church, though it came down in a very attenuated fashion.

The Dominicans—traditionally the theological scholars of the Church—produced a number of outstanding men but on the whole their record in the United States has been undistinguished. The order has turned out devoted, hard-working parish priests and earnest teachers, yet the Dominicans as such have not made the impression on the American Church that might have been expected of a group with such a powerful intellectual tradition. The same sort of thing might be said of such groups as the Carmelites, with their historic emphasis on the virtues of contemplation, and the Augustinians, the order which produced Martin Luther and Gregor Mendel.

New orders were founded in America and had to work out their basic character in the novel setting of a democratic, religiously pluralistic environment. Of these the most influential, though always remarkably small in number, have been Father Hecker's Paulists, who now specialize in communications, ecumenism, inner-city work, and especially the ministry to Catholic students on secular campuses. The Maryknoll Fathers, founded in 1911 in Ossining, New York, send their members to foreign missions around the world. The Servants of the Paraclete, a later American foundation, are devoted to the care of priests having difficulties of one kind or another.

Of the 58,000 American Catholic priests active in the ministry in 1970, more than 21,000 were members of the various orders and congregations, engaged in a wide variety of works. The Vincentians and Sulpicians, for example, man seminaries for the training of diocesan clergy. The Friars of the Atonement, originally an Anglican group, are primarily concerned with Christian unity. The Glenmary Fathers are dedicated to work in the remote rural areas of Appalachia. The Fathers of Saint Camilus work in hospitals. The Salesians specialize in trade schools. The Passionists and Redemptorists emphasize preaching. Almost all these congregations, and dozens of others which might be named, also conduct parishes. But they have made their best contribution by undertaking a wide assortment of specialized assignments, made possible above all by their mobility and the distinct spirit that gives each one of them its own particular identity.

CHAPTER TEN

CHURCH AND STATE

Few would have predicted two hundred years ago that the authoritarian Roman Catholic Church and the democratic government of the United States could coexist without constant turmoil and recriminations against one another; yet in no place in the world have Catholics felt more secure in practicing their faith than in America, and in only few places have relations between Church and state been as stable.

This happy situation has long been taken for granted but it actually represents a historic accomplishment. It points up not only the extraordinary capacity of Catholicism to adapt to the political facts of life wherever it is found, but the ability of American democracy to accommodate itself to the needs of all its citizens. Had either Church or state failed along the way, American history might have been marked by religious strife rivaling the outbursts that have marred Church-state relations elsewhere.

In the long run, it is also a tribute to American Protestantism.

The first generation of Americans had every reason to claim that their new nation was not only basically Protestant in its original inspiration but Protestant in its cultural spirit and essential principles. If today the United States is truly a pluralistic nation, it is only because earlier generations of Protestants were finally impelled by their devotion to religious liberty to permit other faiths, particularly Roman Catholicism, to take solid root in "Protestant" soil. It seems necessary to say this lest the history of Protestant harassment of Catholics in the United States overshadow the fact that for years American Catholicism in the final analysis was dependent for its survival on Protestant devotion to freedom of conscience. Without it, the Church of Rome might have been legally proscribed or at least placed under severe disabilities (as Protestantism was in Spain).

The prosperity of American Catholicism, then, has not been

a single-handed achievement. Above all, it must be attributed to the men who wrote the First Amendment to the Constitution, with its double provision that "Congress shall make no law respecting an establishment of religion, or prohibiting the free exercise thereof. . . ."

The guarantee of religious liberty would have been easier to fulfill of course had the nation remained as overwhelmingly Protestant as it still was when the Constitution was being drafted, for the presence in the United States of a supranational, hierarchical Church, with cultural traditions rooted in medieval thought, inevitably created legal difficulties. They were not made any easier by the fact that hostility toward Catholic Christianity was part and parcel of the tradition which the Protestant brought with him to the New World—a hostility that had been toughened by the experience of Europe's murderous religious wars and political intrigue.

The first significant Church-state problems were centered on control over ecclesiastical property. They were made more difficult because of the bitter controversy over trusteeism within Catholicism itself and the fact that the force of civil law strengthened the position of those trustees who, at least in the hierarchy's own view, were set on depriving the bishops of their God-given rights. For example, a law was drawn up in New York in 1813 which provided that before any religious congregation could be legally incorporated, a board of trustees would have to be elected from among its lay members "to take charge of the estate and property . . . and to transact all affairs relative to the temporalities [of the parish]." The law in effect deprived the bishops of their historic right to appoint and remove pastors without the consent of the laity. As such, it conflicted not only with important provisions of Canon Law but with Catholic doctrine on the authority of a diocesan Ordinary.

The New York law and others like it were disturbing to the reigning Pontiff, Pius VII. In 1822 he wrote to the American hierarchy that the polity then arising in America was "totally unheard of in the Church"; it amounted to a subversion of laws "not only ecclesiastical but divine." With it, the Pope stated, "the Church would be governed, not by Bishops but by laymen; the shepherd would be made subject to the flock." The bishops heartily agreed and most of them set out to eradicate lay trusteeism root and branch.

There was no more fierce opponent of the system than Archbishop John Hughes, who soon after he took over in New York appealed to the parishes within his jurisdiction to give up voluntarily their undoubted civil right to hold Church property, out of loyalty to Catholic doctrine. Every church in the New York archdiocese but one complied with the request. The Church of Saint Louis, in Buffalo, the single parish which held out against Hughes, was put under interdict and its trustees were excommunicated. Then the Archbishop arranged to have a bill presented to the state legislature which would allow ecclesiastical authorities to hold Church property in their own names. Protestant opposition to the bill was predictably successful; the measure was roundly defeated.

In 1855 when the trustees of the rebellious Buffalo parish appealed to the political authorities to take up their case against the Bishop, the legislature responded lavishly by passing a measure (the Putnam Bill) which made it actually illegal for Hughes or any other cleric to hold ecclesiastical property. The Putnam Bill was never enforced, however, and was repealed eight years later. Had it or similar legislation been allowed to stand, American Catholics would have been forced to choose between the civil law of the land and the Canon Law of their Church.

An even stormier case had developed in Philadelphia in 1820 when Bishop Henry Conwell attempted to remove Father William Hogan from the pastorate of Saint Mary's Cathedral, though Hogan had been duly appointed by the lay trustees of the parish. Hogan, claiming the protection of the civil law, refused to budge, and the cathedral trustees, standing by him, petitioned the authorities to draw up legislation prohibiting bishops from interfering in the election of pastors. Again, the legislature obliged, but the law that came out of their deliberations was stillborn, since it was immediately vetoed by the Governor of Pennsylvania.

The legal problems arising out of lay trusteeism were settled once and for all when the principle was established in American law that property conveyed for religious purposes is to be held in accordance with the appropriate ecclesiastical or

Canon Law. In most states, in line with this principle, diocesan property is now held by the Bishop as a "corporation sole." Elsewhere the state still requires that a certain number of the incorporators be laymen. But since the laymen are not democratically chosen but named by the Bishop and other Church officials, this vestige of the congregationalism that was once forced upon American Catholicism by law has long since become only a *pro forma* requirement.

A second crucial problem arising from Catholic doctrine was settled very early. It concerned the seal of the confessional —or the obligation of a priest not to reveal to any other party anything he has heard in his capacity as confessor. The classic case involved a New York Jesuit, Father Anthony Kohlmann, pastor of Saint Peter's Church.

In 1813 Kohlmann was asked by a penitent to return some stolen goods to a man named James Keating, a resident of the city. After Keating informed the authorities that his property had been returned, the police summoned Father Kohlmann to tell them what he knew of the case. Because the priest gained his information through the confessional, he courteously refused to cooperate.

The case was submitted to the grand jury, and Kohlmann was subpoenaed to appear before it. He complied but again declined to answer any questions. After a couple of suspects were put on trial for the crime, he found it necessary to refuse a third time. It was finally decided that the trial should be interrupted until the confessional question—a much more basic issue—was settled.

A distinguished panel of Protestant judges was chosen, which included the scholarly mayor of the city, DeWitt Clinton. Father Kohlmann, in court, testified eloquently, not about the crime but about his reasons for refusing to cooperate with the law. "I must declare to this honorable court that I cannot, I must not answer any question that has a bearing on the restitution in question; and that it would be my duty to prefer instantaneous death or any temporal misfortune, rather than disclose the name of the penitent in question. For, were I to act otherwise, I should become a traitor to my Church, to my sacred ministry, and my God."

After a great deal of quasi-legal, quasi-theological argument pro and con, the priest was upheld. Later the decision was incorporated into the law of New York when it was enacted that "no minister of the Gospel or priest of any denomination whatsoever shall be allowed to disclose any confession made to him in his professional character in the course of discipline enjoined by the rules or practices of such denomination." The ruling was ultimately extended to other states and is now generally accepted as an American legal principle.

The most persistent Church-state problem has involved the juridical status of parochial schools. It still remains to be determined exactly.

From the beginning, the first and foremost issue was the right of the Church schools to exist at all. It was not definitively settled until 1925, when the Supreme Court struck down as unconstitutional an Oregon statute that required parents to send their children to public schools between the ages of eight and sixteen. The Oregon legislation was directed against all private schools but its primary target was the parochial school system. The authors of the statute based their formal case on the need for children to be instructed in the principles of patriotism, as defined by the government, and the necessity for the state to avoid the possibility of young persons being trained to subvert the nation's political or economic system. Had the law been allowed to stand, full-time Catholic schools would have been outlawed in Oregon—and perhaps elsewhere if similar legislation were drawn up by other states. Since the issue was brought to court by a group of Oregon nuns, the case went down in history as *Pierce vs. the Society of Sisters*.

In an historic decision—later called the Magna Charta of the parochial school system—the Supreme Court declared that the act "unreasonably interferes with the liberty of parents and guardians to direct the upbringing and education of children under their control. . . . Rights guaranteed by the Constitution may not be abridged by legislation which has no reasonable relation to some purpose within the competency of the state. The fundamental theory of liberty upon which all governments in this Union repose excludes any power of the

state to standardize its children by forcing them to accept instructions from public school teachers only. The child is not
the mere creature of the state; those who nurture him and
direct his destiny have the right, coupled with the high duty,
to recognize and prepare him for additional obligations."

The decision not only insured the continuance of parochial
schools in the United States but put the Court's imprimatur
on a central point of traditional Catholic thinking about educational matters. For American Catholics the Court's words
"the child is not the mere creature of the state" became the
most treasured of judicial dicta.

After the parochial schools' right to exist was firmly established, the argument about their claim on public support got
under way in earnest. It went on for years, leading to such
heated exchanges as the one between Eleanor Roosevelt and
Cardinal Spellman. Both sides in the perennial dispute invoked
the First Amendment—one claiming that the parochial school
has a right in justice to share in the public funds allotted
to education by virtue of the "free exercise of religion" clause,
the other claiming that since the avowed purpose of parochial
education is to relate religion to every other discipline, public
support is permanently foreclosed by the anti-establishment
clause. When the Supreme Court has dealt with the issue it
has put its emphasis on the latter point. A goodly number
of American Catholics over the years have agreed with the
Court (as John F. Kennedy apparently did), but the Catholic
community by and large, especially after World War II, continued to press for support, claiming that parents who send
their children to parochial schools are exercising both their
claim on religious liberty and a personal right specifically recognized by the Court in *Pierce vs. the Society of Sisters;* they
should not, then, be penalized by having to support two school
systems to do so. The argument, though, has never been accepted by the Court.

John Courtney Murray, who shaped the most sophisticated
version of the standard Catholic argument in *We Hold These
Truths* (Sheed & Ward, 1960), acknowledged that it is never
easy to determine where legitimate governmental support of
religious freedom ends and where illegitimate establishment
of religion begins. He concluded that clarification of the consti-

tutional issue would have to be reached step by step, case by case, through *ad hoc* legislation in the years ahead.

Father Murray wrote before any significant number of parochial schools were shut down for want of cash. Since that has happened, there has been increasing support in the community at large for keeping the Catholic system afloat by providing it with a measure of public support, and in some States grants have been made for the purchase of books and other necessities.* This change of heart is understandable in view of the fact that, if all the Catholic schools operating in 1970 were closed down, nine billion dollars would have been added to the taxpayers' burden. Ironically, however, the present receptive attitude toward state aid is coming at a time when American Catholics themselves, in their eagerness to assimilate to secular society, seem to have less and less enthusiasm for the very idea of parochial education. In increasing numbers they are ready to let it go by the boards. To many of the new generation of Catholics, then, the tortuous litigation Murray envisioned does not seem to be worth the candle.

An issue replete with emotion from the earliest days of the Republic has been focused on sending an American diplomatic representative to the Vatican. When President Harry S Truman nominated General Mark Clark to be ambassador to the State of Vatican City in 1951, the move was fiercely denounced from Protestant and Jewish pulpits throughout the land. Congressmen were flooded with protesting letters, and the President was charged with flouting the Constitution in order to win Catholic support for the Democratic Party in the 1952 election.

The show of displeasure was so massive that after a decent interval, at General Clark's own request, Mr. Truman withdrew the nomination. He did so "reluctantly," he said, adding that he still approved the idea and would name someone else later. He never did, however, and apparently no President

* The Supreme Court has consistently outlawed state support for the teaching of religion per se. On June 25, 1973, the Supreme Court struck down provisions in New York and Pennsylvania laws which would have granted partial reimbursements to parents who paid tuition to non-public schools.

since Truman has even entertained the idea, though Henry Cabot Lodge served during the Nixon administration as a private link between the White House and the Vatican, as Myron C. Taylor, President Roosevelt's "personal representative," did on a more formal basis during the war years.

In the standard anti-Catholic rhetoric of his day John Adams, in a letter to the Continental Congress, once predicted that "Congress will probably never send a minister to His Holiness who can do them no service, upon condition of receiving a Catholic legate or nuncio; or in other words, an ecclesiastical tyrant which, it is to be hoped, the United States will be too wise ever to admit in their territories." Actually over a seventy-three-year span—1797–1870—the United States supported a consul in Rome, then part of the Papal States. Again, between 1848 and 1868, during the reign of Pius IX, an American *chargé d'affaires* was accredited at the papal court. The appointment was politically feasible at that time because Pio Nono, when he first took office, was thought to be a liberal set on modernizing the Papal States, and there was an outpouring of support for him among Americans of all creeds. Later, however, this same Pope became one of the most intransigent of rulers, forbidding public Protestant worship in the city of Rome, issuing the reactionary *Syllabus of Errors,* and otherwise disappointing the hopes that had been placed in him. In response to his intolerant policies the United States Congress in 1868 flatly refused to appropriate the funds necessary to keep the Roman operation going.

At least one part of John Adams' unecumenically worded warning, though, has been fully observed. The Vatican has never had a diplomat accredited to the United States government. The Pope has been represented in Washington by an Apostolic Delegate since January 1893,* but the Delegate's authority extends only to ecclesiastical affairs, and those who have held the office have generally kept silent on political matters.

* Bishop Spalding and a few other bishops strongly opposed the move to name a Delegate. Others in the hierarchy urged the Pope to name an American citizen to the post. But the Vatican, deciding that only an Italian could be an impartial arbiter between the rival national groups in the American Church, chose Archbishop Francesco Sattoli, a curial official. His eight successors have all been Europeans.

The recurrent controversy over diplomatic relations with the Vatican never failed to engender a great deal of heat and Protestant passion every time it came up, which in turn led to a certain amount of bruising polemics. Yet the issue never seemed to be particularly crucial to Catholics themselves. Even at the height of the brouhaha in 1951, there was no significant pressure to counter the opposition to Mark Clark's nomination. Actually a good number of Catholics quietly agreed that, whatever case non-Catholic nations like England and Japan might make for maintaining formal relations with the Vatican, the temper of the American people is such that it would not be a good idea for the United States.

The Second Vatican Council called into question the whole apparatus of Vatican diplomacy. Many in the Church, it turned out, would like to see it dismantled completely because in the postconciliar Church it appears unseemly and anachronistic. There is, then, probably less support now for naming an American ambassador to the Holy See than there ever was.

A problem which bedeviled the Catholic Church in the United States for years was once summed up by John Courtney Murray in the simple question, Should there be a law? Should there, for example, ever have been such a law as the statute passed in 1879 by the State of Connecticut which provided that "any person who shall use any drug, medical article, or instrument for the purpose of preventing conception shall be fined not less than fifty dollars or imprisoned not less than sixty days nor more than one year or be both fined and imprisoned"? For almost ninety years that statute and others similar to it remained as monuments to the puritanical "Comstock era" in American life. Though they were originally passed by legislators responding to Protestant pressure, they became the source of recurrent Catholic-Protestant tension after American Protestants came around to the support of planned parenthood. Catholics, however, had not yet changed *their* minds and were determined to keep them on the books, though practically every other major group of Americans was set on abolishing them. Whenever attempts were made to be rid of the laws, Catholics, as legislators and voters, rallied to keep them intact.

In the New England states, whether or not anti-birth-control laws would be retained was turned into a rough test of Catholic prestige and power. The Catholic argument of course was never shaped in such crass sociological terms; rather it was stated solemnly that, since contraception was forbidden by the Natural Law, the prohibition against it bound all men; therefore Catholics—contrary to what the Yankees charged—were not really using their power to "impose" Catholic morality on others when they carried on political campaigns to uphold the old Protestant morality. In that spirit, Catholic support for the laws was carried out as a kind of religious duty.

Father Murray was probably more responsible than anyone else for finally changing Catholic minds on the subject—an example, incidentally, of how a scholar's work, for all its limited circulation, can indirectly influence masses of people. In the 1950s Murray began to argue that the New England laws failed utterly to distinguish between a "private sin" and a "public crime" and that they represented legislation at its worst, if only because they were unenforceable short of police invasion of the bedroom. There is reason to believe that the Murray argument, which was presented in an idiom understandable to the people caught up in the "clerical culture"—as the American Church still was—was more effective with Catholics than the appeals of the earnest civil libertarians who spoke the language of Tom Paine. In any case, by the midsixties, when the laws were struck down by the Supreme Court as unconstitutional, it was difficult for the press to find a highly placed Catholic cleric willing to mourn for them in public.

Murray also contributed significantly toward tempering the American Catholic readiness to support the methods of censorship—another long-standing source of tension which reached a climax in the years following World War II. In an essay widely distributed among Catholic leaders in the late fifties he argued that Americans "have constitutionally decided that the presumption is in favor of freedom, and that the advocate of constraint must make a convincing argument for its necessity or utility in a given case." He went on to say that "no society should expect very much in the way of moral uplift from its censorship statutes. . . . Particularly in

the field of sexual morality the expectations are small . . .
a Philip Wylie may have been right in saying that American
society is technically insane in the matter of sex. If so, it cannot
be coerced into sanity by the force of law."

Father Murray was not alone in getting such ideas a hearing
in the Catholic community. A number of lay writers for *Commonweal* shared his views. And many of them went much
further in their permissiveness. Still, the Jesuit was probably
the most effective of all for the simple reason that as a cleric
his theological credentials were in smashing order and his
characteristic device of invoking the tradition of the Church
at the same time that he cautiously attacked its present practices made him a formidable opponent in argument with other
theologians.

Murray, who burst out of his academic shell in the 1950s,
appeared on the public scene at precisely the right time. Just
a few years earlier, in 1948, Mason Wade, a well-known historian, complained at a meeting of Catholic writers in Boston: "In recent years there have been certain signs that we
Catholics, who once hailed the American tradition of tolerance
and freedom because they enabled us to exist as a tiny minority
in an overwhelming Protestant U.S.A., are becoming somewhat bumptious. . . . We seem to be adopting the Puritan
attitude of 'I will not. Thou shalt not.'"

The next year Paul Blanshard's blockbuster attack, *American Freedom and Catholic Power,* hit the best-seller lists—
an indication that there were many others who shared Professor Wade's concern. Blanshard detailed some of the "signs"
the professor had noted. As one, he cited a case involving
a Washington newspaper and the Sisters of the Good Shepherd
in that city. A young girl died while trying to escape from
the upper window of a home for delinquents run by the sisters. After the newspaper account appeared, the paper published some letters from its readers criticizing the nuns. Catholics, all too predictably, reacted with anger and indignation
and immediately set out to make their feelings known where
it would do the most good. According to a report in *America* by a Jesuit priest, the most effective action was taken by
the Catholic Truth Society of Washington, a tiny society of
four or five priests and laymen. Their efforts were aimed at

the financial rather than the editorial offices of the paper. Members of the society undertook a campaign to interview merchants who advertised in the offending paper and suggest that they put pressure on the publisher to get the editorial policy changed. A number of advertisers complied. In addition, priests of the city were advised to tell their parishioners: "I do not know what kind of Catholics each of you may be, but as for me, I will fight insults to Holy Mother Church. I do not know what you will do; I will fling any offending newspaper from my house and I will never buy it again." A good number of parishioners responded obediently. In two weeks the paper lost 40 per cent of its circulation.

The same year Cardinal Dougherty of Philadelphia wrote to two theater owners telling them that he was so upset by the showing of *Forever Amber* and *The Outlaw,* films condemned by the Legion of Decency, that if the pictures were not immediately withdrawn he would direct all Catholics to boycott their theaters for one year.

Actions of this kind, not uncommon in the 1940s and 1950s, were quite successful in keeping out of magazines, newspapers, and films material which was considered either anti-Catholic in tone or immoral in character. To earnest Catholics of the time they may have seemed to represent a perfectly legitimate use of political and economic powers being put in the service of noble ends. But to increasing numbers of other Americans they represented nothing less than a slow undermining of American principles of free speech and artistic freedom.

The most spectacular case involved Cardinal Spellman and the showing of an Italian film called *The Miracle.* The plot of the film is simple. It is about a deranged peasant girl who comes across a bearded stranger on a lonely hilltop. The girl takes the stranger to be Saint Joseph and herself the object of a heavenly visitation. The stranger plies her with wine until she becomes drunk and then seduces her. Later, despite the mockery of the villagers, she believes that the child she has given birth to is the Christ.

The story was taken by Cardinal Spellman to be a sacrilegious assault on the doctrine of the Virgin Birth, and he preached against it in Saint Patrick's Cathedral—one of the half-dozen times the Cardinal appeared in the cathedral pulpit during his years in New York.

For a time the film was shown at the Paris Theater, an East Side art house, without incident. Then the theater abruptly lost its license after Commissioner Edward McCaffrey, a leading layman, informed its management that he found the picture "officially and personally to be a blasphemous affront to a great many citizens of our city." The license was quickly restored, however, and the picture shown again after Joseph Burstyn, its American distributor, obtained an injunction against McCaffrey. This time the Paris Theater was picketed by members of the Catholic War Veterans carrying such signs as "Don't enter that cesspool" and "This is a communist film."

The New York courts upheld McCaffrey, and the film was withdrawn from circulation. But Burstyn pushed the case to the top, despite personal threats and intimidation from anonymous people. Finally, in May 1952, the Supreme Court handed down a unanimous decision which reversed the lower courts. "It is not the business of government in our nation to suppress real or imagined attacks upon a particular religious doctrine, whether they appear in publications, speeches, or motion pictures," the Court concluded.

In his cathedral utterance Cardinal Spellman had urged all "right-thinking citizens" to strengthen laws which would make it "impossible for anyone to profit financially by blasphemy, immorality, and sacrilege." The decision, then, represented a blow to his prestige. It also dampened Catholic enthusiasm for boycotts, picket lines, and other pressure tactics. Though such practices did not disappear overnight, American Catholics today are far removed from the fearsome moral crusaders of the past who fought against birth control, picketed theaters, and put the fear of the Church if not the fear of the Lord into publishers and movie makers.

Some now attribute the change in attitude to a loss of conviction and a general moral debilitation—in a word, as a show of weakness more than a sign of conversion. There may be some basis for this claim. However, it is probably more important that there has been a profound change in the average Catholic's perception of the Church's role in the world—a byproduct of the Vatican Council. After all, there are no signs of either a lack of conviction or sense of mission among the radical priests, nuns, and young laymen who joined the opposition to the Vietnam war and have protested against racial injustices since the Council was brought to a close.

Actually the Council may have timidly anticipated the cultural revolution and realignment of values that burst upon America in the middle of the 1960s. The legalism, triumphalism, and clericalism which were excoriated in Rome have their secular counterparts, and these are precisely what have been under recent attack in the United States—the "legalism" that protects institutions even when they are not working, the "triumphalism" that heralds every American venture as virtuous precisely because it is American, and the "clericalism" represented by unbudgeable establishments. That so many of the most articulate members of the new generation of Catholics have been caught up in the movement to undo this trinity, whether in Church or state, may yet radically transform the relations between the Catholic Church and American democracy.

One reason that relationship was always vaguely uneasy in the past was that Catholics freely granted to ecclesiastical authorities powers Americans constitutionally withheld from their own government—for example, the right to proscribe books, plays, and movies and to control the dissemination of ideas. Catholics were ready to abide by the Index of Forbidden Books, for example, even though very, very few of them ever actually saw a copy of it and even fewer knew what titles were on it. Students were taught to get special permission before they could read books which they had reason to believe were found on the Index. Librarians in Catholic schools and managers of Catholic book stores were quick to withdraw from circulation any books that Church authorities thought might undermine faith or morals. Students were taught that excommunication was incurred *ipso facto* by those who knowingly read or kept such books without permission.

Such practices made non-Catholics understandably uneasy. And inevitably every Catholic attempt to use pressure and boycott to prevent ideas from being propagated or to keep

material unfavorable to the Church out of the press was taken
to be part of a grand papal design to impose on all Americans
the kind of censorship members of the Church mysteriously
accepted for themselves. Dr. Robert J. McCracken, the influential minister of Riverside Church in New York, spoke for
many others when he said in a sermon in 1951: "Roman
Catholicism is engaged in a ceaselessly surreptitious pressure
to obtain a position of preference in the New World. Nor
can there be any doubts as to the success attending its efforts."

The Church's spokesmen of course flatly denied charges of
this kind. Just three years before the McCracken warning the
American hierarchy had issued a statement on the subject:
"We deny absolutely and without qualification that the Catholic Bishops of the United States are seeking a union of
Church and State by any endeavor whatsoever, either prox-
imately or remotely. If tomorrow Catholics constituted a majority in our country, they would not seek a union of Church
and State. They would, then and now, uphold the Constitution
and all its Amendments." But such reassurances were not convincing as long as the "error has no rights" philosophy was
still upheld in the official Roman texts and American Catholics
were given to using pressure tactics in order to bring the press
and the movie industry around to their point of view.

The fear Dr. McCracken voiced was not really stilled for
another decade or more. By that time Catholics themselves
were beginning to rebel openly against ecclesiastical censorship.

Shortly before the Vatican Council opened, Hans Küng,
the brilliant young Swiss theologian who led the way, went
on a lecture tour throughout the United States. Küng was
not yet well known in the United States but, surprisingly, thousands of Catholics turned out wherever he spoke. From New
York to San Francisco, they applauded vigorously every time
he called for an end to "unfreedom" in the Church and the
abolition of ecclesiastical censorship and secrecy. The movement to exorcise the censorious mentality in the Church began
in earnest then, under the leadership of a non-American. It
gained increasing momentum as the Ecumenical Council proceeded. With the *National Catholic Reporter* leading the way,
the Catholic press itself was soon publishing stories about the

inner workings of the Church that no secular paper would have dared to run a few years earlier. By the time the Council ended, nothing in the Church seemed to be too sacred for public criticism and debate. Ecclesiastical leaders, to be sure, were not overjoyed by losing their immunity to public criticism. Many of them stoutly resisted the trend toward openness. But by the early seventies even the Vatican appeared to be coming around. In May 1971 the Holy See issued an official endorsement of full freedom of information: "It is absolutely essential that there be freedom to express ideas and attitudes," the pastoral declared. "Freedom of opinion and the right to be informed go hand in hand." Several years earlier the Index had been quietly abolished.

But if this change in thinking eliminated one old source of friction between Catholics and other Americans, new ones may have been created by the Vatican Council. The issue of conscientious objection to specific wars is a particularly striking example. The Council did not issue a call to pacifism but it did insist that individual citizens have not only the right but the duty to resist wars they regard as unjust—a definite change from the position taken during the nation's earlier wars, when Catholics were encouraged to answer the call to arms without hesitation. With the Council's authority to go on, a large number of Catholic conscientious objectors appeared during the Vietnam hostilities, and in 1968 the American hierarchy issued a statement of support for them. "As witnesses to a spirited tradition which accepts enlightened conscience, even when honestly mistaken, as the immediate arbiter of moral decisions, we can only feel reassured by this evidence of individual responsibility and the decline of uncritical conformism to patterns, some of which included strong moral elements to be sure, but also included political, social, cultural, and like controls not necessarily in conformity with the mind and heart of the Church." This conflict between Catholic moral principles and the law of the land, which did not yet provide for selective objection, led to serious Church-state problems; others may follow.

Again, the Council's thundering denunciation of racism and social inequality has already inspired a certain number of priests, nuns, and laymen to rebel against the status quo who at an earlier period in American Catholic history might have been counted on to conform readily to social inertia in either Church or state. After they were jailed, Fathers Philip and Daniel Berrigan—radical pacifists and social revolutionaries— became heroic figures to many of the younger clergy and the idols of thousands of young nuns and seminarians. As more and more Catholics like the Berrigans are caught up in the revolutionary spirit that began to sweep throughout the Church after the Council, the priest or nun behind bars may no longer be a rare sight in America. Catholics may once again seem to be a disruptive force in the United States, but this time the disrupters will not be carrying the discredited banner "Error Has No Rights" but one deeply rooted in the American tradition—"Liberty and Justice for All."

AFTERWORD

It was in the 1940s that D. W. Brogan stated that the intellectual prestige of Catholicism was lower in the United States than in any Western society. A few years later, Evelyn Waugh, after a field study for *Life* magazine, reached a similar conclusion. By the 1950s the same judgment had been made by so many visitors from abroad that even among Catholics themselves it had become a truism that the American Church, for all its wealth and the size of its educational establishment, was riddled with anti-intellectualism and was far from holding its own in the cultural arena.

It was widely noted, for example, that while a number of established American writers had borne Catholic names— among them Eugene O'Neill, F. Scott Fitzgerald, James T. Farrell, and Theodore Dreiser—they all described themselves as ex-Catholics. Not until J. F. Powers, who concentrated on the foibles of clerical life, was a literary man of high standing identified unambiguously with Catholicism—a situation that Waugh in particular found deplorable. Here and there in the secular universities there were a few outstanding academics who were known to be Catholics—some of them, like the lit-

erary scholars Hugh Kenner and B. G. Harrison, converts
to the faith; but only a handful were conspicuous in the Catholic community itself and an even smaller number were identified in the public mind with the Church.

When, in the fifties, Father John Cavanaugh, a former president of Notre Dame, asked in a Communion breakfast talk,
"Where are the Catholic Salks, Oppenheimers, Einsteins?" his
words brought on a flood of editorials in the Church press.
Most of them were predictably defensive, but others, acknowl-
edging the embarrassing situation, urged the Catholic educational authorities to take the criticism to heart.

Father Cavanaugh's speech was delivered in December
1957. Two years earlier the erudite Monsignor John Tracy
Ellis had published an article in Fordham University's
Thought, in which he charged that American Catholics were
shamefully remiss in upholding the intellectual traditions of
the Church; he ended the study with a cautious plea for more
academic freedom for Catholic scholars. The article was well
timed. After it got around, the leaders of the Catholic community seemed at long last ready to explore the reasons for
their failure. The discussion the Ellis charges provoked went
on for years in books, magazines, and popular forums, and
it led to serious efforts to upgrade the Catholic institutions
of higher learning.

One of the most thoughtful contributions to the discussion
was furnished by Thomas F. O'Dea, a Harvard-trained soci-
ologist then teaching at Columbia. O'Dea argued in *American
Catholic Dilemma* that intellectual life in the Church was being
hampered by four bad habits of thought, all of them deaden-
ing for the life of the mind.

First there was authoritarianism—a readiness to accept statements not so much on their intrinsic merits as on the authority
of those who made them, whether Thomas Aquinas, the reigning Pontiff, or a classroom teacher. Aquinas himself had
treated the argument from authority as the weakest of all,
but in the American Catholic milieu, O'Dea pointed out, it
had somehow gained primacy.

He listed clericalism as the second problem—the tendency
of priests to extend the doctrine of papal infallibility to almost
every statement of their own, and the willingness of so many

of the laity to bow to clerical pronouncements without any further argument. With most of the Catholic colleges and universities under strict clerical control, this handicap extended beyond the pulpit to the lecture hall.

The third characteristic was moralism—the habit of concentrating on the right-or-wrong rather than the true-or-false aspect of reality. O'Dea argued that Catholics spent too much of their energy condemning and anathematizing, frequently in pat formulas that were meaningless to the contemporary world, and the results were sterile and depressingly negative.

Finally he noted a trait that was shot through all of Catholic life—defensiveness, the impulse to protect the Church even at the price of rewriting history, closing one's ears to just criticism, and pulling away from everything that might create doctrinal difficulties or constitute a possible threat to faith.

O'Dea's thesis was bitterly rejected in some quarters, as might have been expected, but in general it was recognized as all too valid. Catholic college graduates coming upon his book experienced the shock of recognition.

However, in less than a decade, with the turn in ecclesiastical history which no one could possibly have anticipated, the charges made in it had become almost completely out of date. The changes following upon the Vatican Council were so drastic that by the late sixties the four fatal flaws O'Dea spotted had been almost completely obliterated.

As late as the reign of John XXIII, for example, a single word from the Sovereign Pontiff was enough to close any argument. Any Catholic who dared question a pronouncement from Rome was quickly reminded that the Pope was the only authorized interpreter of the "mind of the Church," and that was that. William F. Buckley, Jr., for one, was taught the lesson again and again, especially by the liberal Catholic press, when his *National Review* ventured to express reservations about *Mater et Magistra,* John's social encyclical of 1961. And the agonistic Garry Wills, then a vigorous young spokesman for the conservative party in the Church, felt it necessary to come to Buckley's defense with a 260-page, closely reasoned book—*Politics and Catholic Freedom*—which established the theological grounding for the right to dissent even from an encyclical. Six years later, however, some of the very same writers who had castigated Buckley for publishing the quip "Mater, si; Magistra, no" were the most voluble of all in their rejection of Pope Paul's birth-control encyclical *Humanae Vitae*, and from then on, the Pontiff's words have received less deference from them than the pronouncements of a new curate might have commanded before the Vatican Council.

Episcopal authority, once rarely challenged, though it was often accepted with a great deal of grumbling, has also been seriously eroded in the American Church. Even in his own diocese, a bishop's authority today is only as strong as his persuasiveness, and the entire American hierarchy has learned to expect picket lines protesting their general policies every time they convene as a body. Simple priests, who are frequently in a rebellious mood themselves, have had to acknowledge that they have no choice any more but to fall back on pleas for cooperation from their parishioners. Even the heads of religious orders no longer count on automatic obedience from their monks and nuns.

At the higher intellectual reaches, teachings which were once taken to be just short of infallible are now being accepted with extreme caution—when they are accepted at all. With the abolition of the Index of Forbidden Books, ideas from all kinds of sources—Christian, non-Christian, and even anti-Christian—are being treated seriously, and there is no hesitation about rejecting the once sacrosanct philosophical and theological texts which formed the bedrock of Catholic education in the past. Even the *Summa* of Saint Thomas has lost favor, and most of the old papal encyclicals are brushed aside as simply wrongheaded.

Clericalism hangs on in only a few aging priests who are no longer taken seriously by anyone but themselves and frequently find themselves lampooned mercilessly in Catholic publications like *The Critic* and the *National Catholic Reporter*. The younger clergy are so aware of the pitfalls of the clericalist mentality that many of them avoid wearing distinctive clothes, scrupulously delete pieties in their speech, and insist on being called by their first names at all times. And a new Catholic aversion to moralism, at least when it comes from the clergy—the censorious young are quite another matter —has become so pronounced that preachers hesitate to speak

openly about sin or guilt. Finally, the old defensiveness has
been replaced by exaggerated breast-beating for the Church's
failures in the past and a debilitating loss of confidence in
its ability to cope with the problems of the present.

Theories abound as to how this remarkable about-face oc-
curred in so short a time. Certainly Pope John, changing the
style of the papacy and opening the windows to new currents
of thought, had a great deal to do with it. Again, the progressive theologians who had been working quietly in order not
to arouse the Roman watchdogs before the Vatican Council
became important influences after their work was generally
available. The Council itself, introducing structural reforms
and releasing pent-up energies, also had a tremendous effect.

But to this list must be added the crucial political experiences of the American Catholic community itself, for,
through all the years when Catholics were lagging behind their
Continental brethren in providing a characteristically "Catholic" intellectual leadership for America, they were also living
out, day by day, a democratic history unique in the annals
of Catholicism—and doing so precisely as Americans. From
the crucible of that experience, for better or worse, the new-
style Catholic was shaped.

As much as any other force, then, America itself may have
been responsible for the changes in the Church, for it is just
possible that Catholics provided so little intellectual leadership
before the Second Vatican Council because the style of traditional Catholic thinking—which either grew from the experience of a premodern, predemocratic Europe, or was deliberately designed to counteract the influence of contemporary
thought—was basically foreign to Americans, even American
Catholics. Out of a sense of loyalty to Rome, Catholics in
the United States long upheld the philosophical-theological
consensus they had inherited, but in their daily lives were
regulated by quite another way of thinking.

To pull this off, they were required to live in two separate intellectual worlds—the one looking to the Europe of a
past age for its authority, the other to America and the present.
The one upheld the claims of authoritarianism and accepted
a rigidly hierarchical notion of leadership, which was effectively impervious to criticism; the other, individualistic and

egalitarian, was pledged to calling its leaders regularly to account. One emphasized abstract reasoning and put its major emphasis on syllogistic logic; the other, typically American, was heavily pragmatic, skeptical about the exercise of power, and irreverent toward claims that any group of men has a special option on the Truth.

For a long time the switch back and forth between these two worlds seemed to be effortless; but whatever it was that happened at the Vatican Council, things were never the same after it. In the Church as well as out of it, American Catholics abruptly began to behave like other Americans.

The Council was barely concluded, for instance, when laymen were making the kinds of demands on their pastors and bishops that they were long used to making on their political leaders—for candor, a public accounting of stewardship, and above all for the reasons why certain policies were decided upon. The sentimental devotional practices of the past (which grew out of peasant piety) suddenly became the butt of jokes, and Catholic journalists began to write mockingly about such subjects as their youthful experience in the confessional, their former awe of ecclesiastical authority, and their frantic efforts to pile up the indulgences graciously granted by Roman prelates to repentant sinners.

The decisions the clergy made without any consultation or advice from the laity had long been accepted passively. Now there were vociferous demands for active lay participation in ecclesiastical policy making, even at the highest levels. Bishops and priests were asked to present budgets, to justify their expenditures, and to account for their priorities in assigning Church income. Again, the laity and the lower clergy had never seen fit to complain because they were not consulted when Church law was drawn up, but abruptly they began to balk—against the regulations regarding mixed marriages and the imposition of clerical celibacy, to cite two examples.

For years Catholics, against all their democratic instincts as Americans, had stood by the rigidities of the theological exclusiveness which the Church demanded, avoiding any *religious* contact even with the non-Catholic members of their own families, lest the shadow of theological "indifferentism" be cast upon them. But with the first opening to the ecumenical movement, they responded with vast enthusiasm, astounding the Protestant brethren by their willingness to cooperate in interfaith endeavors and even joint worship. After all, they had been prepared for ecumenism by the American experience of living in a pluralistic society where religious tolerance is highly valued, all religions are respected, and none has a claim on the political community. The spirit of ecumenism engendered by Pope John was much more "American," then, than the unbending rigidity and exclusiveness that had earlier been insisted upon.

The "Americanizing" of Catholics, in a word, reached into the internal life of the Church for the first time, and, at least during the early postconciliar period, the experience was as exhilarating as an ex-convict's first hours in the outside world. Indeed, throughout the Church the new catchword was "freedom." It was heard on campuses, in convents, monasteries, and rectories and rang like a call to arms in the parishes.

Around the same time the leading commentators on Catholicism began to write about the sociological changes which marked the full "assimilation" of Catholics into the life of the nation. For example, Philip Gleason of the University of Notre Dame, in an essay published in 1969, traced the history of the Church through its various stages—isolation, ghettoization, and gradual emergence into full participation in American life. He concluded that by the 1960s assimilation on the individual level had not only brought Catholics abreast of their fellow citizens, economically and socially, but had resulted in a new "self-conception" for those who had fully adopted the beliefs and attitudes prevalent in secular society. Andrew Greeley, in *The Catholic Experience*—a sociological interpretation of American Catholic history—held that while the long battle between the "Americanizers" and their opponents was still going on among the clergy, the question had already become purely academic for the laity. The practical problem now, Father Greeley suggested, was how ecclesiastical structures should be reshaped to conform to the new "self-conception" of the Catholic community itself. That problem has still not been solved, though it has been at the core of almost all the recurring crises marking the life of the American Church in recent years.

The American bishops seem to have recognized the problem, or at least most of them have; but it is clear that the solution to it does not appear as simple to them as to those who keep demanding even more radical changes than have already taken place. For the bishops—who are ever aware that they were ordained to be not only pastors of their flocks but the official guardians of Catholic doctrine—the central issue is how far they can go along with the reformers without sacrificing their own obligation to pass on the Faith, pure and undefiled. There is not a theological reductionist in the lot of them. And all of them, one way or another, have asked where *aggiornamento* ends and heresy begins.

Not only the bishops but many other Catholics—among them laymen as learned as Jacques Maritain, the eminent French philosopher, who spent many years in the United States—seem to be convinced that some of the foremost proponents of the "new Catholicism" may have already passed the point of no return, and that those who are charged with preserving the integrity of the Faith have no choice but to resist extreme innovations, whatever the cost. In other days, they point out, those who rejected basic Catholic teaching either left the Church willingly or were formally excommunicated. Today, however, the announcement on a jacket cover that an author "would once have been burned at the stake" for his teachings is widely looked upon as a guarantee of a theologian's concern for Christian relevance.

Martin Luther, who has become a kind of hero to the new Catholics, taught that in the last analysis every man had to be his own priest; but even the great reformer never held that every man should be his own theologian. Yet, what the conservative forces in latterday Catholicism seem to be worried about is that such a principle may gradually win general acceptance among Catholics. They fear that what are put forth as attempts to update the Church may really signify a loss of faith in fundamental Christian doctrine and represent little more than a desire for a religious community which would be "liberated" from the claims of dogma.

The concern appears to be well founded, for it is true that many of the old Catholic teachings which were once put forth as essential to the Faith are now being widely repudiated: belief in Purgatory and Hell, in the efficacy of indulgences, and the sinfulness of contraception, to cite a few examples. Papal infallibility is being publicly challenged by priests who continue to remain in good standing, and such questions as the indissolubility of Christian marriage and the doctrine of Apostolic Succession are being questioned in quite exalted theological circles.

In sum, the "crisis of faith" which disturbs the guardians of contemporary Catholicism is not simply a product of conservative paranoia; it is a very real problem for those who take orthodoxy seriously. Philip Gleason summed it up well when he wrote: ". . . to strive with blinkered singlemindedness for relevance to the contemporary world runs the risk of forgetting that, while the Church must be engaged in the world, it cannot be completely assimilated to the world."

In the past the Church of Rome, in order to hold on to its doctrinal identity, fought against dozens of opponents—the Manichees, the Albigensians, the Protestant reformers, and a long list of political ideologies, to name just a few. Some of these battles certainly did no honor to the Church, but what is significant is that they were made at all. However, the new "enemy" the Church has to confront is not as easy to single out as, say Gnosticism or the Jansenism of Port Royal. It may, rather, be something as intangible as modernity itself— the whole complex of ideas, attitudes, habits of mind, and notions about the good life which, for better or worse, have produced the modern man.

Modernity of course is an amorphous, subtle force, a pervasive influence rather than an identifiable movement, yet it may represent no less a danger to the old Faith than the organized heretical movements of the past. Within what used to be called Christendom for some time now it has operated like a secret gas, odorless, tasteless, undetectable, but imperceptibly changing the whole environment. American Catholics, while they still maintained their own separatist subculture, were capable of a certain resistance to it. However, being assimilated into modern American society may mean that traditional Catholicism has been deprived of its first line of defense. Out-and-out resistance to the *Zeitgeist*, the leaders of the Church know, would throw Catholics into another ghetto, a step backward they are not willing to take. Frank capitulation to the spirit of the times, on the other hand, would mean—as it has to so many individual Catholics—the loss of any definite religious identity, or at least of a specific cultural identity shaped by religious beliefs.

It is becoming increasingly clear that the price now being paid for assimilation into American life is a state of tension and the kind of indecision even in the highest circles that shocks everyone who grew up with the idea that the Church of Rome, whatever else might be said of it, always knew its own mind.

The current ordeal of the American Catholic community has been aptly compared to a nervous breakdown. Until the Church authorities settle upon some strategy for survival that is more promising than any they have attempted so far, the tensions will probably remain. Perhaps, with its remarkable ability to ride out the storms of history, Catholicism will outlast the impact of modernity. (Already some of modernity's central tenets, such as the absolute autonomy of science and the inevitable benefits of technological development, are being called into question by society as a whole.) But until that happens, it is probably too much to await any return to the placid ecclesiastical orderliness of the past. Priests may in time be allowed to marry, most of the suggested ecclesial reforms may be put into effect, Church structures may be "democratized" beyond the wildest dreams of Catholicism's earlier critics—but the tensions created by modernity will not fade out naturally. And as long as they last, many Catholics will give up out of sheer exhaustion, while a new generation—as many of the young are already doing—will simply refuse to accept the burdens entailed in living in two worlds, the one proposed by the ancient Church and the other by modern life.

If it is to survive as a real force in the United States, Catholicism may have no choice but to accept the unpopular and difficult role of the prophet. In sociological jargon, it may have to learn to live more like a "sect" than a "church." At least that seems to be the burden already accepted by the comparatively few American Catholics who have looked squarely at the contradictions between their own beliefs and the challenges of modernity, and have opted for religious principle. Some of them, like the radical priest-brothers Philip and Daniel Berrigan, were put behind bars for being too vehemently right too soon about the immorality of the Vietnam war. Others, like the Milwaukee civil-rights worker, Father James Groppi, have been in and out of jail for protesting too violently against the injustices committed against black America.

As the technological and biological revolutions proceed, perhaps doing new violence to basic Christian notions of human rights, others may feel called upon to make similar protests. But, as has been true throughout Christian history, the dissenters will probably be few and far between. Most Catholics, as always, will go along, whatever the developments, until the pressures become unbearable and the ultimate choice has to be made: Christianity or the *Zeitgeist*?

When the brilliant Jesuit, the late Gustave Weigel, spoke of the "Present Embarrassment of the Church" in 1958, he may have had something like this in mind. "The prophetic function of religion is embarrassing to the secular community," Father Weigel said. "It is disturbing; it is a source of division; it is a distraction from the purely secular. . . . The prophet not only shows the way to salvation; he also utters judgment on the actions of the world."

He might have added that the prophet is also embarrassing to the religious community, whose leaders have always felt more at ease sprinkling holy water on the status quo than denouncing it. The Catholic Church in America, for example, never succeeded in mobilizing its full strength to combat a social evil, whether slavery, poverty, racism, or war. Only when an identifiable, distinctly "Catholic" concern was at issue—such as birth control, divorce, or abortion—was an all-out effort even attempted, and even then, often enough, because Catholic social prestige or political muscle was being tested.

Throughout most of its history in the United States, however, Catholicism carried on in a nation where a diffuse Christianity was "established" by social consensus if not by law. In a certain sense, then, to bless the status quo was to affirm the righteousness of a people who thought of themselves as making up a "Christian country." That situation no longer prevails. More and more, Christianity is being apprehended as just one more option among several, and among the most prestigious leaders of thought it is rarely even given lip service. This situation doesn't seem likely to change in the foreseeable future. There is little in modern education, for instance, to sustain the Christian faith and a great deal to erode its hold on the individual.

Moreover, whatever vitality religion, specifically Christianity, does have in contemporary America is often found more abundantly outside the churches than in them. The churches, not least of all the Roman Catholic Church, are now being denounced not only for propagating obscurantist, superstitious beliefs—a very old charge repeated once more by one important segment of the new generation—but for actually betraying Christianity by their irrelevance—a newer charge made by the religious-minded of a smaller but certainly not negligible segment of the young.

Caught between these two sets of critics—the one charging "too much," the other "too little"—the institutional Church appears to be condemned to a degree of anxiety and insecurity unparalleled in American Catholic history. Oddly enough, this difficult period came only a few years after the complete social "assimilation" of American Catholics was symbolized by the election of John F. Kennedy—whose pivotal Houston speech, incidentally, already reads like a period piece.

The religious community that survived the early onslaught of bigotry, with a certain style; that built up an enormous citadel of protective institutions to protect its identity; and that valiantly fought its way out of a ghetto to achieve acceptance in American life may yet have to face its greatest challenge.

The brothers Berrigan—secure enough in their Americanness to speak out as Americans and at the same time secure enough in their faith to speak in the name of Catholicism— may have provided an example of the duty that before long will fall upon all Catholics who do not give up on either their country or their faith.

The Berrigans (however one might criticize their practical judgment or style) have pointed out that, while Catholicism can coexist very well with separation of Church and state, its best representatives will always refuse to separate religion and life. And that makes all the difference.

BIBLIOGRAPHY

GENERAL WORKS:

ELLIS, JOHN TRACY. *American Catholicism*. Chicago: University of Chicago Press, 1956.

MCAVOY, THOMAS T., C.S.C. *A History of the Catholic Church in America*. Notre Dame: University of Notre Dame Press, 1969.

MAYNARD, THEODORE. *The Story of American Catholicism*, 2 vols. New York: Doubleday Image Books, 1960.

STOKES, ANSON PHELPS. *Church and State in the United States*, 3 vols. New York: Harper and Brothers, 1950.

BAINTON, ROLAND. *Christian Attitudes Toward War and Peace*. Nashville: Abingdon Press, 1960.

BARRY, COLMAN J. *The Catholic Church and German Americans*. Milwaukee: Bruce, 1953.

BLANSHARD, PAUL. *American Freedom and Catholic Power*. Boston: The Beacon Press, 1949.

BLIED, BENJAMIN. *Catholics and the Civil War*. Milwaukee: 1945.

CASEY, W. V., and NOBILE, P., eds. *The Berrigans*. New York: Avon, 1971.

CATHOLIC UNIVERSITY OF AMERICA. *New Catholic Encyclopedia*. New York: McGraw-Hill, 1967.

CATHOLICISM IN AMERICA: A Series of Articles from *The Commonweal*. New York: Harcourt, Brace, 1953.

CHRIST, FRANK L., and SHERRY, GERARD E. *American Catholicism and the Intellectual Ideal*. New York: Appleton, 1961.

DAY, DOROTHY. *House of Hospitality*. London: Sheed & Ward, 1939.

———. *The Long Loneliness*. New York: Harper and Row, 1952.

DEVER, JOSEPH. *Cushing of Boston*. Boston: Humphries, 1965.

DI DONATO, PIETRO. *Immigrant Saint: The Life of Mother Cabrini*. New York: McGraw-Hill, 1960.

ELLIS, JOHN TRACY. *The Life of James Cardinal Gibbons, Archbishop of Baltimore, 1834–1921*, 2 vols. Milwaukee: Bruce, 1952.

FUCHS, LAWRENCE H. *John F. Kennedy and American Catholicism*. Des Moines: Meredith, 1967.

GANNON, ROBERT I., S.J. *The Cardinal Spellman Story*. New York: Doubleday, 1962.

GILBERT, ARTHUR. *The Vatican Council and the Jews*. Cleveland: The World Publishing Company, 1968.

GLEASON, PHILIP, ed. *Contemporary Catholicism in the United States.* Notre Dame: University of Notre Dame Press, 1969.

GREELEY, ANDREW M. *The Catholic Experience.* New York: Doubleday Image Books, 1967.

——, and ROSSI, PETER H. *The Education of American Catholics.* Chicago: Aldine, 1966.

GUILDAY, PETER. *The Life and Times of John Carroll, Archbishop of Baltimore (1735–1815).* New York: Encyclopedia Press, 1922.

——. *The Life and Times of John England, First Bishop of Charleston (1786–1842).* New York: American Press, 1927.

HANDLIN, OSCAR. *Al Smith and His America.* Boston: Little, Brown, 1958.

HOLDEN, VINCENT F., C.S.P. *The Yankee Paul: Isaac Thomas Hecker.* Milwaukee: Bruce, 1958.

HUGHES, EMMETT JOHN. *The Church and Liberal Society.* Princeton: Princeton University Press, 1944.

HURLEY, SISTER HELEN ANGELA. *On Good Ground.* Minneapolis: University of Minnesota Press, 1957.

KÜNG, HANS. *Council, Reform, and Reunion.* London: Sheed & Ward, 1963.

LALLY, FRANCIS J. *The Catholic Church in a Changing America.* Boston: Little, Brown, 1962.

MAIGNAN, CHARLES. *Studies in Americanism: Father Hecker, Is He A Saint?* Paris, 1898.

MAURIN, PETER. *Radical Christian Thought: Easy Essays.* New York: Sheed & Ward, 1936.

MAYNARD, THEODORE. *Orestes Brownson: Yankee, Radical, Catholic.* New York: Macmillan, 1943.

MELVILLE, ANNABELLE. *Elizabeth Bayley Seton, 1774–1821.* New York: Charles Scribner's Sons, 1960.

MOYNIHAN, JAMES. *The Life of Archbishop John Ireland.* New York: Harper, 1953.

MURRAY, JOHN COURTNEY. *We Hold These Truths.* New York: Sheed & Ward, 1960.

NEUWEIN, REGINALD H., ed. *Catholic Schools in Action.* Notre Dame: University of Notre Dame Press, 1966.

NOVAK, MICHAEL. *The Open Church.* New York: Macmillan, 1964.

O'BRIEN, DAVID J. *American Catholics and Social Reform, The New Deal Years.* New York: The Oxford University Press, 1968.

O'DEA, THOMAS F. *American Catholic Dilemma.* New York: Sheed & Ward, 1961.

PFEFFER, LEO. *Church, State, and Freedom.* Boston: Beacon Press, 1953.

RICE, MADELINE HOOK. *American Catholic Opinion in the Slavery Controversy*. New York: Columbia University Press, 1944.

ROCHE, DOUGLAS J. *The Catholic Revolution*. New York: McKay, 1968.

ROVERE, RICHARD. *Senator Joe McCarthy*. New York: Harcourt, Brace, 1959.

RYNNE, XAVIER. *Letters From Vatican City*. New York: Farrar, Straus & Giroux, 1963.

——. *The Second Session*. New York: Farrar, Straus & Giroux, 1964.

——. *The Third Session*. New York: Farrar, Straus & Giroux, 1965.

——. *The Fourth Session*. New York: Farrar, Straus & Giroux, 1966.

SCHLESINGER, ARTHUR M., JR. *Orestes A. Brownson*. New York: Octagon, 1963.

——. *A Thousand Days: John F. Kennedy in the White House*. Boston: Houghton Mifflin, 1965.

SHANNON, WILLIAM V. *The American Irish*. New York: Macmillan, 1963.

SMITH, H. SHELTON, HANDY, ROBERT T., and LOETSCHER, LEFFERTS A. *American Christianity*, 3 vols. New York: Charles Scribner's Sons, 1960.

TULL, CHARLES J. *Father Coughlin and the New Deal*. Syracuse: Syracuse University Press, 1965.

WEIGEL, GUSTAVE, S.J. "The Present Embarrassment of the Church," in John Cogley, ed., *Religion in America*, New York: Meridian Press, 1958.

WILLS, GARRY. *Politics and Catholic Freedom*. Chicago: Regnery, 1964.

INDEX

Acton, Lord, 68
Adams, John, 10, 207
Aggiornamento, 95, 96, 102, 108, 113, 223
Albigensians, 224
Alexander VI, 59
America, 93, 118, 140, 210
American Catholic Dilemma, 217
American Freedom and Catholic Power, 210
American Irish, The, 49
American Party (Know-Nothings), 41
American Protective Association, 178
"Americanism," 60, 62, 63, 64, 122, 158, 177, 178
Anti-Catholic laws, 11–12, 15
Anti-Catholicism, 8, 19, 24, 37, 38, 39, 41, 49, 52, 65, 75, 97, 136, 169, 170, 175, 180, 211
Anticlericalism, 23, 124, 125
Anticommunism, 84, 92, 93, 142, 186
Anti-Semitism, 77, 79, 80–81, 89, 101, 147, 148, 160
Apostolic Delegate, 207
Aquinas, Saint Thomas, 90, 137, 149, 153, 164, 217, 219
Ark, The, 14
Army, U.S., 43, 70
Augustinians, 25, 119, 158, 167, 196, 199
Austrians, 46
Ave Maria, 140
Awful Disclosures, 38–39

Baltimore, Maryland, 22, 25, 28, 33, 100, 156, 157, 171
Baltimore, Lord. See Calvert
Bardstown, Kentucky, 25, 28, 43
Barry, John, 9
Baruch, Bernard, 79
Bay of Pigs, 190
Bay Saint Louis Seminary, 133
Bedini, Archbishop, 41–43, 45
Belgium, 18, 99
Bellarmine College, 158
Belloc, Hilaire, 137
Benedictines, 23, 45, 77, 86, 87, 123, 124, 158, 196, 197, 198
Berrigan, Daniel, 112, 123, 198, 216, 226, 227
Berrigan, Philip, 112, 123, 216, 226, 227

Bill of Rights, 55
Birth control, 91, 104, 106–107, 140, 149, 151, 163, 209, 212, 226
Bishops' Program for Social Reconstruction, 71, 72
Bismarck, 122
Black Clergy Caucus, 134
Blakely, Paul J., 169
Blanshard, Paul, 56, 149, 210
B'nai B'rith, 160
Bohemia Manor, 17
Bonzano, Cardinal, 73
Book of Martyrs, 11
Borgongini-Duca, Cardinal, 183
Boston, Massachusetts, 25, 28, 52, 83, 92, 100, 115, 122, 124, 157, 170, 188, 189, 191
Boston College, 157, 188
Bowers, Bishop, 133
Brazil, 41
Briand, Bishop, 21
Brogan, D. W., 194, 216
Bronx, New York, The, 80, 115
Brook Farm, 61, 138
Brooklyn, New York, 80, 115, 157
Brothers of the Christian Schools, 119, 156, 158
Brothers of Holy Cross, 64, 156, 157
Broun, Heywood, 138
Brownson, Orestes, 49, 138–139
Brownson's Quarterly, 139
Buckley, William F., 119, 123, 218–219
Buffalo, New York, 126, 202
Burke, John J., 70
Burstyn, Joseph, 212
Byzantine Catholics, 128, 129

Cabrini, Mother, 125
Cahensly, Peter Paul, 65, 66, 177
California Missions, 8
Calvert, Cecil (Second Lord Baltimore), 14–15
Calvert, George, 14
Calvert, Sir George, Lord Baltimore, 13
Calvert, Leonard, 14
Camillian Fathers, 199
Campion, Edmund, 11
Cana Conference, 91
Canada, 12, 20–21, 129, 130, 154
Canada, Diplomatic Mission to (1776), 20–21

Canterbury, Archbishop of, 22
Cantor, Eddie, 79
Capuchins, 124
Carbry, Thomas, 31
Carmelite Nuns, 26, 155
Carmelites, 196, 199
Carroll, Archbishop, 9, 16, 18, 20–27, 28, 29, 43, 135, 155, 173, 191, 197
Carroll, Charles, 16, 17
Carroll, Charles (of Carrollton), 16, 17, 18–20, 119
Carroll family, 16, 119, 136
Carthusians, 11
Castro, Fidel, 131, 190
Catholic Digest, 118
Catholic Experience, The, 222
Catholic military chaplains, 52, 69, 88, 176, 177, 185
Catholic organizations (general), 117–118, 136–137
Catholic Rural Life Movement, 153
Catholic Schools in Action, 159
Catholic Theological Union, 167
Catholic Truth Society of Washington, 210
Catholic University of America, 71, 99, 158–159
Catholic War Veterans, 212
Catholic Worker Movement, 81–85, 88, 89, 91, 198
Catholic Worker, The, 81, 82, 83
Catholic World, The, 61, 140
Catholic Youth Organization, 77
Catholicism, statistics, 7, 23, 26, 43, 44, 45–46, 69, 95–96, 126, 132, 152–153, 155, 156, 159–160, 171, 199
Cavanaugh, John, 217
Center for the Study of Democratic Institutions, 157
Charles I, 13, 14
Charleston, South Carolina, 31, 32, 33, 35
"Charleston constitution," 33–34
Charlestown, Massachusetts, 37
Chase, Samuel, 20
Chesapeake Bay, 13
Chesterton, G. K., 137, 153
Cheverus, Bishop, 28
Chicago, Illinois, 44, 73, 74, 77, 83, 86, 89, 92, 100, 112, 118, 124, 125, 126, 132, 157, 167, 176
Chicago, University of, 160, 167
Chicago World's Fair (1893), 64
Chicanos, 115, 131
Chinese, 134
Christian Family Movement, 91
Christian Front, 80, 81
Church and State in the United States, 25
Church of England, 16, 22
Church, State, and Freedom, 171
Cincinnati, Ohio, 41, 44, 113, 122, 156
Civil War, 41, 47–52, 124, 139, 176, 177

Claiborne, William, 14, 15
Clancy, William, 153
Clark, Mark, 206–207, 208
Clinton, De Witt, 203
College of Cardinals, 181, 190
Collegiality, 58
Columbia University, 86, 217
Committee of Correspondence, 19
Committee on Human Rights, 80
Commonweal, 92–93, 118, 141–142, 143, 153, 210
Congress of Industrial Organizations, 77
Congress, United States, 25, 30, 35, 42, 52, 78, 198, 207
Connecticut, 12, 208
Connell, Francis J., 99
Constitution, United States, 30, 46, 175, 201, 206, 214
Continental Congress, 12, 19, 20, 207
Conwell, Bishop, 28, 33, 202
Cooke, Cardinal, 188
Cooke, John, 15
Copley, Thomas, 14–15
Corkery, Dennis, 32
Corrigan, Archbishop, 174, 178
Cotton, John, 8
Coughlin, Charles E., 78–81, 92, 141
Council of Trent, 30, 105
Cowley, Malcolm, 82
Critic, The, 219
Croats, 128
Cromwell, Oliver, 137
Crosby, Bing, 138
Cursillo Movement, 92
Cushing, Cardinal, 100, 119, 173, 188–191
Czechs, 46

Daughters of Charity, 52, 156
Davenport, Iowa, 158
Day, Dorothy, 82, 84, 85, 86
Dayton, University of, 158
De Hueck, Catherine, 86
De Paul University, 157
Declaration of Independence, 11, 19
Delaware, 11
Democratic Party, 49, 52, 74, 93, 98, 178, 206
Denver Register, 140
Detroit, Michigan, 77, 79, 83, 126
Detroit, University of, 157
District of Columbia, 26
Divine Word, Society of the, 132, 133, 167
Dominicans, 25, 31, 119, 153, 158, 167, 196, 197, 199
Dominican Sisters, 156
Dougherty, Cardinal, 211
Douglas, Stephen A., 50
Dove, The, 14
Draft Riots (Civil War), 51
Dreiser, Theodore, 216
Drexel, Mother Katharine, 132

Drinan, Robert, 198
Du Bourg, Bishop, 26, 28
Dubois, Bishop, 29
Dubuque, Iowa, 192
Dulany, Daniel, 18–19
Duquesne University, 158

Eastern Rite Catholics, 128–129
Eastman, Max, 82
Easton, Pennsylvania, 83
Ecclesiastical Review, 99
Education of American Catholics, The, 160
Einstein, Albert, 217
Eisenhower, Dwight D., 93, 94
Elizabeth I, 8, 11
Elliot, Walter, 61
Ellis, John Tracy, 217
Emancipation Proclamation, 50
Emerson, Ralph Waldo, 139
Emmitsburg, Maryland, 156
England, Bishop, 32–35, 48–49, 119, 146
England, Johanna, 32, 34
Enlightenment, The, 54, 149, 153
Episcopalians, 22, 25, 33
Eucharistic Congress (Chicago), 73–74

Faith of Our Fathers, 175–176
Faribault, Minnesota, 179, 180
Farrell, James T., 118, 216
Federal Bureau of Investigation, 81
Fendall, Josias, 15
Fenton, Joseph Clifford, 99
Fisher, John, 11
Fitzgerald, F. Scott, 216
Flaget, Bishop, 26, 28, 44
Flanagan, Edward J., 196
Flanders, 17
Florence, Italy, 126
Fordham University, 71, 80, 115, 157, 182, 217
Forever Amber, 211
Founding Fathers, 18
Foundling, The, 141
Foxe, John, 11
France, 8, 9, 99, 119, 156
Franciscans, 8, 18, 23, 31, 125, 167, 196, 197, 198
Franco, Francisco, 79, 138, 140, 141, 150
Franklin, Benjamin, 20–21
French, 46, 66, 119, 129–130
French Catholic Colleges, 16
Friars of the Atonement, 199
Friendship House, 85–86, 91
Full Vindication of the Measures of Congress, 12

Gazette, The Maryland, 19, 20
George, Henry, 174
George III, 8

Georgetown University, 26, 80
Georgia, 11, 26
German clergy, 42, 64, 123–124, 158, 177
Germans, 7, 27, 28, 44–45, 67, 70, 118, 119, 122–124, 179
Gesu (Church, Milwaukee), 157
Gethsemane Abbey, 90
Ghana, 133
G.I. Bill, 90
Gibbons, Cardinal, 61, 64, 66, 119, 174–176, 177, 180, 182, 184, 185
Gill, Eric, 153
Gillis, James M., 140, 196
Gleason, Philip, 222, 224
Glenmary Fathers, 199
Glenmary Sisters, 113
Gnosticism, 224
Gold, Mike, 82
Golden Gloves Tournament, 77
Greeley, Andrew M., 160, 168, 222
Green Bay, Wiconsin, 158
Greene, Graham, 138
Greenwich Village, 82
Gregory XVI, 48
Grennan, Jacqueline, 112
Groppi, James, 226
Guilday, Peter, 35

Haas, Francis J., 77
Hallinan, Archbishop, 101
Hamilton, Alexander, 7, 12
Handmaids of Mary, 132
Harper's, 51
Harrison, B. G., 217
Harvard University, 71, 75, 159, 217
Hayes, Richard, 31–32
Hecker, Isaac, 61–62, 140, 199
Hennepin, Louis, 8
Henrietta Maria (Queen of England), 13
Henry, Patrick, 29
Henry VIII, 11
Hispanos, 130–131
Hitler, Adolf, 80, 89
Hogan, William, 202
Holy Ghost Fathers, 158
Holy Name Society, 92, 148
Holy Office, 99
Holy See, 22, 180, 215
Hoover, Herbert, 75, 76
House of Representatives, U.S., 50
Houston, Texas, 97, 227
Hoyt, Robert, 144
Hughes, Archbishop, 51, 119, 170, 171, 202
Hughes, Philip, 46
Humanae Vitae, 106–108, 219
Humphrey, Hubert, 98
Hungarians, 46, 128

Immaculate Conception Church (Boston), 157

Immigration to U.S., statistics, 27–28, 45–46, 124
Index of Forbidden Books, 114, 145, 149, 213, 215, 219
Indian (American), 134
Indiana, 124, 157
Integrity, 153
Ireland, 156
Ireland, Archbishop, 61, 63, 64, 119, 173, 176–182, 192
Ireland, Church of, 59
Irish (general), 27–43, 59, 66, 67, 70, 118–122, 170
Irish clergy, 31–32, 42, 120, 121, 129
Irish-French dissension, 28–29, 31–33, 121, 129
Irish-German dissension, 30, 64–66
Italian clergy, 42
Italians, 46, 66, 67, 119, 124–126

Jansenism, 31, 119, 224
Jay, John, 12
Jefferson, Thomas, 30, 53
Jesuits, 8, 15–16, 17, 18, 21, 26, 28, 30, 39, 47, 64, 92, 119, 139, 140, 157, 167, 169, 188, 196, 197–198, 203, 210, 226
Jews, 54, 100–101, 135, 147–148
Jingle, Bob, 12
John Birch Society, 190
John Carroll University, 157
John XXIII, 94–95, 96, 102, 113, 144, 146, 189, 191, 218, 220, 222
Josephites, 132
Jubilee, 118
Julius II, 59

Kansas City, 143
Kavanaugh, James, 105
Keane, Archbishop, 158, 191–192
Keating, James, 203
Kelly, Bishop, 105
Kenrick, Bishop, 39–40
Kennedy, Jacqueline, 190
Kennedy, John, 51
Kennedy, John F., 10, 39, 56, 75, 76, 93, 96–98, 134, 175, 190, 205, 227
Kennedy, Robert F., 98
Kenner, Hugh, 217
Kensington, Pennsylvania, 40
Kent, Corita, 112
Kentucky, 25, 90, 156
Kilkenny, Ireland, 176
King, Martin Luther, Jr., 112
Klein, Felix, 62
Knights of Columbus, 69, 183
Knights of Labor, 64, 174
"Know-Nothings" (American Party), 41
Kohlman, Anthony, 203
Kosciusko, Thaddeus, 9
Koslowsky, Anton, 128–129
Krol, Cardinal, 127
Ku Klux Klan, 75

Kulturkampf, 122
Küng, Hans, 214

"Labor Priests," 55, 76, 77–78
Latin America, 154
Latin Americans, 130–132; Hispanos, 130–131; Mexicans, 130, 131; Puerto Ricans, 118, 130, 131–132; Cubans, 130, 131
Lebanese, 134
Legion of Decency, 114, 142, 149, 211
Lemke, Charles, 79
Leo XIII, 61, 62, 72, 76, 164
Lewis, John, 21
Lewis, John L., 77
Life, 118, 216
Lincoln, Abraham, 50
Lithuanians, 46, 66, 128
Liturgical Weeks, 87
Lodge, Henry Cabot, 207
Lombardy, Italy, 125
Lord, Daniel, 196
Los Angeles, California, 44, 101, 112, 113, 157
Louisiana, 17, 26, 28
Louisville, Kentucky, 158
Lowell, Robert, 89
Loyola, Saint Ignatius, 198
Loyola University, 112, 157
Luce, Clare Boothe, 188
Lucerne Memorial, 65–66
Luther, Martin, 199, 223
Lutherans, 45
Lyons, Daniel, 198

McAvoy, Thomas T., 63, 173
McCaffrey, Edward, 212
McCarthy, Eugene, 98, 123
McCarthy, Joseph R., 71, 92–93, 140, 142, 150, 186
McCloskey, Cardinal, 174
McCracken, Robert J., 214
McDonald, Donald, 157
McGlynn, Edward, 174
McGowan, Raymond A., 77
McIntyre, Cardinal, 101, 188
McNabb, Vincent, 153
McQuaid, Bishop, 64, 174, 178
Maignen, Charles, 62
Manhattan College, 158
Manhattanville College, 158
Manichees, 224
Mann, Horace, 170
Maréchal, Bishop, 28, 30–31, 35
Marianists, 124, 158
Marists, 156
Maritain, Jacques, 223
Marquette, Jacques, 8
Marquette University, 92, 157
Mary, Queen of Scots, 137
Maryknollers, 199
Maryland, 7, 11, 13–16, 23, 24, 26, 47
Maryland, Proprietor of, 15
Maryland General Assembly, 15, 17

Maryland Legislature, 18, 19–20
Maryland Religious Toleration Act, 15
Massachusetts Board of Education, 170
Masses, The, 82
Maurin, Peter, 82, 83, 84
Maynard, Theodore, 29
Mendel, Gregor, 199
Merton, Thomas, 86, 89–90, 198
Meyer, Cardinal, 100 124, 187
Miami, Florida, 131, 132
Michel, Virgil, 77, 87
Milan, Italy, 126
Milwaukee, Wisconsin, 44, 83, 122, 126, 226
Ministerial Association of Greater Houston, 97
Minneapolis, Minnesota, 83
Minnesota, 45, 86, 118, 124, 176, 178, 179
Miracle, The, 211–212
Missionary Sisters of the Sacred Heart, 125
Mississippi, 133
Monk, Maria, 38–39, 75
Montreal, Canada, 38–39
Mooney, Cardinal, 79
More, Saint Thomas, 11
Mount Angel Abbey, 124
Mount Saint Mary's, 26
Mundelein, Cardinal, 73, 77, 80, 124
Murray, John Courtney, 99–100, 205, 206, 208, 209–210
Musial, Stan, 138
Muskie, Edmund, 98
Mussolini, Benito, 58, 183

Nation, The, 118
National Association of Manufacturers, 72
National Catholic Reporter, 143–144, 214, 219
National Catholic War Council, 70, 71
National Catholic Welfare Conference, 71
National Education Association, 180
National Opinion Research Center, 160
National Review, 218
National Union for Social Justice, 79
Nativism, 36–41, 130
Navy, U.S., 9, 43, 69
Nazi Party, 79, 185
Neale, Bishop, 28
Negro Catholics, 132–134
New Deal, 72, 79
New Frontier, 190
New Orleans, 47, 124, 130, 132, 133, 157
New Republic, 118
New York, 12, 22, 23, 158, 201, 202, 204

New York City, 25, 29, 41–42, 52, 83, 92, 93, 100, 122, 124, 125, 131, 132, 136, 156, 157, 170, 173, 174, 178, 203
Newfoundland, 13
Newport, Rhode Island, 190
Newsweek, 133
Newton Center, Massachusetts, 184
Nixon, Richard M., 97, 207
"No Irish Need Apply," 52
No Popery Laws, 8
Norfolk, Virginia, 30
North American College, 182, 193
North Carolina, 12, 26
North Dakota, 79
Notre Dame, University of, 63, 64, 71, 80, 138, 140, 157, 159, 217, 222

Oath of Succession, 13
Oblate Sisters of Providence, 132
O'Boyle, Archbishop, 107
O'Connell, Cardinal, 119, 183
O'Connell, Daniel, 32, 50
O'Connell, Denis, 63
O'Connor, Edwin, 52
O'Dea, Thomas F., 217–218
Old Catholics, 128
O'Neill, Eugene, 82, 216
Oppenheimer, Robert, 317
Oregon, 124, 204
Orthodox Churches, 128, 129
Ossining, New York, 199
Our Sunday Visitor, 140
Outlaw, The, 211

Paine, Tom, 209
Papal Legate, 73
Papal Nuncio, 21, 41, 43
Papal States, 58
Papal States, Consul to, 207
Paris Theater, 212
Parliament, British, 12, 15
Parliament of Religions, 64
Passionists, 167
Pastoral Letter to the Roman Catholics of Norfolk, 30
Patrick Henry Forum, 89
Paul VI, 96, 100, 104, 106–107, 114, 146, 219
Paulists, 61–62, 63, 64, 70, 140, 146, 199
Penitentes, 118
Pennsylvania, 7, 9, 11, 22, 23, 40, 124, 126, 202
Peoria, Illinois, 192
Perry, Bishop, 133
Pfeffer, Leo, 171
Philadelphia, Pennsylvania, 10, 25, 28, 30, 33, 36, 39, 40, 41, 42, 52, 92, 122, 124, 136, 157, 158, 202, 211
Pierce vs. the Society of Sisters, 204, 205
Pilot, The, 183
Pittsburgh, Pennsylvania, 118, 158

Pius VII, 36, 201
Pius IX, 55, 57, 58, 207
Pius XI, 55, 72, 76, 80, 183
Pius XII, 94, 146, 182, 183, 187
Plenary Council, Third, 171–172
Poland, 127–128
Polish Catholics, 9, 46, 66, 118, 119, 126–128
Polish National Catholic Church, 127–128
Polish Roman Catholic Union, 66
Politics and Catholic Freedom, 218
Poor Clares, 155
Port Royal, 224
Portuguese, 134
Power, John, 29
Powers, J. F., 89, 138, 216
Premonstratensians, 158
Private Journal (Benjamin Franklin), 21
Prohme, Rayna, 82
Propaganda University (Rome), 183
Protestant Orphan Society of New York, 136
Protocols of Zion, 79
Providence, Rhode Island, 105
Providence College, 158
Public School Society, 170
Pulaski, Casimir, 9
Puritans, 8, 14, 15
Putnam Bill, 202

Quadragesimo Anno, 72, 76
Quakers, 11, 76
Queens, New York, 80

Reader's Digest, 118
Redemptorists, 124
Reed, John, 82
Reinhold, H. A., 87
Religious orders (general), 67, 89–90, 109–113
Religious Toleration Act, Maryland, 15
Republican Party, 75, 178
Rerum Novarum, 72, 76
Revolution, American, 7, 8, 9, 11, 12, 20, 36, 126
Revolution, French, 24, 56
Revolution of 1688 (England), 15
Rhineland, 44
Rhode Island, 158
Richmond, Virginia, 191
Ritter, Cardinal, 100
Rockne, Knute, 138
Rogers, Will, 72, 75
Roosevelt, Eleanor, 186–187, 205
Roosevelt, Franklin D., 77, 79, 184, 185, 207
Roosevelt, Theodore, 174, 175
Roosevelt family, 185
Rossi, Peter, 160
Royal Oak, Michigan, 78, 80
Rummel, Archbishop, 124

Ruthenians, 128
Ryan, John A., 71–72, 73, 77, 79, 80

Saint Ambrose College, 158
Saint Ansgar's Guild, 134
Saint Catherine's College, 158
Saint Francis of Assisi, 83
Saint Frances Cabrini. *See* Cabrini, Mother
Saint James' Parish (New York City), 74
Saint John's Abbey, 45, 86, 124
Saint John's University (Brooklyn, New York), 157
Saint Louis, Missouri, 44, 87, 112, 122, 157
Saint Louis Church (Buffalo, New York), 202
Saint Louis University, 157
Saint Mary's Cathedral (Philadelphia), 202
Saint Mary's Church (Philadelphia), 36
Saint Mary's College (California), 158
Saint Mary's Seminary (Baltimore), 26
Saint Meinrad's Abbey, 124
Saint Norbert's College, 158
Saint-Omer's College, 17
Saint Patrick's Cathedral (New York City), 211
Saint Paul, Minnesota, 61, 105, 122, 158, 177, 192
Saint Peter's Basilica (Rome), 164
Saint Peter's Church (New York City), 25, 203
Saint Rafael Society, 65
Saint Thomas College, 158
Saint Vincent de Paul, Brothers of, 62
Saint Vincent's Archabbey, 124
Salesians, 125, 199
Salk, Jonas, 217
San Francisco, California, 44
San Francisco, University of, 157
Sanger, Margaret, 140, 149
Satolli, Archbishop, 207
Scalabrini, Bishop, 125
Scalabrinians, 125
Scandinavians, 134
Scholastics, 137
Schools, Catholic, 91, 98, 113, 154–172, 179–181, 204–206
Scotland, 22
Seabury, Bishop, 22
Seattle, Washington, 125
"Second Citizen," 18
Select Body of the Clergy, 21
Selma, Alabama, 112
Senate, U.S., 20
Serra, Junipero, 8
Serra Club, 91
Servants of the Paraclete, 199

Servites, 88, 125, 167
Seton, Mother Elizabeth Ann Bailey, 155–156
Seven-Storey Mountain, 89
Shannon, James P., 105
Shannon, William V., 49
Sheen, Archbishop, 138
Shehan, Cardinal, 100
Sheil, Bishop, 77, 92
Sicily, 118, 126
Single-Tax Movement, 174
Sisters of Loretto, 156
Sisters of Mercy, 52, 156
Sisters of Saint Joseph, 156
Sisters of the Blessed Sacrament, 132
Sisters of the Good Shepherd, 210
Sisters of the Holy Family, 132
Sisters of the Immaculate Heart of Mary, 113
Slavery, 46–50, 139
Slovaks, 128
Smith, Alfred E., 56, 74–76, 97
Social Justice, 79, 80
Socialist Call, 82
Society for the Propagation of the Faith, 188
Society of Saint James, 189
Sons of Italy, 66
South Carolina, 11, 26, 32
Southwark, Pennsylvania, 40
Spain, 8, 141, 175
Spalding, Bishop, 192–193, 207
Spanish, 46, 119, 130
Spanish Civil War, 138, 140, 150
Spanish colonies, 8, 43, 130
Spellman, Cardinal, 58, 93, 99, 100, 119, 141, 142, 182–188, 205, 211, 212
Starkey, Lawrence, 15
Stillwater, Minnesota, 179, 180
Stokes, Anson Phelps, 25
Studs Lonigan, 118
Suffolk Resolves (1774), 12
Sulpicians, 25, 26, 28, 30, 33, 199
Sumter, Fort, 50
Supreme Court, U.S., 43, 133, 204, 205, 206, 209, 212

Tammany, 52, 74
Taney, Roger, 43
Taylor, Myron C., 207
Temperance Movement, 179
Ten Commandments, 146
Thomism, 149, 164
Thought, 217
Trappist Monks, 86, 89–90, 119, 197
Trinity College, 158
Truman, Harry S, 206
Trustee System, 27, 29–30, 33, 35–36, 127–128, 201–203

Ukrainians, 128
Uniate Churches, 129
United States Catholic Miscellany, 34, 35
Urban College of Propaganda, 182
Ursulines, 37, 47

Vatican, 10, 21, 22, 24, 31, 32, 46, 54–55, 75, 106, 174, 178, 181, 182, 183, 184, 207–208, 214–215
Vatican, diplomatic relations with, 206–208
Vatican City, 58, 206
Vatican Council I (1869), 57–58
Vatican Council II, 10, 24, 56, 58, 60, 67, 87, 95–96, 98–104, 105, 107, 108, 109, 110, 112, 113, 143, 146, 152, 153, 155, 162–163, 164, 165–166, 172, 187, 189, 208, 213, 214, 215, 218–219, 220, 221
Vermont, 138
Viereck, Peter, 148
Vietnam war, 85, 150, 215, 226
Villanova University, 158
Vincentians, 157–158, 199
Virginia, 11, 13, 15, 23

Wade, Mason, 210
Wahrheitsfreund, Der, 122
Waldensians, 124
Walmesley, Bishop, 23
Walsh, Michael, 49
Wanderer, Der, 122
Washington, D.C., 26, 42, 86, 107, 158
Washington, George, 9, 25, 126
Waugh, Evelyn, 216
We Hold These Truths, 205
Webster College, 112
Weigel, Gustave, 226
Welch, Robert, 190
Weld, Thomas, 23
West Virginia, 97
White, Andrew, 14
White House, 27, 56, 96, 98, 184, 207
Whitman, Massachusetts, 182
Wills, Garry, 218
Woodstock College, 26, 99
World War I, 45–46, 66, 69–71, 122, 123, 175
World War II, 10, 88–89, 123, 127, 131, 132, 138, 140, 153, 184–185, 205
Wright, Cardinal, 157
Wylie, Philip, 210

Xaverian Brothers, 156
Xavier University, 132

Yale University, 71, 159
Young, Loretta, 138